Celebration Solutions

101 Themes and Decorating Ideas for
Reunions, Parties, Fund-raisers,
Holiday Celebrations, Anniversaries
and Every Other Get-Together

Celebration Solutions:

Themes and Decorating Ideas for Reunions, Parties, Fund-raisers, Holiday Celebrations, Anniversaries and Every Other Get-Together

by Dina C Carson and Risa J Johnson

Published by:

Reunion Solutions Press
P.O. Box 999
Niwot, CO 80544
www.ReunionSolutions.com

Copyright © 2004 Reunion Solutions Press
Printed in the United States of America
    ISBN 0-9724975-6-0
Cover Design by Robin R Meetz
    Imagination Technology, Inc. www.imaginationtechnology.com

Publisher's Cataloging-in-Publication Data

Carson, Dina C, 1961 -
Johnson, Risa J, 1960 -

Celebration Solutions:
101 Themes and Decorating Ideas for Reunions, Parties, Fund-raisers, Holiday Celebrations, Anniversaries and Every Other Get-Together

        p.   cm.
    Includes index.
        ISBN 0-9724975-6-0   LOC 2002096762
        1. Reunions—Planning.
    2. United States—Social life and customs.
    3. Family Reunions—United States—Planning
    4. Class Reunions—Handbooks—Planning
    5. Military Reunions—Handbooks—Planning I. Title.
    LB 3618.C3214 2004
    394.2 Car

Table of Contents

Think about a sunny day at the beach. Take guests back to the early 1960s when Annette Funicello and Frankie Avalon were making beach movies.

Picture a dark, closely-intimate, smoke-filled nightclub. Imagine you and your guests dressed to the nines out for a night in Berlin during the heyday of the 1930s jazz-scene.

Imagine the glamor of the city at night. Make your guests feel as if they've been transported to the deck of a yacht overlooking a sea of lights.

Picture a close, intimate, urban club. Give your guests a night full of laughter at your "comedy club."

Imagine a romantic, English garden. Just the thing to lift your guests' mid-winter spirits.

Picture yourself out for a night at the Oscars. Roll out the red carpet to greet your guests and treat them like stars.

Celebration Solutions

Table of Contents

Table of Contents

Celebration Solutions

Table of Contents

Table of Contents

Celebration Solutions

Table of Contents

Table of Contents

Celebration Solutions

Table of Contents

Table of Contents

Celebration Solutions

Checklists

Creating a Theme

Celebration Solutions

Introduction

Why host a theme party? Why not just put out the food and gather the guests? Because we enjoy theme parties for the same reason we enjoy books, movies and theme parks. They allow us to take an imaginative trip to a different time, place, or location. They satisfy our inner spirit of adventure. They play to our fascination with the unknown, the mysterious — even the frightening. We love to see colorful characters in exotic settings, winding their way through the twists and turns of surprising, inventive plots.

You can have all of these things in a theme party as well — only one step better. With a well-planned theme party, you can give your guests a chance to place themselves in the action, in the location, or as characters in the scene.

For a theme party to be successful, you need three things:
1) to suspend reality for a little while;
2) to satisfy guests' essential needs; and
3) to engage guests in the celebration.

Success Secret #1 — Suspend Reality

In order to suspend reality, you need to do what books and movies do well — to make the situation feel *real*. Good *movies* make viewers forget that they're sitting in the movie theater. Good *themes parties* make people forget that they're in your dining room or a hotel ballroom. The best themes suspend reality by creating an ambiance that satisfies each of the senses — sight, sound, taste, touch and smell — and they help guests put what they're experiencing into context. In other words, there should be just enough reality in the scene to make the setting plausible.

Success Secret #2 — Satisfy Guests' Essential Needs

Let guests know what to expect. Some people are uncertain about how they'll fit into a social situation. Use the words and the images in your invitation to convey the essence of the party. This will help alleviate any apprehension. Give guests more than enough information to answer their questions. Tell them what the dress code is so there will be no worries about showing up over- or under-dressed. If you're holding a fund raiser, say so. That way, guests won't be embarrassed if they can't participate because they have left their wallets at home. Supply driving directions, parking instructions, and what amenities might be available in public venues, like an ATM machine or a block of rooms reserved at a discount for guests who would not wish to drive home after the celebration.

Success Secret #3 — Engage Guests in the Theme

Use an activity to engage guests in the theme. Play a game, hold a contest, have a demonstration or teach your guests something about your theme subject.

Introduction

Even if you're planning more traditional entertainment like music and dancing, plan an activity that engages everyone in the theme.

No matter what the theme, if you can apply each of the three theme-party success secrets, you'll have a hit on your hands. If you don't find the theme of your dreams in these pages, don't worry. We're going to tell you how we build our best theme ideas, so you can take one of our themes, in whole or in part, and make it your own.

Creating a Unique Celebration

When we sat down to write this book, we brainstormed more than 1,000 theme ideas in a very short period of time. We found that just about any idea could become a good theme with a little bit of help, *and,* that any good theme could be turned on its ear and developed into a completely different experience using the same idea but a different look. That's good news for you, because themes are incredibly flexible. You can take any one of these theme ideas, put a little twist on it and make it a unique experience for your guests.

One of the biggest challenges this book presented was envisioning how the details of the themes would work for all gatherings, from birthdays to reunions to gala fund raisers. We found that to be difficult. We also found that it's much easier to start with a picture of a big celebration like a reunion or a corporate holiday party, and then scale the idea down for a more intimate gathering like a birthday or anniversary. As a result, in this book we've given each theme as much information as possible, as if it will be used for an all-out, corporate-funded, fully-catered event for a large, adult audience. We realize that many celebrations won't fit this model. Not to worry. There are many ways to make these theme ideas work for a small budget or a small group, for children or teenagers, and with or without help of a caterer or decorating consultant.

Creating a Theme on a Small Budget

For those of you who have a huge budget to work with, go for it. For those of you who don't, use your decorating dollars where they will have the most impact. The goal of any theme is to create an *impression* with the guest, not necessarily to land him or her smack in the middle of a deep, dark jungle with heat, humidity and bugs! More often than not, it's the little things, the finishing touches, that take an average theme idea and turn it into an extraordinary experience. The upcoming decorating section will give you suggestions for maximizing the impression you're trying to create without "busting your budget."

Another way to stretch your budget is to create strategic partnerships with groups or businesses that might lend, donate or help you pay for items that you need. If, for example, you want to create more permanent, bigger-impact decorations, talk to a local theater group that might be interested in purchasing the materials for the "sets" if you'll donate them to the theater after your production is over. Or, talk to local parents' groups that sponsor after-prom events. Spending a few dollars on elaborate decorations may be just what these groups need to keep their children off the roads and out of trouble after the prom ends.

Talk to local businesses. Businesses may donate items, materials or the help that you need in exchange for advertising or name recognition at the event. Offer to do something that not only will give the business a positive image, but will bring people in to the business. That's what is important to the business owner. For example, if a photographer is willing to lend you photographic prints to decorate the walls, instead of just putting a small business card at the bottom edge of each print, ask the photographer to give your guests a percentage-off coupon for any purchase they make in the next 30 days. This is a win-win-win situation. You get the prints you want, the photographer gets to show off his work to a captive audience, and the guests are given a limited-time discount which is an incentive to visit the photographer's studio.

Making Themes Age-Appropriate

Although the themes in this book were designed with adult audiences in mind, you can translate any theme into something appreciated by a younger crowd. It may take more work to pull off a Teddy Roosevelt theme, for example, with younger children, but you can if you give them the background necessary for *them* to put the theme into context. Stories of the "olden days" work very well for this purpose.

If you need to make your theme age-appropriate, you can generally divide children into three categories: toddlers, school age, and teenagers. The easiest way to change a decorating scheme to fit an age group is to scale the decorations. While it might be difficult to place a large group of adults under a tent in a room, for example, it's fairly easy with small children because they fit. So, instead of decorating a whole room, create a space that fits their size.

Toddlers won't be terribly impressed with elaborate decorations. They will be more interested in things they can play with, so structure the theme around kid-safe activities. You can still host an incredible prehistoric theme party, for example, but instead of decorating for a Jurassic Park experience, use blowup or stuffed dinosaurs that the kids can hug, bump into and interact with.

For school-aged children, activities are more important than the decorations. Young children like to role play. They love the idea of putting on a costume and stepping into a storybook. For this age group, you don't need to rebuild the castle walls of Camelot, for example. Instead, plan activities that teach the children about what it might have been like to be a kid back then. A group of princesses might like to make some silk-flower hair wreaths or a group of princes might like to watch a film about sword fighting or jousting.

How to Use this Book

Teenagers are a tougher group to please. Most teenagers like to imagine themselves exploring places of magic and mystery. This is easy to achieve with a theme, but you may need to sell the *fun* behind the idea before you will get enthusiastic participation. The easiest way to overcome teenagers' reluctance is to involve them in the planning and decision-making. Let *them* sell the idea to their peers. You almost can't overdo decorations with this group, either. No project is too big or grandiose. Fortunately, the enthusiasm of teenagers for a good idea often translates into lots and lots of volunteer help. Make use of all of their talents. In almost every teenaged group, you will find natural leaders who can direct the efforts of other volunteers, as well as entertainers, artists, and multimedia whiz kids who will be anxious to show-off their talents for a theme party. Let them!

Traditional Celebrations

There are a few celebrations that play a unique role in our lives — weddings, anniversaries, retirements and reunions. These celebrations have traditions associated with them that makes using a theme a bit more difficult in some situations and easier in others.

Weddings are one of society's oldest and most important celebrations. We realize that there are purists out there who won't entertain the idea of a theme wedding, but for those of you who will, theme weddings are a lot of fun. The wedding ceremony itself should focus on the couple, but the reception is as much for the guests as it is for the bride and groom, and therefore ripe for a good theme.

Anniversaries are occasions to celebrate continuity while nurturing and renewing family bonds. At an anniversary party, you're not just celebrating the couple today, you're celebrating their history together. Pick out something about the couple's married life and focus on that. If, for example, the couple eloped, consider a destination theme about the place they got married. Or, if the couple got married in the '50s, use a '50s theme.

Retirements shouldn't be *just* a farewell. They should be a celebration of the contribution of the person who is retiring. Forget about the sheet cake and mystery punch. Send the retiree off with an acknowledgment of who he or she is and the activities he or she participates in or enjoys. Celebrate the retiree's profession or hobbies. Talk to the family. You might be surprised to find out that your co-worker or boss is a watercolor painter or a train enthusiast.

Reunions of all types can use themes very effectively. Reunions are popular with family members who want to reconnect with their relatives and learn about their ancestors. Celebrate your family's unique heritage with an ethnic theme. Family trees, genealogies, heirlooms, photographs, and ancestral legends passed on from generation to generation should be an important part of the celebration. Families also can use themes to celebrate the experiences of their ancestors. If, for example, your family came west in a wagon train, an Old West theme might be perfect.

School classes share a common history as well. Drag out the yearbooks, pick through the pictures, search out the scrapbooks and gather reminders of the time period you shared. These are the things that will awaken some fond memories.

The same goes for military reunion groups. Choose a theme that will make the most of your memorabilia and recognize the time period in which you served. Military reunion groups could use a theme to celebrate your branch of the service, to remember a favorite spot for shore leave, or to showcase the movies or music popular way back when.

Every group that gathers to celebrate is unique — unique in its experience, likes and dislikes. Every celebration should be unique, too. You know your guest list. Put that knowledge to work to create an extraordinary experience for your guests.

How to Use this Book

This book has three sections: Creating a Theme, Themes and Checklists. Part I, Creating a Theme, is an introduction to the different elements it takes to create a theme. Part II, The Themes, is themes and more themes — 101 of them. Part III, The Checklists, is a group of tools you should find helpful while planning and carrying out your theme celebration.

Part I — Creating a Theme

We want to show you how we construct themes, so that you can use the same methods to create themes of your own, or change these themes to better fit your celebration.

When we create a theme, we start by getting a good visual picture of the ambiance we want to create. Sometimes this involves a little research to get enough background information to be able to construct a realistic scene. Next we choose a color scheme. In order to get a scene to look right, we try to choose colors that are not only right for the theme, but right for the context of the theme or the era that's being represented. The suggested attire usually comes next. We choose a suggested attire that will allow guests to fit in with the theme, in other words, to look right in the scene, as well as to be comfortable participating in the celebration. Next we choose the graphics or gift that we'll send with the invitation. Invitations should convey the essence of the celebration to the guest.

Once we have these basic elements, we add in the decorations, focusing on items that are not only spectacular and will make an impression with the guests, but practical to find or construct. Next comes the menu. For some themes, choosing a menu is easy because some foods naturally go with some themes. For oth-

How to Use this Book

ers, we focus more on a well-balanced, crowd-pleasing menu and on the way the food will be presented. We look at the entertainment in three parts: 1) things that will play in the background, either sounds or music that reinforce the theme; 2) entertainers we might hire to perform for the group; and 3) activities that will involve the entire group in the theme. We look at souvenirs of the celebration as a finishing touch. They're not absolutely necessary, but for some events like a reunion, they're a lasting reminder of the gathering. Fund raisers are a high priority if they are the purpose of the event, but for most celebrations, fund raisers are a way to provide a cushion in case ticket sales are not what is expected, or as a way for the group to give a gift or make a donation to a charity.

There you have it, the elements we use to put together a theme. In the sections that follow, we'll give you more ideas and 101 themes to choose from!

Part II — The Themes

In the themes section, you'll find all 101 themes. They are organized into twelve broad categories — ambiance, decoration, destination, entertainment, ethnic, government, holiday, professional, progressive, regional, transportation and yesteryear. Each category has unique characteristics.

Ambiance themes are about a specific place like a sidewalk cafe, a mountain retreat, or a Pullman train car with all of the sounds and feel of speeding down the tracks.

Decoration themes use a single decorating scheme throughout, such as balloons, umbrellas, colors, clowns, animals, hearts, masks, crayons, transportation, playing cards, games or kites. Decoration themes work best with a single idea that permeates the decor.

Destination themes use any place you would consider for a vacation like Hawaii, Alaska, Yellowstone, Jamaica, Paris or New York. Wouldn't your guests like an afternoon on a beach in Hawaii, an evening stroll along the "great white way" of Broadway, or a sunset cruise along the canals of Venice?

Entertainment themes focus on anything to do for amusement. These themes can be about the *people* who entertain us (actors, comedians, authors, composers, artists, musicians, or sports figures), about the *productions* themselves (ballet, books, cartoons, games, musicals, sporting events, television or theatre) or the *characters* of the production (fictional places, or cartoon, literary or television characters). The possibilities for these themes are endless. (Before you plan an Entertainment Theme, read the copyright discussion at the end of this section.)

Ethnic cultures are particularly good for themes because it's easy to coordinate food and decorations according to custom or location. Ethnic themes could be *continental*, such as African or Asian, or they could be *specific*, such as Italian or Native American.

Celebration Solutions

Government themes aren't just about politicians. One of the biggest branches of government is the military. Besides the four major branches of the military (Army, Navy, Air Force, and Marines), don't forget the Coast Guard, the Merchant Marine, and former military groups such as the Cavalry or the Russian Imperial Guard. There are also some quasi-governmental groups that fall under this category such as NASA or the French Foreign Legion.

Holiday themes can be built around any holiday or combination of holidays. Among the many holidays are: New Years, President's Day, Valentine's Day, Mardi Gras, St. Patrick's Day, Passover, Easter, Memorial Day, 4th of July, Labor Day, Rosh Hashana, Yom Kippur, Columbus Day, Veterans' Day, Thanksgiving, Hanukkah, Kwaanzaa, and Christmas. Combining holidays can be quite amusing — 4th of July and New Years — St. Patrick's Day and Thanksgiving. See what kind of interesting combinations you can come up with!

Professional themes are fun if you're celebrating in honor of someone who practices in a particular field or if all of your guests are from the same profession. Professional themes could include journalists, doctors, lawyers, miners, truckers, nurses, teachers, farmers or sports. Most professions have equipment, symbols, lingo or uniforms that could be used as a part of the theme.

Progressive themes ... well ... progress. The party evolves as it moves from place to place or from time to time. Progressive themes can use changing times of day, changing seasons, changing holidays, changing places — anything that moves along.

Regional themes capture the unique characteristics of different parts of the country, such as New England, coastal, Midwest, South, Pacific northwest, southwest, West, the Rockies, Maritimes, the Everglades, the Appalachians, Amish country or the Great Lakes. Regional themes are less specific than destination themes.

Transportation themes focus on a mode of transportation such as cars, trains, planes, boats, or bicycles. Or, you could use transportation modes of the past or the future such as, space travel, stagecoaches, carriages or tall ships.

Yesteryear themes come from any time period in the past. Think about *ancient civilizations* (i.e. Byzantine, Egyptians, Greeks, Mayan, Romans), *time periods* (i.e. medieval, Renaissance, colonial, pioneer, British empire, gold rush, old west, turn of the century, postwar), *decades* (i.e. 1920s, 1950s, 1970s), or *historical events* (i.e. Civil War, Revolutionary War, first man on the Moon, Lewis and Clark Expedition, the Alamo). Costumes, architecture, furniture and transportation are all era-dependent, so using these things can help make yesteryear themes come alive.

The themes we've chosen in this book are representative of each of these major theme categories. There are not an equal number of themes for each category

How to Use this Book

because some categories have so many possibilities than others, so you'll find many more entertainment themes, for example, than government themes.

How to Use Each Theme

On each theme page you'll find our ideas for the theme, but you'll also find some resources you can use to make the theme your own. On each page in this section you'll find: online resources, visual examples, keywords, research, ambiance, colors, suggested attire, invitations, decorations, menu, entertainment, souvenirs/party favors and fund raisers. These are all the tools you'll need to brainstorm a unique celebration and plenty of ideas to jumpstart your creativity.

Online Resources

At the end of each keywords section in bold print, you'll find a web page address. We set up a web page for each theme so we can better show you what we describe in this book, and so we can update our recommendations for items you might need for the theme.

Illustrations

One of the easiest ways we found to jumpstart a theme idea was to look at images that depict elements of the theme. On every two-page spread, there are a dozen line art pictures. While it's true that a picture is worth a thousand words. It's also true that a picture can spark a thousand ideas.

Keywords

We also found that by looking through a list of items associated with a theme idea, we could generate many more ideas than looking at pictures alone. Reading through the keywords list may help you better visualize what's possible for the theme.

Introduction

Every theme starts off with an introduction to the subject. One of the first things we do when preparing a theme is to gather background information. We get most of our research from books and movies. Movie studios have some of the best research departments in the world to get time-period details correct. Watching movies is a great way to get ideas for props, decorating, suggested attire and sound effects.

Ambiance

The ambiance is the complete picture — the sum total of what will go into the theme. This section will give you a synopsis of the theme — a description of the place, time period, lighting, sounds, and smells to help create the ambiance.

Celebration Solutions

Creating a Theme

Color

For every theme, we give you a suggested color scheme. Color helps to set the mood because people react to the colors around them. Color also helps to provide visual continuity when planning decorations. You'll find color examples on the inside front and back cover of the book.

Suggested Attire

The usual categories assigned to the dress code — casual, cocktail, business and formal — are too broad in our opinion, and subject to misinterpretation. So, we have given each theme a more descriptive suggested attire. There's little doubt about what to wear if you're told to come to the celebration in "don't mind if you get it dirty" casual, "James Bond" black tie or "vampire costume" chic, is there?

Invitations

Your invitation will tell the guest a tremendous amount about what to expect during the celebration. In this section, we'll give you ideas for invitation graphics as well as a more elaborate invitation gift. Think of these gifts as attention getters, before-the-event souvenirs, or an added incentive to attend.

Decorations

There is literally no end to the universe of decorating ideas you can use for each theme. To get you started, we'll give you some ideas for decorating the tables, the walls, the ceiling, the floors, and the props you might use to fill any empty spaces in the room.

Menu

There's only one rule of thumb when it comes to feeding guests — don't send them home hungry! We'll give you menu suggestions to get you thinking, but your menu will very much depend upon the tastes of your guests. We also suggest a specialty drink with each menu. Let guests try these concoctions because they fit into the theme, but be prepared with alternatives. These drinks are probably not what guests will prefer during the entire celebration.

Entertainment

Entertainment is also a matter of taste. In some cases, all you might need is background music so guests can talk and enjoy each other's company. In other situations, you might want a full orchestra for nostalgic ballroom dancing. In most situations, you'll want to engage guests in the theme by planning an activity that involves everyone.

Suspend Reality

Souvenirs/Party Favors

Send your guests home with something to remember the celebration by, or give them something they can use during the event. A good souvenir can be something as simple as a handwritten menu or as elaborate as a weekend getaway for two.

Fund-raisers

If you need to raise funds during your event, we'll give you suggestions for incorporating the fund-raiser into the theme. The most important part of fund-raising, though, is to choose a method appropriate to your financial goals.

Part III — The Checklists

The final section of this book is the Checklists section. To help you stay organized and on track, we've given you some checklists to help you plan and worksheets you can fill out as you're budgeting and conducting interviews with vendors.

Success Secret #1 — Suspend Reality

In order to effectively suspend reality, a theme must appeal to all five senses — sight, sound, taste, touch and smell. The ambiance is the tool you'll use to suspend reality. The ambiance will help you plan out the rest of the details and explain your vision of the event to any vendors or volunteers who might be helping you.

Creating an Ambiance

Creating an ambiance is about creating an illusion. When you create an ambiance, you're the storyteller and the setting for the story is the impression guests will get when they step into the room after it's decorated. You may be bringing an outdoor setting indoors, or an indoor setting outdoors. To be effective, you need to recreate the elements necessary to make the scene believable.

To get a feel for creating an ambiance, close your eyes and imagine you're actually in the setting you're trying to create. To conduct this exercise, think about a place that's familiar to you — a ballpark, a beach, a museum, a theater, etc.

What does the scene look like?

The sense of sight may seem like the simplest of the five senses to satisfy, but it's more complex that you might think. There are quite a few visual elements to consider.

Creating a Theme

What colors do you see? Is there one color in different shades, colors that blend, or colors that clash? Are you looking at a garden that's primarily green with little splashes of reds and yellows? Or, are you looking at an explosion of color? Color helps define the atmosphere and set the mood.

What time of day is it? Is it midnight or dawn? High noon or sunset? The time of day appropriate for the theme will affect the lighting. Lighting, like color, is a powerful way to establish mood.

What objects do you see? Is there a recognizable architectural style in the scene? Are you seeing whitewashed walls against an azure blue sky, or are you indoors? Does the room have exposed brick, wood paneling, or paint? The objects in the setting will help determine how you will decorate surfaces (walls, tables, floors or ceilings), or fill spaces (props or 3-dimensional decorations).

Who are the people in the scene? Are they dressed in 1940s fashions and dancing to a lively swing band, or are they quiet couples walking hand in hand on Broadway? Are they in costume? Are they other-worldly? The people in the setting will help you determine the suggested attire for the celebration.

What does the scene sound like?

Sound reinforces what we see. Lack of sound is also quite noticeable. For example, in a movie scene, if an actor threw a punch and there was no sound of the fist connecting, you would notice. Is the noise in your scene a crowd cheering on a favorite team, or the wind whistling through a hollow? Is there music playing? Sounds explain a lot, which is why sound effects are used so often in television and movies.

What does the scene smell like?

Smell is one of our most powerful senses. Do you smell the scent of pine in the forest, the earthy smell of a garden, or the salty smell of ocean spray? You can create smells with potpourri pots or scented objects like candles or soap. Don't get too carried away with smells, though. You don't want to overpower the guests or trigger any allergies.

What does the scene feel like?

Satisfying the sense of touch is partially about the atmosphere and partially about the objects guests will interact with. What's the weather like in the scene? Are you in the soupy fog of London or the bright sun of Honolulu? Raising or lowering the ambient temperature or using a fog machine or fan, can simulate weather.

What will guests touch? To satisfy the sense of touch, maybe you'll cover the tables with fuzzy smiley faces, line the walls with textured fabric, or hang beads that guests will brush past as they move throughout the room.

Suspend Reality

What does the food in the scene taste like?

Taste can be the easiest sense to satisfy with a theme because some foods go naturally with some themes, such as ethnic or holiday themes. In the scene, are you eating corn dogs on a stick or indulging in a fabulous gourmet dinner? If you choose a theme where food choices aren't obvious, think about how you can use the menu to add to the overall ambiance by the presentation. Serve gourmet boxed meals in a popcorn bucket from the theater, soup in a cartoon character thermos, or put sandwiches in a canvas knapsack.

Once you have the ambiance thought out, ask yourself whether what you have envisioned is consistent throughout the theme. Don't try too hard to make an idea fit. If an element doesn't work just right, don't use it. When evaluating an idea for consistency, imagine a haunted house. Haunted houses have scary background sounds, low lighting, areas of complete darkness, spider webs that give visitors the creeps as they brush by and a faint smell of something musty. The best haunted houses do a good job creating a complete illusion. A complete illusion is what we're after when we create a theme.

Choosing a Facility

Where you hold your celebration will go a long way to helping you establish an ambiance even before you start decorating. It's hard to recreate the enormous space of an airplane hangar without actually being in an airplane hangar. So, think about the dozens of creative and clever places to host a theme party. Some of the following are tried and true, some are a little out of the ordinary — and that's our point. When it comes to hosting a celebration, any place can be a great place. It all depends upon your event idea. You can create an event around an unusual location or try something totally unexpected. There are a few limits, though. Some people just *will not* go down into a cave or up into a hot air balloon!

Aircraft Hangar	Botanic Gardens	Country Clubs
Amusement Parks	Bowling Alleys	Cruiseships
Aquariums	Breweries & Pubs	Docks/Marinas
Arboretums/Parks	Business Clubs/ Sites	Double Decker Bus
Arcades/Fun Centers		Embassies
Arenas/Stadiums	Camps/ Campgrounds	Fairgrounds
Art Galleries	Casinos	Farms/Ranches
Auditoriums/Halls	Church Halls	Fraternal Organizations
Ballrooms	Civic Sites	Government Buildings
Banquet Facilities	Comedy Clubs	Guest Houses
Bed & Breakfasts	Community Centers	Guest Ranches
Boats/Yachts	Conference Centers	Historic Homes

Celebration Solutions

Choosing a Facility, cont.

Hotels	Race/Polo Grounds	Steamships
Houseboats	Railroads	Tea Rooms
Libraries	Recreation Centers	Teen Centers
Motels	Resorts	Theaters
Movie/Television Set	Restaurants	Trolleys
Museums	Retail Centers	Vacation Rentals
National/State Parks	Retreat Facilities	Vineyards
Nature Centers	RV Parks	Visitor Attractions
Night Clubs	Schools	Waterparks
Opera Houses	Service Clubs	Wilderness Areas
Planetariums	Skating Rinks	Zoos
Private Estates	Ski Centers	

Satisfying Sight — Decorating

Think of the undecorated room as a composition. In its simplest form, there are only two elements to consider — harmony and contrast. Harmony is continuity. Contrast is discontinuity. Pretty simple.

Picture a simple table setting. If you set all of the places alike — same plates, same silverware, same glasses in the same order for every place at the table — that's harmony. Add a centerpiece, you have contrast. Now step back and take a look at the bigger picture. If you set all of the tables with the same color tablecloths, you have color harmony. Use tablecloths of different colors, you have contrast.

Harmony and contrast are more interesting in combination. If every element of the decorations is harmonious, the setting will be dull because there will be nothing to catch your attention or draw your eye. The same is true if every element of the decorations contrasts. Again, nothing in particular will get your attention or draw your eye because there is too much to see. A combination of harmony and contrast is much more interesting because it creates tension and eye movement.

There are five major elements in theme decorating you can affect by harmony or contrast: lighting, color, placement, coverage, and proportion.

Lighting

An integral part of decorating is the lighting. Lighting helps set the mood by establishing time of day in an outdoor scene or reinforcing the setting in an indoor scene.

Suspend Reality

Lighting in harmony is even lighting. The light levels are the same or roughly the same throughout the room, although you may want to raise or lower the ambient light or cast a colored tint over the room.

If you need to brighten the ambient lighting, like you might for a summer beach scene, add high-wattage spot lights overhead to simulate noontime sun or use a combination of overhead lighting and floor spot lights. Remember that light equals heat, so don't go overboard with spot lights.

If you need to lower the ambient light, like you might need for a nightclub theme, use string lighting, luminaria or lamps. String lighting is common — Christmas lights, twinkle lights, tube lighting or light strings that come in shapes like stars, chili peppers or boots. Luminaria are made in a wide range of shapes, sizes and materials — paper, ceramic, tin and terra cotta. Use table lamps with low-wattage lightbulbs or candles, or freestanding lamps in areas that won't get heavy foot traffic. You might want diffuse lighting if you want guests to feel as if they're under a canopy of trees. Diffuse lighting by covering the light source with see-through material in a neutral color.

If you want to change the color in the scene, use colorine-dyed lightbulbs or shine-through lamp shades, cover spot lights with colored gels, or hang see-through, colored gauze material over the ceiling lighting.

Lighting in contrast uses areas of light and shadow to give the atmosphere texture, depth, dimension or movement. Use sharp beams of light to create strong contrast or strong shadows, like you would find in a creaky old mansion. Or, shine spotlights on wall decorations but leave the ambient lighting low to make the room feel like a museum or gallery. Create silhouettes by backlighting a decoration, or a moon and stars effect by using fiber optic or twinkling lights behind a black backdrop with small holes in it.

Use lighting to create movement. If you need to change the impression of the time of day, raise and lower the lighting slowly by putting them on a timer.

Lighting can be used for effect as well as illumination. Consider using glow-in-the dark objects, neon, fiber-optics, a floodlight that shines a logo, robotic lighting or laserlight. Pyrotechnics are also a form of effects lighting but you'll need the help of a professional to use them.

Color

Color is not only something that we see, it's something we feel. According to Jim Krause the author of *Color Index,* "we are all persuaded, moved, aroused, challenged, inspired, repulsed, warned and informed by color and combinations of colors."

Colors have temperature based upon where they appear in the color spectrum and colors with similar temperatures will feel harmonious. Cold colors — shades

Celebration Solutions

of blue, blue-green and green — remind us of ice. Hot colors, like intense red, make us think of fire. Warm colors, like reds, oranges and yellows, are sensuous and emotional. Cool colors — purples, greens and blues — are soothing and peaceful.

In most situations, the greatest amount of solid color in the room will come from the tablecloths. You can emphasize and reinforce that color by using place settings and napkins that are the same or a shade of the tablecloth color.

Solid colors are harmonious. Disrupt a solid color block by adding texture and you have contrast. You can de-emphasize a large block of color like tablecloths by adding objects to the table surface like centerpieces, placemats or confetti to distract the eye from the color, or by using a pattern in the tablecloth fabric.

Color can also be used to create the illusion of movement. Light colors — mostly white and shades of white — open up spaces and make them feel more expansive. Mirrors do this as well. Dark colors — browns, deep blues and green — are sobering and makes spaces seem smaller. Cover the walls with large areas of dark or light color if you need to bring the space in or open the space up.

Placement

You can create harmony or contrast with how you place your decorations. Use a pattern with repetition if you want harmony or a pattern without repetition if you want contrast. The easiest way to illustrate this is with wall decorations. Imagine a wall where you might hang a dozen posters. Hang the posters at the same height and equidistant from each other and you have harmony. Hang the posters in groupings of two at different heights and you have contrast.

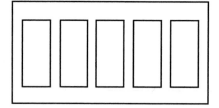 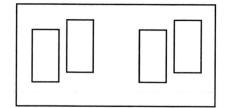

Coverage

You can create harmony or contrast with how much of an area you cover with decorations. Cover an area completely, you have harmony. Partially cover an area, you have contrast. Take the ceiling for example. If you wanted to create a nighttime sky, you might cover the ceiling completely with midnight blue balloons with small specks of white glitter glue on them. Or, if you wanted to cover only a small area of the ceiling, you might hang a single chandelier.

Suspend Reality

Coverage applies to wall decorations, table decorations and floor decorations, as well. We often speak of the size of wall or ceiling decorations in the themes. Mural-sized decorations provide lots of coverage, but not necessarily complete coverage. You might want to completely cover a wall with fabric that looks like brickwork for a back alley look, or hang photographs of 8' tall Nutcrackers as an army of toy soldiers for a Nutcracker theme. Poster-sized coverage might be as small as a standard 24" by 36" poster or a floor to ceiling scroll that's only a foot wide. Photograph-sized coverage might be as small as 4"x6" prints to as large as a 12"x16" print.

You might also use coverage in combination. For example, you might create a wall-sized mural using postage stamps or High School yearbook photos.

Creating large graphics is fairly simple but you need to start with a high quality or high resolution graphic or photograph to begin with. Most Kinko's copy centers can create mural-sized posters in full color. They're not cheap, but the color is spectacular and they're printed on paper or vinyl that is very durable. This would be the best option if you want to use the decorations more than once.

Another possibility is to create the decorations on fabric or butcher paper. You can find fabric in sheets as big as a theater backdrop or butcher paper up to eight feet wide and as long as the roll. Remember, you don't necessarily have to create true-to-life paintings. Look at how theater sets are painted. They're not terribly precise as far as the artwork goes, because they won't be seen up close. Your decorations might be seen closer than a backdrop for a stage, but they still may not need to be highly detailed. You can use a projector to enlarge a small graphic onto a larger surface and then draw or paint on to the bigger surface. This is not as difficult as you might think. Look at clip art graphics. They're often nothing more than a combination of simple shapes like squares, circles, triangles and lines. Even if you think you don't have any artistic talent, you can create simple graphics.

Proportion

Proportion is all about the ratio of the object or picture to human scale. Scale that is equal to the size of normal people is harmonious. Scale that is too big or too small compared to normal-sized people creates contrast.

Creating a decoration in harmony with human scale might be as simple as finding an object that is proportional such as a photograph where the subject in the photograph looks in proportion to the landscape around it.

A way to use large decorations while keeping them in proportion to human size, is to show only part of the scene or object. For example, if you want your guests to feel like they're standing on the deck of an historic sailing ship, all you might need is a mural of a scene looking out to sea, and a section of railing like you might find on the fantail of the ship. This would be a big decoration that completely covers one wall, but would be in proportion to the people in the room.

Creating decorations out of proportion to human scale can be fun, too. If you want to make your guests feel *really* large against the decorations, scale them down in proportion to the guests' size. Use large packing boxes wrapped in Christmas wrap to make your guests feel like small children next to the pile of presents, or create a small city of Lego™ that will make guests feel like Godzilla walking through Gotham.

You can get this same effect using pictures. Use a close-up photograph of something small, like a flower, blown up to a size dramatically bigger than the real thing. Or, hang prints showing objects that are large in real life, like an Egyptian pyramid, as a small print mounted to a large matte. The effect makes the print look like a miniature.

Practical Matters

The materials you choose to decorate with depend upon four things: how you plan to use the decorations, the size of the area you need to decorate, safety considerations, and your budget.

Durability

What materials you create your decorations with depends upon whether you need throwaway or durable decorations. Most celebrations are unique events and need only temporary decorations that will last until the end of the event. In this case, you can use cheap, throwaway materials to construct your decorations. There are a few celebrations, like after-proms, reunions, fund-raisers or corporate events that might want to make a bigger initial investment in the decorations so they can be used again and again. In this case, use materials such as fabric or vinyl instead of paper, or metal or plastic props instead of cardboard.

Area Size

The size of the area you need to decorate may also dictate what type of materials you use. For example, if you need to cover an entire wall of an airplane hangar it would be impractical to try to use fabric. Fabric would be expensive and heavy to hang. An alternative might be a balloon mural. You could still get the coverage you want using a cheaper, lighter material.

Safety

Safety is an issue with hanging, placing or choosing decorations. You certainly wouldn't want to do anything that would cause an injury to a guest or facility employee. You also may be facing rules from the facility about materials that are allowed, where you can put decorations, or the method you can use to hang items from ceilings or walls.

Suspend Reality

Of course, you won't want to use flammable materials if they will hang around or near open flames, electrical boxes or lighting that will give off heat.

Any cords or materials used on the floor must be made of nonslip material and taped down to prevent tripping.

The heavier the material hanging from ceilings or walls, the sturdier the hangar you'll need, or you might need to build a framework upon which to hang the decorations. You can create freestanding frameworks for wall decorations using simple PVC piping with T-connectors and elbow joints. You can build sections that stand alone, or sections that are connected together along an entire wall. The framework will need a base adequate to the weight of the material that will hang from the frame. Either give the base a big footing to make it steady or fill the base piping with sand to make it heavier than the material hanging from the frame.

Many facilities have rules against hanging decorations directly from the walls because of the damage tape or sticky substances cause to paint or wallpaper. One way to avoid sticking anything directly to the walls is to use hangars specially designed to fit onto the framework so commonly found in acoustic ceilings used in businesses. There is usually a metal frame edge at the intersection of the ceiling and the walls. This part of the ceiling framework can be used to hang decorations very close to the walls.

Another safety factor is stress that may be put on the materials themselves. Make sure the materials you choose can stand up to any activities you have planned for them. For example, canvas stretched over a wooden frame would be very strong and durable for a door prop or a table to hold a small object, but might not be strong enough if a guest is supposed to stand on it.

Budget

The final factor, and often the most important, in choosing materials to decorate with is your budget. If you have a large budget, you can paint Times Square with polka dots if you like, but if your budget is limited, you may have to be clever to stretch your decorating dollars as far as you can and still get the ambiance you want.

One of our favorite sources of decorative art and photographs are calendars and art books. After the first few weeks of January, most calendars are dramatically discounted. Calendar publishers may also want to get rid of any overstock they have. Find a calendar that suits your needs and make the publisher an offer. Oversized art books are another source. As long as you don't mind having to destroy the book in the process, you can make beautiful decorations out of the pages.

Creating a Theme

Postage stamps are also a good source of incredibly detailed art. Look at the stamps that were made by lithography. Before stamps were printed in full color, they were printed by the same technology as currency. An engraver made a plate. Ink was added to the plate and transferred to paper. The detail in some of these early stamps is phenomenal. To be appreciated, though, the stamp may have to be blown up to a bigger size.

Copyright-free art is another source of relatively inexpensive, high-quality art. Dover Publications at www.doverpublications.com has hundreds of titles of copyright-free art in nearly every subject. There are hundreds of online sources as well. Three of the biggest are www.clipart.com, www.photos.com and www.fotosearch.com. You may have to pay a fee to get the photograph or graphic you need, but if you want to create poster- or mural-sized prints, you may need a high-resolution file to get good results.

Outlet stores are a good place to find decorations, objects or props you might want. Restaurant supply outlets are a good place to start if you need linens, place settings, glasses, utensils or tabletop lamps. Fabric remnant outlets are a good source for material, although you may not find large amounts of any one fabric pattern unless it has been discontinued. Flea markets can net incredible finds at just the right price, as well.

Decorating, in its simplest elements, is nothing more than covering surfaces and filling spaces. Now let's take a look at some of the areas where you would want decorations to create the ambiance of your theme.

Wall Decorations

Look at the walls of your facility as a blank canvas. You can hang just about anything on them. At many celebrations, the tables are decorated but the walls are left as an afterthought. Wall decorations can go a long way to establishing an ambiance. Here is a list of ideas to get you thinking about the infinite variety of wall decorations you could create.

Create a mural from a photograph. Buy some out of date calendars and create a colorful collage. Mount or frame photographs or posters. You can give photos or posters a more expensive look by adding a fabric border or frame. Matte boards come in nearly every color. You can use matte boards to mount photographs, or you could add a design using colorful construction paper or fancy wrapping paper.

Stamp a design on a cheap beach mat. Choose a printed fabric. Add paint to a foam sheet using a brush or sponge. Stamp a pattern onto plain fabric to create a Navajo rug, brickwork, or a stone wall.

Hang a wreath. Plain vine or pine bough wreaths are beautiful. Or, if you want something a little more elegant, cover them with silk or dried flowers.

Suspend Reality

Use balloons. Put them together in a mural like a Monet painting or create a string of balloons like bubbles rising through water. Use them to add texture to the walls. Use a balloon sculpture to create a character that looks like it's stepping right through the wall.

Fashion a window. Create a lightweight window frame and fill it with a scenic photograph. If you're trying to create a log cabin look, for example, use a picture of hewn logs outside of the window's frame to help create the impression. Leave the edges ragged and uneven rather than leaving the outer area of the logs square.

Hang a banner — give guests a welcome message, identify your group, repeat a design into a border pattern or cut holes in a solid-color banner for a different look. Weave a bunch of streamers together. Weave them together flat like a mat or weave them together loosely for more dimension.

Use butcher paper for large blocks of color. It comes in a wide variety of colors. Break up the color by affixing photographs or other graphic art to the butcher paper.

Hang mirrors or create a mirrorlike effect by using silver metallic paper.

Table Decorations

Look at your tables as display space. When most people think of table decorations they think of centerpieces — objects to occupy that big, empty spot in the middle of the table. Whatever you place on your tables, make it functional first and beautiful second. Avoid anything that will interfere with service or socializing.

Tablecloths

Tablecloths are a good place to start. Tablecloth linens are standard fare although you could cover the tables in cloths of more than one color, a cloth with a pattern, a smaller overcloth of a different color, or a transparent plastic cloth under which you could place memorabilia such as magazine covers, photographs or postcards. You can break up the solid color of a tablecloth by using confetti or mirror chips. Confetti comes in all shapes, colors and sizes. Another way to jazz up a plain tablecloth is to decorate the edges. Add a ribbon weaving around the edges, stitch a pattern or use fabric paint to add a design. If you want to personalize your tablecloths, use transfer solution or paper to add photographs to the tablecloth material.

Napkins

If you want to reinforce the color of the tablecloths, use napkins of the same color but a different shade or use colorful napkins to add visual interest to the tabletop. Use a fancy napkin fold to add height or dimension. Use a clever napkin ring. Everything from a candybar wrapper to a piece of jewelry to a fancy, jewel-encrusted antique will work. Small souvenir items such as pins or emblems can also make nice napkin rings.

Centerpieces

The options for centerpieces are nearly unending. Make them conversation pieces — funny, striking, eclectic, or edible. Floral arrangements are commonly used as centerpieces although bud vases are an inexpensive alternative and often just as elegant. Dried or silk flowers are another alternative although they can be as expensive as fresh flowers. Use unusual or inventive vases, such as tennis ball cans, cookie tins, jars, or wine bottles to hold floral arrangements. Or, pick an unusual object, like a pair of high-heeled shoes, fill them with floral foam and stick flowers in the foam.

Balloon bouquets make good centerpieces. They're inexpensive for the size of the arrangement and heights can be varied to keep them from interfering with dinner conversation. Use a decorative weight or container to secure the balloons to the center of the table. Mylar and latex balloons can be easily hand-decorated, or you can order balloons preprinted at very little cost.

Just about any object can be turned into a centerpiece — popcorn buckets, baskets, tin cups, wine bottles — you name it. Fill fish bowls, glasses or vases with candy, colorful marbles, flower buds, candy, dried fruit, pine cones, shells, sand or tissue. Use memorabilia to turn your tables into an elaborate display. Fill the tables with miniature sculptures made of ice, paper maché, pastry, cake, confectionery or chocolate. In fact, anything in miniature might make a nice centerpiece. You can do some amazing things with candles, as well. Use candle markers or wax add-ons to turn a plain candle into a masterpiece.

Use centerpieces to fill your guests' stomachs! Arrange vegetables and dips in colorful displays. Decorate dessert cakes just big enough to feed the people at the table. A cornucopia or bread ring would dress up any table or carve fruit or cheese into shapes such as a watermelon boat to fit a nautical theme.

Placemats

Enlarge photographs or printed memorabilia and laminate or cover them in clear contact paper to create decorative placemats for you table settings. Another option, depending upon you theme, may be to purchase placemats from a restaurants, hotel or resort. These businesses often print scenic or decorative placemats as advertising.

Floor Decorations

Decorating floors is a bit more tricky than decorating other surfaces in the room, although it can be done effectively. Any materials you use must be nonslip or able to be tacked down securely.

Suspend Reality

Use thin craft foam to create a checkerboard pattern or vinyl sheets to create a life-size gameboard or design. Oz wouldn't be Oz without the yellow brick road, would it? Let your wall or ceiling decorations carry out onto the floor. For example, if you have a tree graphic up on the wall, create a tree-shaped silhouette shadow for the floor. If you have something more ambitious in mind, there is hardly a fraternity in America that hasn't trucked in a ton of sand for a midwinter beach party, but the cleanup can be difficult for such an elaborate and realistic floor decoration.

Ceiling Decorations

Ceiling decorations are important to some themes because they help complete the illusion — a star-filled sky, falling snow, a cathedral ceiling or big, puffy clouds. A balloon mural would work for any of these effects. Create a decorative chandelier out of beads or balloons. Create a metal frame to attach the balloons or beads to, and secure the frame to the ceiling. Use fabric to create a tent-like effect, to diffuse high intensity lighting or to cover up plain ceiling tiles. Use a trellis to create a gazebo, garden, or patio look.

Whatever you hang from the ceiling, make sure it hangs high enough so that the tallest guest won't bump into them. And make sure anything that will hang near lighting is made of fire-retardant material.

3D Decorations/Props

If there are any empty spaces in the room that are unimportant to traffic flow, you might want to use freestanding decorations to fill them. Take a trip to the local party store for ideas. We've seen cardboard turned into incredible decorations — old fashioned street lamps, giant candy bouquets, saloon doors — just about anything you can imagine. Make sure these decorations have sturdy bases and are not too top heavy. If they fall, they'll become decorating disasters. You can also use fishing line from the ceiling to secure these decorations in place.

Create a tower out of objects like hat boxes or champagne glasses. Prop open a few suitcases and fill them with clothes or tourist souvenirs. Create a balloon sculpture of a cartoon character, an animal, a building, or a giant shape. Hang clothing on dressmaker's forms or stuff them to create life-size dummies.

Buy or create some life-sized cardboard stand-ups. These are popular during new movie premiers and often feature the stars of the film in costume or in character. Create a character cutout that guests can have their pictures taken with. Use a large graphic of people dressed in period-costume or doing something extraordinary and cut out the faces in the pictures. Creating a picture cutout is as easy as creating a mural-sized poster, but you'll need to either mount it to something sturdy so it will stand up, or hang it in such a way that guests will be able to reach the "open faces" easily.

Celebration Solutions

Creating a Theme

Put together a collection of period-specific artifacts. For example, a '50s-era collection might include an Edsel, a hoola hoop, a band or cheerleader uniform, poodle skirts and saddle shoes. Contact hobby groups that might want to participate in an exhibit of their hobby items such as trains, classic cars, historical reproduction items or memorabilia.

You can also make just about any item that you want out of: celiastic (a cheese-cloth material impregnated with cellulose nitrate and a fire retardant which when softened in acetone becomes pliable); paper maché (a mixture of glue or paper maché paste and paper); cast plastics, paper, soap, candles or plaster; or urethane (a high density, rigid foam that can be carved, then painted).

Fresh greenery adds a natural element and often a pleasant smell to your decorations. Hang lights on them. Large plants are expensive to buy, but they can be borrowed or rented. Silk or plastic plants are another possibility.

Costumes

Let the guests or the facility staff provide some of the decoration. Ask them to come dressed in period costume, in uniform, or as fantastical, alien creatures. Another option is to give guests a costume as they enter. Hand each guest a colorful mask, or top hats for the gentlemen and long, white gloves for the ladies. Makeup is another form of costume. Maybe your guests or the staff would like to be made up like silent film stars or Egyptian pharaohs.

Print Materials

Don't forget your print materials. They're part of the look, too. Think about how you might design informational or directional signs, menus, place cards, programs or table numbers. Fonts come in thousands of different looks. Make sure the font you choose fits the look you're trying to create.

After you've created a plan for decorating the tables, walls, ceilings, floors and empty spaces, you will have created a nearly complete transformation of a plain-Jane space into a world of its own.

Working with the Facility

Before you get too far along with a decorating plan, consult the facility where you plan to hold the event. They may have rules for what you can or cannot hang, place or do. Facility owners or operators have understandable concerns for the safety of their guests and the security of their property. If you're proposing something they've never tried, show them how you plan to do it. Bring examples. Test your methods out. If you can demonstrate that nonpermanent double-sided tape won't peel paint, or that the ceiling hangers won't bend the framework, chances are pretty good you'll be able to go ahead with your plans.

Suspend Reality

While it's fun to let the imagination run wild with a theme, you still have to balance fun with functionality. The facility you choose will be the biggest factor in how your party will function. Choose a facility big enough to accommodate your guests comfortably with enough room for the free flow of traffic to important areas of the room, such as buffet tables or bars, and space for your decorations, all without compromising the level of service you want for the caliber of event you're planning.

Decorating Out-of-Doors

Just a few words about decorating out-of-doors. Outdoor decorating is only limited by space and materials that can withstand sun, wind and inclement weather. If it's possible to recreate an outdoor scene indoors, it's also possible to recreate an indoor scene out-of-doors. Anything you use to decorate out-of-doors, however, should be friendly to the environment in case anything blows away and is left behind after cleanup.

Create an elegant atmosphere out-of-doors by using crystal and china on linen picnic tablecloths or create an Italian restaurant atmosphere by using checked table cloths and bottles of Chianti on cabaret tables. Put up a large party tent and create a rustic log cabin scene. It's fun to be creative out-of-doors. Give it a try! It's easier than you think.

Outdoor decorations can help delineate boundaries. If your group is meeting in a large area such as a city park, decorating can be one way to identify where the members of your group are supposed to meet. Set out beach umbrellas or balloons in a large circle or rectangle. Hang a banner to welcome or identify your group. Use metal signs, whirligigs, wire-frame characters or lawn art at the edges of the area.

Most table decorations that will work indoors will work out-of-doors as well. The one exception might be edible centerpieces — where there is food out-of-doors, there are bugs. If you want to use something edible for centerpieces, rather than setting them up ahead of time, wait until guests are seated, then have the centerpieces delivered to the tables.

Freestanding decorations such as balloon bouquets are perfect for outdoor decorating. Since there aren't walls out-of-doors, items such as banners must be hung on whatever is available or on stands. Freestanding decorations need to be secured very well — a sudden breeze can undo your hard work quickly.

Satisfying Sound — Audio

Sound is important to creating a complete ambiance. Well-planned background sounds can make your guests sense something that they aren't seeing by making their imagination do the work. Play mortar blasts and gunfire and you're in a war zone, use the sound of flowing water and crickets and you're sitting by a stream on a lazy summer evening.

Background music is important, as well. It molds emotion. It can punch up tension or excitement, create a feeling of tranquility or peace, even inspire fear or apprehension. Think of the music behind the movie *Jaws*. Everyone who has seen the film has a reaction when they hear the duh-duh, duh-duh sound that signaled the shark's approach.

Play by the rules, though. If your celebration is strictly for a group of close personal friends and is held in a non-public venue, you probably don't have to worry about infringing anyone's copyright to music. But generally speaking, you can't play music or show clips of movies or television to a public audience without buying a license to do so.

You can rent the rights to countless thousands of songs, from the latest hits to 11th Century Gregorian chant. Look on the websites of ASCAP, BMI or SESAC, the agencies that manage the copyrights of most available music, and follow the instructions. You'll end up with the right to use the rented piece for your celebration.

Music becomes copyright-free by virtue of the license you buy to use it. A buyout license, also known as a royalty-free license, is a one-time, flat fee to use the selection as often as you want for almost all time. Many people use this type of license because of its simplicity. There are no additional fees to worry about and after purchasing the initial license, there is no more paperwork. A per-use license, also known as a needle drop or laser drop license, allows you to lease tracks for a one-time use on a single project.

For celebrations that will be held in a public place, or celebrations that charge a fee to attend, you'll need public performance rights to the music. Public performance, also known as broadcast rights, allows you to play the work on television, radio, cable or in front of a paying audience. Non-broadcast groups, like events and celebrations, pay considerably less than major producers of motion pictures, advertising or television.

Music and sound effects libraries offer an easy, affordable and copyright legal way to get good quality background sounds for your celebration. With so many companies now offering these libraries at affordable prices, it's easier than ever to find one that fits the style of the celebration you're planning and your budget. You can read more about copyrights at the end of this section.

An alternative to purchasing a license for music, is to create some of your own. Music authoring software lets you compose your own original soundtrack — even if you have no musical talent. There are software packages that can help you create original music with nothing more than a modest computer and an inexpensive sound card. Some of these audio creation software packages will

Suspend Reality

create a whole song for you in less than a second, add a solo melody on top and suggest a title for the tune. Some of them allow you to change the instrument playing as easily as changing fonts in a document. Amazing.

If you have absolutely no musical inclination, contact a college music department. You can commission a music student to make music for you. Some schools even have full classes devoted to movie soundtracks and audio-for-video expertise. Perhaps the background music for your celebration could become a student's project.

You can create sound effects of your own with nothing more than a quiet place, a good microphone and a digital recorder. You don't need to create the actual sound you're after, either. Rather, you can create what your audience thinks the sound will sound like. For example, jiggling a sheet of aluminum sounds remarkably like thunder and squishing pasta through your hands sounds like slogging through a swamp. Background sounds are as easy to create as going to a similar location and turning on the recorder.

Satisfying Smell — Aroma

Smell can also help establish a location or ambiance. Go easy on the scents. There are some people who are sensitive to them, and you don't want to overpower the room with any smell, no matter how pleasant.

You can incorporate something scented into your decorations, such as plants, flowers, soap or candles. Or, you can hide the scented object, such as bath salts, sea salts or aromatherapy essential oils, underneath tables or within other decorations. You can also use sprays like perfume or room fresheners that plug into outlets.

Some themes need distinct but not necessarily sweet smells, like the salt-sea air for a nautical theme or oily rags for an inventor's garage workshop. If you want to use a strong smell, use it only near the entrance to the room. Guests will get a sensation of remembering or recognition when they enter, but they'll only smell it for a moment. Once they are in the room, the scent will fade.

Satisfying Touch — Atmosphere

Atmosphere is one of the simple touches that can create mood by generating an all-encompassing feeling. Raising or lowering the temperature in the room is one simple way to help set the scene, but go easy with the thermometer. If guests are uncomfortable, they won't enjoy the celebration.

Use a fog machine if you're setting a mysterious scene or want your guests to think they're in London. Dry ice is one method for creating fog, but a fog machine is usually cheaper in the long run. Fog machines create their magic using pure glycol and water based fog fluid. Haze machines work in a similar way but you can change the quality of the haze by changing how the machine spits out the haze and the fluid used to make it.

If you want a winter wonderland, you might need a snow machine. Many of these units work with dry flakes of snow, material which will not melt or evaporate. These snowflakes can be used over and over again. Aerosnow is plastic and quite realistic looking. Aerosnow can also be packed into a small confetti cannon rather than a snow machine.

If you need a carnival or campaign atmosphere, use a confetti cannon to spit out a wide variety of fun — mylarfetti, aerostreamers, aerofetti, jumbofetti, circles, stars, butterflies, hearts, cannon cash (it looks like money), iridescent, flash coins, aerosnow, mylar streamers or curly Qs.

An underwater theme might need a bubble machine. These machines use the same soap as blowing bubbles for kids, but they can spit them out in many shapes and sizes and as slow or quickly as you like.

Satisfying Taste — The Menu

Food is an area where you can do a lot with a little. What can we say about food? Everyone loves to eat! At wedding receptions, you eat. At most elegant parties, you eat. Even most cocktail receptions offer something to munch on. Keep the style, feel and atmosphere of the event in mind when planning the menu and the level of service you will need to serve the menu well. It's disappointing to spoil an elegant setting with dry, rubber chicken. Likewise, it's frustrating to manage escargot forks at a windy picnic table. Make the menu you choose convenient for the guest, as well. It may be difficult to manage a sit-down menu in an alien costume or food with drippy sauces while standing.

If guests are paying to attend the event, food is an important measure of value. Most people know how much a nice restaurant meal will cost them, and that's what they'll use to evaluate whether what they've paid for the event was a good deal. The more you can do to sell the whole event as a package — the food, atmosphere, decorations and souvenirs — the more likely your guests will be satisfied. After all, it's hard to convince people that any event is a good deal if they're eating dull, bland food. It's better to "wow 'em" a bit.

Success Secret #2 — Meet Guests' Essential Needs

The goal of Success Secret #2 is to alleviate any worries or apprehension the guest might have about the event. You will do this through an informative and creative invitation, a helpful and descriptive suggested attire and by arranging any amenities the guest might appreciate while they're attending the event.

Meet Guests' Essential Needs

Invitations

Think of your invitation as the ambassador for the event. The wording, the pictures or graphics, even the layout and typestyle will leave an impression. The goal of any invitation is to get the guest to act — to accept your invitation and attend the celebration. In order to do that, you need to convince the guest that the event will be fun, entertaining and worth their time.

The first challenge is to get the envelope opened. There's so much junk mail out there today, that unless you get the guest's attention with the envelope, your invitation might end up in the circular file along with the junk. One way to make an impact is to use color. A colored envelope or an envelope with colored ink on it will get more attention than a plain, white envelope. The shape of the envelope matters, as well. Have you noticed that wedding invitations are slightly more square than most other envelopes? The size and shape plus the formal lettering on a wedding invitation is sure to get attention.

One method that marketers use to grab a reader's attention is to use wording on the envelope. While "You're Invited ..." works, making the guest imagine themselves already at the event works, as well. Here are a couple of examples: "Your presence is requested at audience with the Czar," or "Set sail aboard a royal Man-o-War," or "Can't you just feel the sea breeze?" If you back up the words with an illustrative picture, you're helping the guest get a feel for what they will experience, which goes a long way toward selling the whole idea of the event. Your invitation should plant the idea that the guest already wants to attend.

Another method sure to get your invitation opened, is to send a box or a gift. It's almost impossible to resist opening a box arriving in the mail. Send the invitation in an interesting container — a tube, a bag, a popcorn tub, a decorative tin, a cup, a lunch box, a picture frame, or a folder.

Getting the envelope or container open is only half the battle. You still need to put some effort into the invitation itself. More often than not, we see invitations that have the basics covered — the time, the place and a brief description of the event — but we like to take it one step further. Use a good photograph and a quote. Use a cartoon character that speaks directly to the reader. Write the invitation on an apron if your guest of honor is a good cook, or imprint the message on a piece of leather for an Old West theme.

There are a couple of things, though, you don't want to do with your invitation. Don't go too wild with the type (font) you choose. Guests should be able to read the invitation easily. Don't try to pack too much information into the invitation itself. Stick to the information that pertains directly to the event. For example, guests will want information about parking and driving directions. As we will discuss shortly, they might also want information about the area, if they're traveling to join your celebration, or other amenities of the facility where the event will be held. Use a neatly-organized information sheet for extra "nice-to-know" information.

Think about a theme-appropriate gift to send with the invitation. Use these gifts as attention getters, before-the-event souvenirs, or an added incentive to attend. These gifts don't have to be elaborate. You could send plastic bugs for a jungle theme, silk leaves in fall colors for an autumn theme, or a small bag of mini marshmallows and cocoa mix for a winter theme. There are times when a more elaborate (and often more expensive) pre-celebration gift might be appropriate. For example, in the first theme in this book, a beach theme, we set the scene in 1965 on Malibu Beach and we suggest that you send a DVD of the movie *Beach Blanket Bingo* starring Annette Funicello and Frankie Avalon to get guests in the mood. If your budget won't withstand such a gift, perhaps you could send a certificate for the movie rental instead.

Suggested Attire

In your invitation, give guests a suggested attire. We believe that the usual categories for the event dress code — casual, cocktail, business and formal — are too broad, and leave guests wondering whether what they've chosen to wear will be similar to what other guests will be wearing. So, we like to use a more descriptive suggested attire. There's little doubt about what to wear if you're told to come to the celebration in "don't mind if you get it dirty" casual, "James Bond" black tie or "vampire costume" chic, is there?

If you want to have guests dress in period-clothing or costume, give them an idea of what they're supposed to look like in the invitation. Send a photograph or a picture of the suggested attire. Look in costume books, art cards showing people in native or period dress, or magazines from the time period. If you can, also give the guest the names of businesses where they can get the things they might need for a costume or period attire.

Amenities

Amenities are the little extras that help guests relax and enjoy the celebration. Many of the following are particularly nice for guests who may be coming in from out-of-town.

Baby-sitting/Child Care

If you're holding an adults-only event, provide baby-sitting services. Ask parents to pick up the tab for the service, but if you can take the worry out of finding a service and making sure it is bonded, licensed and has instructors certified in CPR, parents will love you. If guests will remain for more than one day, you

Meet Guests' Essential Needs

could also arrange for a half or all-day event for the kids. Many day care centers can provide transportation and meals or snacks for kids during these events.

Concierge Services

A concierge service might be helpful if guests are in an unfamiliar city and want to fill their free time before or after the event. Concierge services can make recommendations for outings and line up tickets to local attractions as well as transportation. Contact a concierge service to see what they offer and whether your guests could call them for help or whether a representative of the company could be available during the event to answer questions.

Emergency Information

Anytime you host activities in an unfamiliar location or in remote areas, you should become familiar with the emergency services in the area. Call the local emergency services group to find out about response times and the qualifications of emergency medical responders. You may be surprised to find out that it might take an ambulance an hour or more to reach you, if you have an emergency. Many rural areas are not served by 911, so find out how to contact the emergency dispatcher for the area. In urban areas, you might want to contact police and inquire about the crime rate in the area where you'll be hosting your event. Chances are good guests will be safe within your facility, but you might want to consider how safe it is to walk to and from parking areas.

Group Discounts

Look around the area for attractions or venues where your guests might like to spend their free time and see whether you can negotiate a group discount. Tell guests about the discount and what they need to say at the ticket counter to get the negotiated group price.

Parking

If you will hold an event in an area where parking is at a premium, make arrangements for prepaid parking at a nearby lot. Or, hire a parking service to watch over or secure vehicles in public lots. If you host an event where there will be a large number of cars, you might need parking services for traffic control.

Security

You may want to hire security if there will be valuable items on display during the event or to keep cash safe if you'll hosting any fund-raisers. If there will be a significant amount of cash changing hands, don't take chances with the safety of the people responsible for it. Hire some security help.

Celebration Solutions

Creating a Theme

Temporary Help

Some events need a significant number of people to help with registration, ticket taking or sales. Hire temporary hospitality help to get guests through the door quickly and so you don't miss parts of the event yourself.

Transportation

You may need to arrange for transportation if the venue you've chosen has limited parking or is remote. You also might want to arrange for transportation to keep guests from drinking and driving after the event. Call a car or taxi service so that they can have cars available as your event ends.

Success Secret #3 — Engage Guests in the Theme

The goal of Success Secret #3 is to engage guests in the theme. It's one thing to walk into a fully-decorated room and be delighted and surprised by the look, but there's so much more you can do to make guests feel like they're a part of the theme.

Party Favors and Souvenirs

Souvenirs are a thank-you to guests for attending, and they increase the perceived value of the event. They're a tangible reminder not only of the theme, but of the fun time guests had during the celebration and of the people who participated in the event.

Some souvenirs are best given to the guest as they enter the celebration. These might be items they could use or wear during the event. If you're going to hold a contest or play a trivia game, you might give guests the playing sheets or pieces as they enter. Or, maybe you'll give guests a part of their costume — hats, gloves, mustaches, masks, flasks, or even toy Tommy guns if they're all supposed to be gangsters.

Other items you might put at place settings that you wouldn't mind if guests took home, such as printed menus, glasses etched with the party's name, or something more personal to the guest. You may want to make a souvenir out of guests' names, pictures or initials. You could then use these souvenirs to direct guests where to sit during the meal.

Some souvenirs are more appropriate to send home with the guest. One of our favorite souvenir suggestions is our parting gift for the Katherine Hepburn theme — a celebration of famous lovers. We suggest that you wrap gifts for him to give to her, and for her to give to him — a nice touch for the end of an already romantic evening. Other souvenirs you might want to send guests home with would be items like books or movies about the theme. Or, they could be something more personal to the guest like a picture of themselves in costume.

Engage Guests in the Theme

Reunion Souvenirs

Reunions have different needs than other celebrations when it comes to souvenirs. A Memory Book or Reunion Book that includes memorabilia, updated member information, photographs from the past or the present reunion, tends to be the most popular souvenir at reunions. A Reunion Book is a great way to help guests catch up with each other, a chance to reconnect, a way to show off their families today, and a terrific way to include those members who can't attend in the reunion's memories and fun. A Reunion Book can be as simple as a list of names and addresses or as elaborate as a beautiful, full-color, coffee-table book.

CD- or DVD-ROMs are dynamic, visual souvenirs. They're a way to collect and display photographs, memorabilia, graphics, video, audio, the reunion's website all in one place. CD- or DVD-ROMs are also a good way to preserve memories for future reunions.

Some things are better seen in motion. Shoot video during the reunion or compile clips sent in from guests. Include interviews, still pictures or footage of places guests might not be able to visit for themselves.

Photographs are memorabilia in the making. Take plenty of photographs during the reunion. They can be used in other reunion souvenirs, such as a video or CD-ROM, or put up on the reunion's website for everyone to see after the reunion.

Ice Breakers

Even though ice breakers aren't necessarily a way to get guests involved in the theme, they are a way to help them ease their way into the celebration. Not everyone is comfortable in social situations where they don't know everyone, so take steps to break the ice so guests can get acquainted.

Use nametags if you need to. In situations like reunions, it's embarrassing to forget someone's name *and* it's embarrassing to have your name forgotten. Nametags solve this.

At some celebrations, though, nametags are not a good option. In this situation, plan an activity that encourages guests to mingle. For example, you could go to a local souvenir business and buy a different local postcard for each guest who will attend. Cut the postcards into five or six geometric shapes. Tell guests that they have to complete a whole postcard by exchanging pieces with other guests to claim a prize or a special souvenir.

Entertainment

What would a celebration be without entertainment? Most celebrations include one or more of the following types of traditional entertainment — bands, comedians, dancing, DJs, fireworks, music, speakers, tributes, honors, memorials, recognition or toasts. The entertainment might also include things you would find at a carnival — clowns, fortune tellers, hypnotists, jugglers, handwriting analysis, carnival games, psychics, puppet shows, stilt walkers, unicyclists, fire eaters, acrobats, ventriloquists, or magicians. We think you should include traditional entertainment in your celebration, but we want you to think about some of the following forms of entertainment to help guests become involved in the theme.

Actors

Actors can help play a role in scripted entertainment like enacting a mystery story, but you could also use them as celebrity look-alikes or cartoon characters. You might also ask them to dress in period costume and speak in period language for a yesteryear theme. Actors make good storytellers. Hire an actor to regale the guests with fantastic tales of high adventure, if that fits your theme.

Artists

You might need an artist if you want to paint children's faces, or create caricatures or silhouettes for guests to take home as souvenirs.

Bazaars

Host a bazaar if your theme might take place in a market, like the open-air markets popular in Mexico, or for themes like Oktoberfest where guests, were they at the actual celebration, would walk from tent to tent or booth to booth buying beer and food. A bazaar is also an opportunity to raise funds by selling products, crafts or services to the guests at the celebration. Not all booths need to generate sales, either — display or demonstration booths are popular, too.

Contests

Contests are a way to foster friendly competition and team spirit. If you have a big group, split the room in two and use representatives of each group to play. Or, pit one table against another, or one half of a table against the other half.

Talent contests can come in many forms, even a few that don't include a performance on *American Idol*. In the politician's theme, for example, we suggest that each table be given the materials to make up a campaign sign and that they come up with a candidate and a slogan from the table. The table's representative then must come before the group and give a convincing speech about why his slogan should win.

Can you imagine a 1970s theme without disco? We can't. Hold a *Saturday Night Fever* dance contest. Widely popular since the release of the game *Trivial Pursuit*, trivia contests are perfect for theme celebrations. There are some themes that people don't know much about. Trivia contests are a way to provide background information to the guests.

Engage Guests in the Theme

Devise a contest that requires teams to construct an object that they will race against other tables. Can you figure out what you might be building for a Beer Can Regata? Check out the Australian theme.

Although contests held during theme celebrations should be all in the spirit of fun, it is a good idea to provide judges and prizes for the winners. Prizes don't have to be elaborate; they could be simple paper certificates or a bottle of wine for the winning table.

Demonstrations

Demonstrations can be very good entertainment. If you're using a regional or ethnic theme, many cultures have distinctive dances that guests might like to watch or learn. Think also about salsa, swing, Charleston, samba, step, tap or ballroom dancing. Formal dancing isn't as common with the younger generations, so a lesson might put reluctant dancers at ease before they take to the floor with their favorite guy or gal.

Games

People of all ages love games. Did you know that you can have a Monopoly™ game made for your hometown? You can. There are also an abundance of games that are played in other places around the world or that have been popular for centuries that guests might like a chance to learn, such as *Mah Jong* from China or *Mancala* from Africa.

Use a game show format, such as *Jeopardy, Family Feud, To Tell the Truth, What's My Line, Who Wants to Be a Millionaire* or a *Trivia Bowl*, to pit individuals or teams against each other and the clock.

Group Photographs

For themes where all guests are in period dress or costume, take a group photograph. Taking a photograph of a large group requires an experienced photographer, a place for everyone to stand and a plan to assemble the group quickly.

Multimedia Presentations

Multimedia means bringing together multiple media types — text, illustrations, photographs, sounds, animations or video. Multimedia presentations are incredibly simple to create on a computer. A multimedia presentation may be an easy way for you to make the room feel like a train chugging down the tracks by playing a video at the front of the room, or to show guests a slide show on multiple screens set up around the room. The copyright rules for showing video clips are similar for playing music as a public performance. Secure public performance rights if you plan to show the video clips in a public place or to guests who have paid to attend the event. Read more about copyrights below.

Copyrights

According to current copyright laws, the minute an author starts writing, a musician starts playing or a painter starts painting — that person becomes the holder of a copyright for that work. The rights belong to the creator of the work for the rest of his or her life unless he or she sells the copyright or assigns the copyright to another person or company. Upon the death of the creator of the work, the copyright will be assigned to the creator's heirs for 50 years after the author's or artist's death. Movie and television rights belong to the company that produced the show as long as they renew their rights or until the rights are sold.

Just to add to the confusion, different copyright laws apply depending upon when the work was created. Under the copyright laws in effect until 1978, a copyright holder could lose his or her rights by neglecting to include a copyright notice on the work, or by failing to renew the copyright, thereby allowing the work to fall into the public domain. Under the old law, all works published prior to 1978 were protected for only 28 years without copyright renewal. After the initial 28 years, an additional 47 years could be obtained if the copyright was renewed during the 28th year of the original copyright. If no renewal was sought, works published as recently as 1960 may have entered the public domain and are available for use without fear of infringing a copyright. Even if a renewal was obtained, works published more than 75 years ago are more than likely in the public domain. After 1978 but before 1989, works that contained a copyright symbol were protected as were works that contained no copyright symbol but had been registered with the U.S. Copyright Office. Since 1989, all works are copyrighted whether or not they include a copyright symbol or are registered. Don't assume! Contact the U.S. Copyright Office at the Library of Congress and check out the copyright status of the work you're interested in using.

There are a number of places where you may run into the possibility of infringing a copyright when hosting a theme party. The following are some of the more common situations in which you might encounter copyright questions.

If you use images when creating your invitations, decorations, entertainment or souvenirs, be sure not to use copyrighted material. The internet is a good source to find copyright-free collections of images, video clips, music clips, sound bites, animated images or photographs. Because there is an ample supply of copyright-free images out there available for purchase, you shouldn't have to use copyrighted images. This includes the images of actors, cartoon characters or animated characters. You should use licensed images if you want to incorporate these images into your theme.

The internet is also rife with copyright infringement. Images, video clips, animated images and text are all easily available to snatch right off the web. Be

Copyrights

wary, though, many of the graphics found online have embedded copyright information that could cause you trouble if the copyright owner detects you using their images.

Memorabilia is common for some themes. Any magazines, newspapers, album covers or movie posters that you own a legal copy of, you may display. You may not, however, make copies of these items and display the copies. Even though you might think of these images as just decorations, the owners of the copyright might not. According to Lloyd Rich, an attorney with the Publishing Law Center:

> "The Copyright Act permits the owner of a lawfully made copy to display it publicly without permission from the copyright owner as long as both of the following conditions are satisfied:
>
> 1) The display must be at the place where the physical copy is located.
>
> 2) The viewers of the copy must be in the same place where the physical copy being displayed is located.
>
> Therefore, assuming that the conditions for public display are satisfied, the purchaser of a movie poster, book, magazine, newspapers, etc. has the right to publicly display these items without obtaining permission from the copyright owner."

Music played during theme parties can also be a source of copyright infringement. Even if you own a legal copy of a song, without paying a licensing fee you can't play it for a crowd of people because that constitutes a public performance which is prohibited. There are some *exceptions* to the public performance rule for an intimate circle of family or friends and veterans groups, but class, association, fund raising or corporate groups don't qualify. The American Society for Composers and Publishers (ASCAP) and Broadcast Music, Inc. (BMI) manage the copyrights and fees paid to use copyrighted music. When you're inquiring about copyright status of songs, inform ASCAP or BMI what type of celebration you're planning. For most celebrations, the charges will be negligible.

You may want to hire vendors (or use volunteers) for photography, videography, or multimedia presentations and each of these vendors will be creating works that are copyrighted — copyrights that the *vendor* controls unless you negotiate the issue when you hire them. You might pay a slightly higher fee for services initially if the vendor is willing to assign his or her copyright to you, but it may be worth it in the long run to avoid having to pay for distribution or licensing fees if you want to use the work again later. Most of the time, you'll just be paying for a single use of the work anyway.

Writers, artists and performers make their living by their art and they deserve to have their work protected. They've created something that belongs to them, and for others to appropriate it without paying for it is stealing. Now that you're aware of the areas where copyrights can affect your celebration, it should be easy to avoid infringing a copyright holder's rights and causing yourself unnecessary legal headaches.

Now that you have our secrets for creating themes, we're certain you'll enjoy reading the rest of this book. Pick out a theme — twist it, turn it, stand it on its head if you want to — and make it your own. We wish you our *very* best at your next extraordinary celebration!

Dina C. Carson

Risa J. Johnson

P.S. We're always looking for new ideas for planning theme celebrations. If you would like to send us suggestions for improving this book, or if you would like to tell us about an extraordinary celebration you have planned, contact us at:

Reunion Solutions Press

P.O. Box 999, Niwot, CO 80544
E-mail: BookNews@ReunionSolutions.com
www.ReunionSolutions.com

Themes

Ambiance Themes

Introduction

Beaches are popular recreational spots for a little fun in the sun. Beaches are so intriguing because they change shape from day to day and season to season. Whether you choose a fun summer scene with lots of beach-goers or a windswept winter shoreline, the beach is a beautiful setting for a party. Take your guests back to the early 1960s when Annette Funicello and Frankie Avalon were making beach movies such as *Beach Blanket Bingo* and singing songs like the very popular *Venus*.

Ambiance

Think about a sunny day at the beach. Turn up the lighting as if it were high noon in Malibu. Don't forget the background sounds that you would hear on the beach, such as the surf, seagulls, boat horns or steel drums. Give the room an oceanside smell of salt, sea air to complete the effect.

Colors

Use "beachball" colors for this theme of orange, green, blue, pink and yellow.

Suggested Attire

The suggested attire is "1960s beach casual" … very casual.

Invitations

"Meet you on the Beach!" Extend your invitation on a blown-up beach ball or send a copy of the movie *Beach Blanket Bingo* on DVD to get your guests in the mood.

Decorations

Set the table with beach blankets for tablecloths and use brightly colored plasticware for the place settings. In the center of the table place clam buckets with umbrellas, big beach hats filled with shell chocolates, driftwood on mirrored tiles, coconut shells with clear glass "bubbles" or hurricane lanterns. Make each table's centerpiece different.

From the ceiling, hang a few large but light beach umbrellas upside down, and fill the umbrellas with helium-filled beach balls or balloons. Use clear fishing line to pull the umbrellas slightly off center so that the beach balls can be seen in the scoop of the umbrellas. Caution: make sure that the point of the umbrellas are above even the tallest person's head height to avoid injury.

Keywords

sand, surf, umbrella, surfboard, bathing suit, sunscreen, sunglasses, lifeguard, palm trees, sun, sky, starfish, seashells, life ring, sand castle, beach ball, sand toys, sand bucket, shovel, beach blanket, sea gulls, waves, volleyball, snorkel, fins, fishnet, hammock, lifeguard stands, palm fronds, beach blankets, beach umbrellas, lounge chairs, sunshine, life preservers, driftwood, mermaid, pearls, sand dollar, dolphins, hurricane lamps, airplane towing a banner, colors: blues, greens, iridescent, silver, cream, apricot, yellow, Hawaiian shirts, shorts,

Beach

On the walls, create a mural of a shoreline with life guard towers every so often or use travel posters of famous beaches from around the world.

Throughout the room place a few freestanding paper palm trees, tiki torches (unlit), kiddie pools filled with sand, treasure chests and beach chairs.

Menu

Consider this "seaside resort" menu.
- appetizers: crab-stuffed lobster
- main course: surf 'n turf (lobster and filet mignon) with green salad
- dessert: pineapple tarts with mango ice cream
- specialty drinks: Blue Hawaiis (rum, blue curacao, coconut, pineapple juice and maraschino cherry) or Beach Bums (light rum, triple sec, fresh lime juice, grenadine)

Entertainment

Hire a DJ or put together a collection of music that would have been played on the beach in 1965 when the movie *Beach Blanket Bingo* was released. Play some of the songs from the movie to get everyone dancing and hold a contest to decide who makes the best Annette or Frankie impression. As the judges are surveying the crowd, ask them to find the person who is wearing the best Bermuda shorts, the wildest shirt, the cutest bikini, the best tan — or the worst!

Souvenirs/Party Favors

Give each of your guests a pair of funky sunglasses and a beach ball as they enter the party. Make cutouts of muscle men and bikini girls that each guest can have their picture taken with. As guests leave, give them with their picture in a fun, beach-themed frame. The frame can be added directly to the photograph if you're using a digital camera.

Fund Raisers

If you need to raise funds, set up a tournament of rapid-fire beach ball in the basket. As light as beach balls are, it's harder than you think. Ask guests to pay for a "play" of 10 shots. Pit groups of 4 to 8 players against each other. The player who scores the highest from each group, moves on to the next round. Make each successive round more difficult until you have a winner. Award a prize to the winner of each round and to the big winner.

Keywords

beach balls, fruity drinks, lobster, Beach Boys music, straw hats, beach comber, swim, parasail, banana boats, jet ski, bonfire, Bay Watch, beach hut, watermelon, pebbles, shells, beach critters, waves, starfish, sand castles, octopus, saltwater taffy, tropical, coconut, shark, guppy, sandals, boardwalk, snack bar, limbo games, steel drums, parasols, leis, flowers, buffed out beach dudes, beautiful girls, bikinis, swimsuits, cabanas, parasol drinks, lifeguards, flip flops, splash, breaking waves, surf boards, **www.celebration-solutions.com/beach.html**

Celebration Solutions

Ambiance Themes

Introduction

Cabaret is a well-known musical set against the rise of Nazism in Germany during the 1930s. The story covers the people, the relationships and the politics of the famous (or infamous) Kit-Kat Club in Berlin. A typical Cabaret "revue" was a lavish production emphasizing cleverness, wit and satire in this style of nightclub entertainment. Imagine you and your guests dressed to the nines, out for a night in Berlin during the heyday of the 1930s jazz-scene.

Ambiance

Picture a dark, closely-intimate, smoke-filled nightclub. To achieve the smoke-filled effect without the cigarettes, use dried ice or a smoke machine along with a fan to keep the "smoke" moving. Keep the lighting low except for the spot-lights on the stage area.

Colors

Use deep, rich, "nightclub" colors of red, black and bronze.

Suggested Attire

The suggested attire is 1930s-era clothing, so suggest that guests come attired in double breasted suits with wingtip shoes or beaded dresses with long, elegant gloves. Send a picture of people dressed for clubbing in the '30s so guests will have something on which to model their attire.

Invitations

"Come to the Cabaret." Find an old Cabaret or club poster from the '30s. The poster style of that era was very distinctive and will make good graphics for your invitation. Or, find some inexpensive top hats and white, cotton gloves. Use cardboard hand cutouts to make the gloves stiff enough to hold the invitation and stand them inside the top hat.

Decorations

Set the tables with black table cloths and white china. For centerpieces, use lamps with bronze-colored shades and red bulbs or red candles. Around the base of the lamps use bronze, metallic confetti for shine and color.

Keywords

Berlin, Germany, nightclub, dancers, feather boa, old-fashioned microphone, Marlena Dietrich, Liza Minnelli, bistro, black leather corset, fish net stockings, hot pants, thick mascara, red lipstick, rouge, guys in whiteface makeup, black pants, white shirts, suspenders, nightclub atmosphere: glasses clinking, cigarette smoke, long cigarette holders, red velvet curtains, red and black linens, lamps on each table, lounge singer, piano player, diamond rings, hats with veils, wide-brimmed hats, feather boas, long black gloves, fur coats, off-the shoulder

DANCING

Cabaret

For the walls, create murals that look like exposed-brick. On the murals, place a few '30s style posters or cigarette ads that were popular at the time.

Menu

Consider this "bistro" menu. Serve your guests dinner-theater style with waiters in tuxedos and have cigarette girls (commonly seen in clubs of the day) walk the room with after dinner mints.

- appetizers: tomato and cucumber salad
- main course: couscous with lamb and chicken
- dessert: black velvet cake (chocolate icebox cake)
- specialty drinks: Cabaret (gin, Dubonnet rouge, bitters, Pernod, maraschino cherry)

Entertainment

Hire a good lounge singer who can imitate the style of music that would have been popular in a cabaret during the 1930s. Make sure you have an old-fashioned microphone for the soloist to perform with. Some of the classics songs of that era were: *On the Sunny Side of the Street*, *I've Got the World On a String*, *It's Only a Paper Moon*, *The Lady is a Tramp*, and *Moonlight Serenade*.

Souvenirs/Party Favors

As your guests enter the event, give each female guest a feather boa and a long-cigarette holder (popular accessories for women back in the day). Give each male guest a pocket handkerchief (as gentlemen would have worn, properly folded with points showing).

As guests leave, give them a music CD of the songs popular during the height of the Cabaret scene.

Fund Raisers

If you need to raise funds, designate a smoking area (preferably outside) and send a "cigarette girl" through the crowd selling cigars and cigarettes.

Keywords

dresses, black tie, beaded dresses, silk stockings, velvet shoes, close-fitting hats, short, wavy hair, long cigarette holders, Lucky Strike cigarettes, women in tuxedos, red lipstick, top hat and cane, chorus-line dancers, glamour, Pierce Arrow, Stutz Bearcat, jazzy, bluesy piano solos, lounge singers, comedians in blackface, vamp, seduction, flirtatious, fast and loose, alcohol, liquor, spirits, booze, taproom, dance hall, ratskeller, tavern, bistro, honky-tonk, dive, joint, microphone, piano man, giggle water, **www.celebration-solutions.com/cabaret.html**

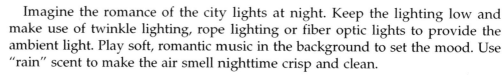

Ambiance Themes

Introduction

Glamour ... the allure of the city ... the lights, the sights, the sounds. Modern cityscapes are a collection of geometric shapes. Buildings form squares, rectangles, sophisticated curves or triangles. Some of the most recognizable skylines have buildings with distinctive shapes that let the viewer know what city they're seeing, even if all they can see are the lights. Choose a famous skyline or design a distinctive skyline of your own. Give your guests a sophisticated night on the deck of a yacht overlooking a sea of city lights.

Ambiance

Imagine the romance of the city lights at night. Keep the lighting low and make use of twinkle lighting, rope lighting or fiber optic lights to provide the ambient light. Play soft, romantic music in the background to set the mood. Use "rain" scent to make the air smell nighttime crisp and clean.

Colors

Use colors of "just-after-sunset" purple and white.

Suggested Attire

The suggested attire is "night-on-the town" semi-formal or theatre attire.

Invitations

"Join us for a night out in the city." For your invitation graphics, use a photograph of a famous skyline like New York City with easily recognizable buildings such as the Empire State building, or a silhouette of a famous building against a night sky. Pin I love NY buttons to the invitations.

Decorations

Set the tables with white linens and black-rimmed china. Use a fancy napkin fold or iridescent ribbon for napkin rings. For centerpieces, place large-diameter white candles with black or deep purple cityscape motifs around the edges on diamond-shaped mirrors. It's easy to add a design to a plain candle by cutting thinly-poured colored wax to shape and wrapping the pattern around the candle.

Keywords

skyline, lights, windows, bustling streets, hustle, street vendors, sky scrapers, brownstones, citizens, density, sidewalks, traffic, horns sounding, train whistles blowing, art museums, theaters, stadiums, department stores, shopping district, financial district, ethnic neighborhoods, overcrowding, sirens, community, urban, bustling marketplace, street hawkers, street artists, street musicians, trade, commerce, finance, stock exchange, steel workers, apartments, hotels, clubs, Bellmen, door man, chauffeurs, elevators, lights, subway, taxis, bridges,

Cityscapes

To add interest to the ceiling, use a planetarium ball to shine small lights on the ceiling that look like stars. On the walls, build a skyline using dark, geometric shapes against a purple background. Add twinkle lights for motion, light and color or add a harvest moon for a more romantic scene. Place street signs throughout the room with the names of famous streets such as Broadway, 5th Avenue, the Strand, or the Champs d'Elysées.

Menu

Consider this "city-style sophisticated" menu. Create food stations as famous city squares such as Place de la Concorde in Paris, Trafalgar Square in London, Times Square in New York and the Ginza in Tokyo.

- appetizers: Vegetarian wanton soup on the Ginza
- main course: English meat pies in Trafalgar Square and Salad Nicoise in the Place de la Concorde
- dessert: New York-style cheesecake in Times Square
- specialty drinks: Manhattans (rye, sweet vermouth, bitters, maraschino cherry)

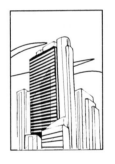

Entertainment

Hire a band or DJ to play soft jazz. Play a city guessing game. Show pictures on a projector and ask guests to guess the skyline or aerial photo. Play a game of street map maze. Take a local street map and ask guests to place different attractions correctly on the map. It will be your job to find funny or unusual local "attractions" to keep your guests guessing.

Souvenirs/Party Favors

Create some of London's distinctive "Tube" (subway) signs using guests' names as station names (e.g. Jones Station). You can use these for place cards. Give each guest a black and silver pen and pencil set.

Fund Raisers

If you need to raise funds, hold a silent auction of the prints you used for the city guessing game. Offer a variety of sizes from 8x10 to poster size.

Keywords

Twin Towers, World Trade Center, Empire State Building, Sears Tower, Bank of America Building, Chrysler Building, architects, neighborhood, vicinity, precinct, quarter, locale, district, stamping grounds, events, getaways, attractions, excursions, motion, movement, ornate, decorated, adorned, embellished, chic, smart, elegant, sophisticated, style, fashionable, intellectual, finely experienced, chichi, connoisseur, good taste, cosmopolitan, cultivated, cultured, urbane, metropolitan, cosmopolitan, urbane, cultured, **www.celebration-solutions.com/city.html**

Ambiance Themes

Introduction

Stand-up comedy has its roots in Vaudeville. Vaudeville shows were made up of individual acts of acrobats, musicians, comedians, jugglers, magicians, trained animals and so on. From the Vaudeville review came the modern stand-up comedy act. Give your guests a night full of laughter at your "comedy club."

Ambiance

Picture a close, intimate, urban club. Keep the lighting low. Use strip lighting on the floor to illuminate the aisles and spot lights for the performer on stage. Light the front of the stage with long-burning votive candles in tall, clear glasses. Play light jazz music in the background between comedy acts.

Colors

Use high-contrast "theatrical" colors of plum, white and gold.

Suggested Attire

The suggested attire is "club-going" cocktail attire.

Invitations

"Laugh it up." Send an audio invitation. Record your invitation as a digital file. Burn the invitation onto a CD that can be played in any CD player or on any computer. Put a label on the disk using the comedy symbol (tragedy/comedy masks). On the CD label, let guests know that it's a party invitation.

Decorations

If you can, set the room with small, two- or four-person tables. Set the tables with deep plum table cloths, white china and gold-stemmed glassware. Use gold metallic ribbon for napkin rings, and plum and gold confetti to give the table some sparkle. For centerpieces, use small candle lamps. Place trivia cards on the table to entertain guests until dinner is served.

Use the symbol of comedy for your wall decorations. Use metallic gold wrapping paper with a subtle pattern for texture to create the masks, and spray mount them to large deep purple matte boards.

Keywords

comedy, comedian, humor, comic, drollery, funny, witty, nightclub, café, hot spot, nightery, night spot, watering hole, liquor, hooch, booze, entertainment, headline act, monologue, Jack Benny, Mel Brooks, Lenny Bruce, Johnny Carson, Jimmy Durante, Whoopi Goldberg, Jay Leno, Joan Rivers, Lily Tomlin, Robin Williams, Vaudeville, farce, travesty, comedy of errors, satire, lampoon, pantomime, mimicry, slapstick, fun, wit, foolery, jesting, joking, jocularity, frivolity, joviality, hilarity, levity, ludicrous, tom foolery, silliness, shenanigan, giddiness, humorist, funny

Comedy Club

Menu

Consider this "club-style grazing" menu.

- appetizers are the main course for this theme: on each table, place a brie wheel with good bread along with a sampler platter of red potatoes with sour cream and caviar, cucumber slices with salmon mousse, pretzel bites with an assortment of toppings, black bean dip with chips, hot crab dip with crackers and tropical fruit salsa.
- dessert: chocolate-mocha mousse souffle
- specialty drinks: Algonquins (whiskey, dry vermouth, pineapple juice)

Entertainment

Hire a stand-up comedian or let your guests try their hand at comedy on stage. If you're going to ask guests to perform, let them know about your plans well in advance so you can get commitments from the people who want to "ham it up." Set rules for the comedy acts, though, because what's funny to some might be vulgar to others.

Before the show begins, play a trivia game of famous one-liners. See how many people can guess the correct comedian for the line. Look at the works of the classic comedians — Jack Benny or Johnny Carson — as well as today's popular comedians.

Souvenirs/Party Favors

As guests depart, give them a lapel pin of the comedy masks and a set of "word" or "phrase" magnets. On the cover of the magnet box, create a label that looks like the magnets with the party's information (e.g. Martinez 50th Wedding Anniversary, Friday August 12th, 8 PM, Excelsior Hotel).

Fund Raisers

If you need to raise funds, hire a caricature artist to create caricatures of the guests. Pay the artist generously for his or her time, but make the artwork available for sale. Or, arrange to split the proceeds of each sale with the artist.

Keywords

man, jokesmith, impersonator, pantaloon, farceur, Punchinello, zany, quizzical, facetious, absurd, amusing, laughable, banter, jest, joke, parody, caricature, rhyme, limerick, good spirits, laughs, ridiculousness, prank, practical joke, whim, whimsy, gag, parodist, scaramouche, wisecracker, punster, cutup, madcap, antic, mimic, sharp, sarcastic, ironical, satirical, mischievous, waggish, pranks, clowning around, schtick, monkey business, mischief, glee, jollity, jugglers, magicians, repartee, ha ha, snicker, **www.celebration-solutions.com/comedy.html**

Ambiance Themes

Introduction

There's just something about a garden when the weather is ideal. In fact, a perfect place for a celebration. "Heaven is not merely over our heads but under our feet" — Henry D. Thoreau (1817-1862). But what if you're hosting a party during the doldrums of February? A garden theme makes for a perfect midwinter party. Just the thing to lift the spirits.

Ambiance

Imagine a romantic, English garden. Make it fragrant. If it's off-season for real flowers, use silk or paper flowers and create a floral scent with potpourri pots. Use live, potted plants as well to give the room an earthy, garden smell. Dim lights just a little as if there is a heavy haze of summer humidity.

If you're going to hold this party out of doors, give the ambiance an *Alice in Wonderland* feel by greatly oversizing the decorations. Create huge flowers using tissue paper and wire. They don't have to look like real flowers, either. Use whatever colorful tissue paper you can find … plaid, paisley or striped … it's all right if they look surreal.

Colors

Use soft "pastel" colors of lavender, light green and peach. If you want a bolder look, use brilliant red, violet and green.

Suggested Attire

The suggested attire is "get your hands dirty" casual if you're holding the event in the afternoon, or "take off your tie" business casual if the event will take place in the evening.

Invitations

"Mary, Mary … will not be contrary … if you'll join us for a garden party." Use a botanical illustration for your invitation graphics or make a trip to the garden shop and pick up an assortment of seed packets to paste to the front of your invitations. Or, hand deliver your invitations attached to fresh-cut flowers.

Keywords

flowers, plants, bugs, shelter, benches, walks, paths, birds, bees, insects, herbs , English garden, Japanese garden, arboretum, recreation, grounds, lawn, yard, horticulture, flower, shrub, trees, flora, vegetation, plantation, sow, reap, scatter, annual, perennial, foliage , cacti, succulents, water lilies, dahlias, tulips, daffodils, bulbs, peony, chrysanthemums, bromeliads, carnations, roses, orchids, violets, begonias, hostas, fuchsias, rhododendrons, azaleas, camellias, clematis, ivies, ferns, delphiniums, irises, pansies, columns, pillars, bricks, steps,

Gardens

Decorations

Set the tables with lavender, light green or peach table cloths. Mix them up throughout the room so there is a lot of color. Use place settings in the same color as the tablecloths but a darker shade. For centerpieces, place a low, flat bowl with votive candles and rose petals floating in them.

Stand a few trellises along the walls intertwined with silk flowers and ivy garlands. To steady the trellises, use freshly-potted plants or garden statuary — snails, rabbits or frogs — at the base. Create a garden path along the floor. Cut foam squares so that they are irregularly shaped like stepping stones, and use paint on a sponge to make the foam look like stone.

Menu

Consider a "high Cornwall tea" menu.
- appetizers: cherry tomato and watercress salad
- main course: cucumber and cream cheese finger sandwiches
- dessert: scones with clotted cream and jam
- specialty drinks: English tea or Panache (a British pub drink of amber beer and lemonade)

Entertainment

Hire a string quartet or chamber music group to play. Teach your guests to play the ancient game of *Pachisi*. This game, first introduced in the 15th Century, was often played by noble women while enjoying their gardens. You'll find a game board and instructions on the web page for this theme.

Souvenirs/Party Favors

Give each guest a plant — lucky bamboo or amaryllis — that they can take with them and enjoy at home. Send along plant care instructions, as well.

Fund Raisers

If you need to raise funds, buy a few exotic orchids and put them up for bid or sell floral products (e.g. bouquets of flowers, dried flower wreaths, gift cards with floral motifs, or framed prints of flowers or other botanicals).

Keywords

pots, planters, bonsai, fencing, harmony, trellis, stones, proportion, border, height, color, curves, lines, spring, summer, juxtapose, climbers, rock plants, conifers, magnolia, hibiscus, lavender, lilac, gardenia, columbine, star-cluster, heather, seeds, berries, variegated, foxglove, tea roses, jasmine, calico, bougainvillea, grasses, bamboo, aster, poppies, lilies, indigo, geranium, mums, fountains, water gardens, sweet-scented orchids, exotics, living sculpture, Monet's garden, alpine, romantic, shady, **www.celebration-solutions.com/garden.html**

Ambiance Themes

Introduction

Hollywood ... one of the most magical places in the world. The first movie studio was established there in 1911 on the site of an old citrus farm. During the 1920s and '30s, many popular radio shows originated in Hollywood and today, many television shows and movies are made there. Hollywood has become a synonym for glitz and glamor. Roll out the red carpet to greet your guests and treat them like stars!

Ambiance

Picture yourself out for a night at the Oscars. Park a couple of limousines at the entrance and roll out the red carpet. Use plenty of paparazzi with flashes going off to capture the arrival of each guest, and herald each guest to the crowd with a formal announcement.

Colors

Use "glitz and glamour" colors of black, white and gold.

Suggested Attire

The suggested attire is pure Hollywood ... black tie, evening gowns and the ever-present sunglasses. If you want to turn this into a costume party, ask your guests to come as their favorite movie star.

Invitations

"And the Winner is ... You ... If you join us for a night in Hollywood." Cover your invitations with gold stars and glitter or buy some fan magazines. Paste pictures of your guests in the magazine and place your invitation on the cover.

Decorations

Set the tables with white linens, white china and gold "Oscar" statuettes. You may be able to have a confectioner create these statuettes for you in chocolate and wrap them in gold foil. Around the statuettes, sprinkle gold and black confetti, gold film spools and black and white film clappers.

Roll out the red carpet and use theater-style crowd barriers to frame the entrance to the room. Honor your guests with their own star on the "Wall of Fame."

Keywords

Oscars, Academy Awards, lights, fame, stars, starlets, producers, actors, directors, film, walk of stars, glitz, glitter, gala, balloons, cameras, "Cut!," "Action!," microphones, dollies, spot lights, move slates, movie posters, directors chairs, cameras, paparazzi, film crew, ceremony "And the Winner Is ..." statuette, tabloids, sparkly gowns, black tie, evening wear, glamour, HOLLYWOOD sign on the hill, champagne, ritzy hors d'oerves, Tinsel Town, orchestra, clips, trailers, Hollywood and Vine, Sunset Boulevard, Hollywood Bowl, broadcasting studio,

6

Hollywood

Create large gold stars using metallic paper and print each guest's name in large bold letters. Pick some famous films and assign each one of your guests a role, then "roll the credits" on the wall using a projector. Use cutouts of famous actors or director's chairs to fill any empty spaces in the room.

Menu

Consider this "not your average Hollywood & Vine" menu.
- appetizers: *Doctor Zhivago* blini with caviar and crème fraiche
- main course: *Godfather* pasta and *Gladiator* antipasto salad
- dessert: *Forrest Gump* chocolates, *Driving Miss Daisy* praline ice cream
- specialty drinks: *Casablanca* champagne, *French Connection* biscotti and coffee

Entertainment

Hire celebrity look alikes to make an appearance. Use these actors to help you officiate an "Oscar" style awards ceremony. Nominate each guest for a prize but draw the winners at random. Make the awards funny like "Best Shopper" or "Most likely to …".

Give guests a chance to have their own video screen test. Set up small video booths, give the guest(s) a script from a famous movie or play and have them act out the part(s). Let the camera operators decide which clips should be in the running for the best screen test and play the winners for the crowd.

Souvenirs/Party Favors

At each place setting, place a tabloid sheet that describes the guest starring in a role in a major motion picture. Look at the cover of Variety (a movie industry magazine) for ideas. As guests leave, give them a DVD of a classic Hollywood film. Wrap the DVD in metallic gold wrapping paper and tie the ribbon in the shape of a black bow tie.

Fund Raisers

If you need to raise funds, raffle off a romantic limousine ride around the city to see the lights after the celebration.

Keywords

celebrity, gossip, fashion, the biz, critics, execs, directors, promoters, made-fors (made for TV movies), agents, writers, scribblers, treatments, scripts, cliches, Variety, backstage, playbill, box office, drama, thriller, romantic comedy, epic, Screen Actors Guild, new release, coming soon, film shorts, screening, grand opening, screenwriter, cinematography, awards ceremony, casting couch, film festival, casting director, day player, extras, grip, makeup, on location, props, shoot, stand-in, wardrobe, costumes, **www.celebration-solutions.com/hollyw.html**

Ambiance Themes

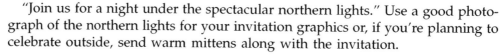

Introduction

The *Aurora Borealis* or northern lights is a luminous atmospheric phenomenon consisting of rapidly shifting patches and dancing columns of light across the night sky. The auroras can take almost any shape including an auroral arch, an auroral bend, filaments and streamers, a corona, auroral clouds, nebulous masses and an auroral glow. Invite your guests for an evening under the spectacular northern lights.

Ambiance

Picture the porch of a lodge, deep in the Alaskan wilderness. Lower the temperature in the room so that the air is crisp and cool. Use a fog machine and create a little movement with a slow-moving fan. Use scented candles or potpourri to give the room a pine scent and keep the lighting low to show off the "aurora" effects. Don't forget the occasional sound of feet crunching through the snow or a wolf howling in the distance.

If you're going to hold this party out of doors, don't let your guests get too cold! Bring along lap blankets and pocket warmers.

Colors

Use "shimmering" colors of metallic gold, metallic silver and midnight blue.

Suggested Attire

The suggested attire is "keep yourself warm" attire — flannel shirts anyone?

Invitations

"Join us for a night under the spectacular northern lights." Use a good photograph of the northern lights for your invitation graphics or, if you're planning to celebrate outside, send warm mittens along with the invitation.

Decorations

Set the tables with midnight blue table cloths and white china. Fill the center of the table with big white candles, greenery and pine cones. Scatter multicolored glitter in the greenery and add small gold and silver balls near the candles.

Keywords

Aurora Borealis, Aurora Australis, Aurora Polaris, colorful, magnetic poles, white, yellow, red, and green sky, solar wind, luminous expanding arcs, quiet glow, fog-like, vertical streamers, protons and electrons in the magnetic field, atmospheric phenomenon, terrestrial, corona, clouds, nebula, masses, glow, arch, bend, ray-filled curtains, filaments, converging rays, north country, twilight curtain, substorm, banded rays, satellite streaks, curtain edge, astronomical midnight, geomagnetic disturbance, great magnetic storm, ultraviolet, magneto-

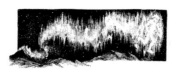

Northern Lights

To create the northern lights effect, drape long lengths of colored, sparkly gauze material in streamers across the ceiling. Aim rotating spot lights with colored gels on the streamers to simulate the changing colors of the aurora lights.

For the walls, create silhouettes of pine trees. You can make the branches look like they have snow on them by using white glitter paint. Make the trees in different sizes and place the smaller ones higher up on the walls to create the illusion of distance.

Menu

Consider this hearty "warm you to the core" menu.
- appetizers: hot artichoke dip on toasted bread
- main course: hearty beef stew in sour dough bread bowls
- dessert: hot honey-roasted almonds in waffle cones
- specialty drinks: hot buttered rum and hot chocolate or Alaskas (gin, green Chartreuse, orange bitters, lemon twist)

Entertainment

Hire a storyteller to tell an adventure tale of the northern wilderness or to read parts of *The Call of the Wild* by Jack London. Teach your kids to play *Grizzly*. This is a game based upon the 16th Century game *Goose*. To win the game, you must traverse the wilderness and reach the cozy cabin without encountering too many grizzly bears. You'll find a gameboard and instructions on the web page for this theme.

Souvenirs/Party Favors

Serve hot drinks in a big mug that your guests can take home, or give each guest a copy of *Northern Lights* by Calvin Hall (photographer) or *Secrets of the Aurora Borealis* by Syun-Ichi Akasofu (photographer).

Fund Raisers

If you need to raise funds, sell tickets to the planetarium or hold a silent auction for a personal tour of an observatory.

Keywords

sphere, telemetry, spectral emissions, solar wind, charged particles, upper atmosphere, ionosphere, oxygen = yellow and green, high-altitude oxygen = red, nitrogen = blue, neutral nitrogen = purple, dazzling, bright, brilliant, vivid, splendent, stunning, beaming, sparkling, gleaming, awestruck, amazed, speechless, wonder, Alaska, cold, polar bears, grizzly bears, Eskimo, snowshoe, salmon, moose, eagle, stars, clouds, river ice, snowshoes, mittens, hats, hot cocoa, roaring fire, Hot Toddy, cool, **www.celebration-solutions.com/northern.html**

Celebration Solutions

Ambiance Themes

Introduction

Astronomy is the oldest science, dating back thousands of years to a time when primitive peoples catalogued objects in the night sky. Constellations are named after religious or mythological figures, animals, or objects. Although they were named by astronomers and poets as long as 4,000 years ago, the real reason for naming the constellations was to help tell one star from another.

The great hunter *Orion* is one of the most popular constellations. He is always accompanied by *Canus Major*, his faithful dog, who is forever chasing *Lepus*, the hare. Take your guests back to a time when the nighttime sky had no competition from city lights and the 10,000 stars shone brightly.

Ambiance

Spend an evening stargazing. Use twinkle lights to give the room a planetarium feel and play the soundtracks from popular television shows or movies about outer space in the background.

Colors

Use "deep space" colors of black, white, metallic silver and metallic gold.

Suggested Attire

The suggested attire is "under the stars" casual.

Invitations

"Star light, star bright …" Create your own constellation to give guests directions to the party or use real star charts. A beautiful star chart would be a good souvenir of the party as well as a good invitation.

Decorations

Set the tables with black tablecloths and white china. For centerpieces, gather gold and silver starburst garland in a bouquet and scatter silver and gold confetti stars of all different sizes around the table.

Laminate photographs of stellar phenomena like spiral galaxies or nebulas for placemats.

Keywords

stars, Sun, solar system, Mercury, Venus, Earth, Mars, Jupiter, Saturn, Uranus, Neptune, Pluto, Milky Way, Andromeda, Cassiopeia, galaxy, Terrestrial, Jovian, Moon, constellations, eclipse, Big Dipper, Sirius, Orion, Perseus, Pegasus, Medusa, Ursa Minor, Ursa Major, Hercules, meteor, meteorite, meteor shower, astronomical, planets, celestial, Zodiac, comet, star projector, reclining seats, night sky, seasonal changes, sun, moon, planets, supernova, telescope, NASA, space exploration, starlit dome, "star citizen," orbit, astronomer, cosmic,

Planetarium

On the walls, hang posters of constellations or you can create them by using midnight blue poster board with glow-in-the-dark stars.

Menu

Since the harvest was the time when ancient peoples looked to the stars for guidance, consider this "celebration of the harvest" menu.
- appetizers: butternut squash soup and pepitas (seasoned pumpkin seeds)
- main course: turkey and dressing with cranberry sauce
- dessert: pumpkin pie
- specialty drinks: Xeres (manzanilla sherry, bitters and orange twist) or Jupiters (gin, dry vermouth, crème de violette, orange juice)

Entertainment

If you are unable to hold your celebration in an actual planetarium, use a star projector to create a planetarium show on the ceiling. Give guests a chance to mingle awhile before you ask them to be seated and lower the lights. Play "celestial" music in the background while a master of ceremonies narrates the show. Or, arrange for a showing of video clips from famous space events, such as the first landing on the moon, or one of the popular IMAX productions.

Afterward the show, set up a telescope(s) and ask a knowledgeable "star-gazer" to give your guests a guided tour of the skies.

Souvenirs/Party Favors

Give each guest a constellation chart, photographs from the Hubble telescope, or a screen saver of stellar phenomenon.

Fund Raisers

If you need to raise funds, sell stars! There are services that will let you name your own star and give you a star chart of where the star is in space. Or, sell star machines that shine constellations on the ceiling or the Stellarscope Portable Planetarium — a hand-held telescope that identifies the 40 brightest stars and 70 major constellations.

Keywords

soar, blackness of space, "All systems are go," "Houston ... we have lift-off," space race, space exploration, Sputnik, rocket launch, satellites, capsules, space shuttle, astrophysicist, phases of the Moon, navigation, axis, solar, lunar, asterisms, celestial sphere, prime meridian, vernal equinox, asteroid, solar flare, magnetic field, pulsar, black hole, brown dwarf, red giant, constellation, Greek heroes, argonauts, centaur, heavenly, astronomical, extraterrestrial, stellar, starry, planetary, asteroidal, lunar, **www.celebration-solutions.com/planet.html**

Celebration Solutions

Decoration Themes

Introduction

Art Deco was a style popular in the 1920s and '30s used primarily in the design of buildings, furniture, jewelry, and interiors. Art Deco is characterized by sleek, streamlined forms and geometric patterns. Two of the most famous of all of the Art Deco buildings are the Chrysler Building and the Empire State Building in New York City.

Art Deco often borrowed design forms from archaeology. King Tut was discovered during the period and many Egyptian motifs found their way into Art Deco designs. Take your guests back to the '30s with sleek, geometric designs.

Ambiance

Picture a romantic night out at a traditional jazz club. Keep the lighting low by using track lighting along the walls or spot lights aimed at the wall decorations.

Colors

Use rich, '30s colors of Italian marble green, sensuous peach and shiny chrome.

Suggested Attire

The suggested attire is "sophisticated" cocktail.

Invitations

"Please join us for an evening in high Art Deco style." The Chrysler building is the one of the most recognizable Art Deco buildings, so you could use this distinctive shape for your invitations, or create an invitation out of thin, colored metal that can be worked easily into an Art Deco-style shape.

Decorations

Set the tables with marble green fabric, chrome place settings and fancy cut-glass glassware. For centerpieces, fill clear, square vases three quarters full with peach colored glass beads. Place a single, large flower blossom just below the top edge of the vase and place the vase on a round mirror.

On the walls, create large, bold, geometric shapes like diamonds filled with squares and circles. Rather than use solid colors, cut the geometric shapes from

Keywords

geometric, sleek, streamlined, chrome, glass, repetition of forms, clean lines, symmetry, Tiffany glass, metal, porcelain, enamel, exotic woods, black and gold, Chrysler Building, Empire State Building, American Radiator Building, Rockefeller Center, Roxy Theater, Waldorf-Astoria Hotel, New York Daily News Building, Radio City Music Hall, seamless surfaces, aerodynamic horizontal lines, linoleum, glass bricks, eclectic, elegant style, cool sophistication, graciousness of form, jazz, tap dancing, Hollywood musicals, Bakelite radios, tiered buildings,

Art Deco

wrapping paper with subtle patterns to give the shapes a little texture. Choose three to four shapes to create a pattern and repeat the pattern around the room.

Menu

Consider this "sophisticated bistro" menu.

- appetizers: Caesar salad
- main course: roast beef sandwiches with a choice of dips — au jous, spicy mustard, honey mustard, fajita-spice mayonnaise and onion-garlic cream cheese
- dessert: a variety of cheesecakes with fruit or chocolate toppings
- specialty drinks: Millionaires (bourbon, curacao, egg white, grenadine)

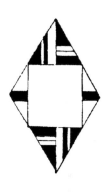

Entertainment

Play romantic instrumental music from the '30s. Harlem jazz had its own sound. Hire a DJ who has access to an original collection of these records or arrange to play one of the many compilations out on CD.

The Chrysler and Empire State buildings are two of the most famous Art Deco buildings in America. Ask all guests to be seated and deliver a 3D puzzle of either one of these buildings to each table. See which table can put together the puzzle the quickest. Give a nice bottle(s) of wine to the group that wins.

Souvenirs/Party Favors

Give each guest nice Art Deco notecards or one of the many beautiful coffee table books about Tiffany glass (e.g. *Louis Comfort Tiffany at the Metropolitan Museum of Art* by Alice Cooney Frelingheysen or *Tiffany's 20th Century* by John Loring) or Art Deco style (e.g. *Art Deco* by Young Mi Kim, *American Art Deco* by Alastair Duncan or *Essential Art Deco* by Ghislaine Wood).

Fund Raisers

Tiffany-style stained glass, lamp shades and freestanding pieces were all the rage during the Art Deco era. If you need to raise funds, contact a stained glass artist who creates pieces in the Tiffany or Art Deco styles and arrange to sell pieces on consignment.

Keywords

surface ornamentation, exotic building materials, striking facades, cohesive environments, industrial design, aerodynamic, high-speed look, graphic style, furniture, clothing, jewelry, stepped forms, rounded corners, striped elements, black, neon, chrome, terrazzo, clean lines, vivid colors, poster art, modernism, innovation, streamlined, vibrant colors, simple shapes, hallmarks of geometry and simplicity, celebrating technology, intense colors, strong lines, architecture, clothing, industry, jewelry, **www.celebration-solutions.com/artdeco.html**

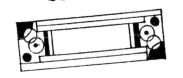

Decoration Themes

Introduction

The colors black and white are contrast in the extreme: one is all colors in the spectrum combined, the other is the absence of color. While it's correct that true black and true white don't occur often in nature except in new fallen snow or a moonless night, the contrast is marvelous for a decorating scheme.

Ambiance

This theme is all about contrast. To make the contrast of black and white dramatic, keep the lighting high. Low lighting will make the black look muddy grey and the white look dull. If you want to add sparkle, use shiny metallic silver in the decorations. Use chocolate in your decorations and you'll give the room a pleasant smell as well.

Colors

Use the only logical colors for this theme ... black and white.

Suggested Attire

The suggested attire is anything from sexy, sophisticated Fred Astaire "white" tie to laid-back Harley Davidson "black" leather. Let your guests decide but instruct guests to wear only black and white. If you want to add a splash of color, give each guest a red rose, purple iris or yellow orchid corsage or boutonniere.

Invitations

Send your guests a "sweet" invitation. Work with a chocolatier to create a block of dark chocolate as a base with "You're Invited" in white chocolate on the top. Affix the invitation details to the lid of a bright white box tied with a black satin ribbon.

Decorations

Set the tables with white tablecloths and white china. Place a black square cloth in the middle of the table to create a diamond shape stretching from edge to edge. In the center of the table use white candles of different heights on a black, shiny tile.

Keywords

checkerboard, reversed out, silhouette, chocolate, vanilla, leather, white tie, B & W pictures, B & W movies, silent films, snow, cotton, yin yang, White House, tuxedo, bow tie, polar bear, black holes, stars, space, night sky, gleaming metal, crows, killer whales, crude oil, pepper, salt, record albums, black sheep, Penny Black, diamonds, bat, blackbird, spiders, bats, black angus cows, oboe, clarinet, bassoon, Tasmanian devil, Beluga whale, clouds, chickens, cream, milk, doves, gardenia, igloo, ghosts, ice, rice, White House, teeth, snowy owl,

Black and White

On the walls, hang long sheets of black butcher paper. Cover some sheets with black and white photographs — portraits, artsy shots, old postcards — anything in black and white. Create a giant piano keyboard or a tuxedo on another sheet. Create a checkerboard from foam squares on another.

In any empty spots throughout the room, place a few huge dice made from packing boxes and fuzzy fabric dots and large stuffed animals like pandas, skunks, zebras, and killer whales.

Menu

Consider this "color coordinated" dessert menu.

- dessert: chocolate, chocolate, chocolate — cream puffs with chocolate sauce, chocolate praline ice cream with white chocolate chips, black and white hazelnut mousse cake, chocolate meringue sandwiches, marble brownies
- specialty drinks: champagne, Irish coffee (whiskey, hot black coffee, whipped cream and sugar), latte drinks

Entertainment

Hire a pianist to play on a black or white grand piano — naturally! After dinner, clear everything from the tables. Bring each table several boxes of dominoes. Instruct each table to work together to create a toppling domino sculpture. When all of the tables are finished, instruct one table after another to start their creations "tumbling." Ask guests to vote for their favorite. Give the guests at that table a nice prize.

Souvenirs/Party Favors

Send each guest home with a box of black and white chocolates. Wrap the chocolates in a black box tied with a white ribbon and bow.

Fund Raisers

If you need to raise funds, conduct a silent auction for nice sets of dominoes, backgammon or chess games and any objects you have used for decorations such as the giant pandas or whales.

Keywords

snowman, swan, bones, cow, dalmatian, marble, dice, panda, piano keyboard, newspaper, penguin, puffin, skunk, zebra, barcode, ermine, lithograph, obsidian, quartz, black widow, witch, haunted house, black belt, martial arts uniform, black walnut, Black and Decker, Black Jack, foam, Black Forest, Black Sea, ink, locomotive, black cat, top hat, black ops, black and white television, black box recorder, White Pages, white collar, white sand beaches, "I'm dreaming of a white Christmas," White Sox, flour, **www.celebration-solutions.com/bandw.html**

Decoration Themes

Introduction

The calendar is a system for measuring time into days, weeks and months. Traditionally, calendars helped to organize life in accordance with the sun and the stars — to determine when to plant, when to harvest and when to hold religious celebrations. The beginnings of the Chinese calendar can be traced back more than 4,000 years with the names of years repeating only once every 60 years. The original Roman calendar had only 304 days. In 1582, the Gregorian calendar corrected inaccuracies by establishing leap years. Today we have calendars on our desks, in our briefcases and on our walls. To put a little twist on this theme, celebrate the 29th day of February which occurs only in leap years.

Ambiance

While many of us bemoan yet another birthday, this theme is a fun, lighthearted look at the passage of time. Keep the lighting high to show off the decorations. Put together a mix of music across the decades to play in the background. Musical tastes and styles changed slowly, so play two or three songs from each decade from the turn of the 20th Century to the present, and play them in order.

Colors

Use "natural" colors of bright blue, tan and purple.

Suggested Attire

The suggested attire is up to the guest. Ask guests to dress to represent the month in which they were born — July babies in shorts and December babies in hats and mittens.

Invitations

"On this day in history … We delighted in your company at our party." Look up pertinent dates in history for the date of your party and include your celebration as one of the "greatest" events to take place on that date.

Decorations

Set the tables with bright blue table tablecloths and white china. Create large "twenty-nines" out of tan felt for the center of the table, and scatter colorful confetti in numbers from 1 to 31 all around the table.

Keywords

Julian, perpetual, Celestial, Eras, Gregorian, Lunar, Hebrew, Islamic, Aztec, Maya, days, weeks, months, years, leap years, celebrations, harvest, moon, sun, winter solstice, summer solstice, chronogram, almanac, chronology, chronicle, annals, register, daybook, ephemeris, date, vernal equinox, autumnal equinox, tropical year, synodic month, phases of the Moon, daylight savings time, spring forward, fall back, rotation of the Earth, Terrestrial Dynamic Time (TDT), liturgical year, civil year, International Atomic Time (IAT), solar calendar, lunar

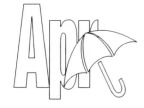

Calendar

Hunt out the bargains in February or March when the big wall calendars go on sale. Display different months on each calendar and ask each guest to sign their name on their birthdate. If you have a large guest list, you may need more than one calendar for each month. Group all of the calendars showing the same month together.

Menu

Consider this "29-course appetizer feast" menu to celebrate the 29 days of February during leap years. Think about things you can serve on bite-sized containers such as spoons, paper cones, waxpaper cups, shot glasses, demitasse cups, on tooth picks or in sake cups.

- appetizers: shrimp, spiced fries, spring rolls, empanaditas, meat balls, wantons, kabobs, mini croissants, gelato, toasted nuts, dips, cucumber canapes, tarts, toast and toppings, mini-muffins, cracker pizza, sushi, grape leaves
- desserts: cheesecake squares, cream puffs, brownie bites
- specialty drinks: Daydreams (passion fruit syrup, orange juice, ground nutmeg) or Blue Mondays (vodka, Cointreau, blue Curacao) or Leap Years (gin, sweet vermouth, Grand Marnier, lemon juice)

Entertainment

Celebrate the birthday of anyone in the crowd who was born on February 29th. Play a game of "ages and numbers." Give each table a tablet and a calculator. Ask each guest to list their birth year. Add the numbers together. Give prizes to the table with the "wisest" guests (oldest), most "youthful" (youngest), greatest "endurance" (greatest number of anniversaries), etc. Give a nice prize to each person at the winning table.

Souvenirs/Party Favors

Personalize calendars using pictures of people in your group. Make the calendar start on the day of the celebration and extend for the remainder of the current year and through the next year. Put milestones on the calendar such as birthdates, anniversaries or events.

Fund Raisers

If you need to raise funds, ask each guest to donate a recipe appropriate for their birth month. Publish and sell a group cookbook made from the recipes.

Keywords

calendar, lunisolar, astronomical clock, Cesium atom, astronomers, stargazer, astrographer, astrochemist, cosmographer, uranographer, soothsayer, astromancer, star diviner, planetary motion, Galileo, Copernicus, observatory, zodiac, solar timepiece, 365 days, 5 hours, 48 minutes, 45 seconds, stardate, Doomsday calendar, Advent calendar, day, week, month, quarter, countdown to the next holiday, calendar converters, sun and moon azimuth and elevation, star charts, agenda, card, schedule, **www.celebration-solutions.com/calendar.html**

Decoration Themes

Introduction

Clowns, jesters or fools have been entertaining party-goers for as long as there have been parties to go to. In the 16th Century, jesters were the "clowns" of the King's court. Clowns in whiteface date back to the 18th Century because the color white was easily achieved by using flour paste. Clowns of the circus and rodeo have been using a variation of the ancient whiteface makeup ever since. Treat your guests to a celebration of those silly jesters dedicated to bringing joy and happiness to audiences worldwide.

Ambiance

Picture the spectacle of a circus Big Top. Make it as bright and colorful, silly and fun as you can. Keep the lighting high to show off the bright colors and think about the sounds you would hear in the background at a circus — elephants, lions or tigers roaring, the crack of a whip, the swing of a trapeze and the crowds laughing and enjoying the clowns.

If you're going to hold this party out of doors, make a few enormous clown hats to mark the corners of the area you'll be using and string colorful pennants on a line in between the hats.

Colors

Use "clowning around" colors of blue, red, yellow and green.

Suggested Attire

The suggested attire is "bring in the clowns" casual.

Invitations

Make a clown face for your invitations. Cut a small, upside down "T" to create a triangle nose that will stand up and attach a red foam clown nose to it. Use red tinsel for hair and glue on rolling eyes and big, fake eyelashes. Attach red, wax lips and a colorful hat with a spiky ball for a pompon.

Decorations

Set the tables with tablecloths, plates and cups of all different colors. Make the

Keywords

balloons, white face, face paint, big shoes, polka dots, entertainment, mimes, circus, jugglers, big top, red nose, miniature car, jester, baggy clothes, funny hair, umbrella, ruffled collar, horn, circus, spotlight, tricks, multi-color, hobo, clown bowler hat, plastic nose and glasses, clown bow ties, clown nose, juggler, circus or carnival, jester, face painting, fool, tricks, buffoon, jester, conjurer, mirthmaker, tumbler, gleeman, mime, actor, harlequin, merry counselor, comic, puppeteer, rustic fool, exaggerated eyebrows, geometrical patterns on the cheeks, tiny

Clowns

room a jumble of color. Use colorful fleece ski hats for centerpieces. Use small wire cone-shaped frames to make the hats stand up at different angles. Use streamers to make the ceiling look like a circus tent. Attach all of the streamers to a small ring (12"-18") that is suspended from the center of the room. Then spread the streamers out in all directions. Leave just a little bit of slack in the streamers before they're attached to the top of the walls to simulate the sag of a tent roof. On the walls, hang light nylon cloth that can be drawn back like the openings in a circus tent. Hang the nylon from a dowel that can be secured to the ceiling tiles right along the walls. Use fishing line to draw the material back as if the tent has a flap open. In other wall areas, place circus posters or clown portraits. Throughout the room place pairs of oversized clown shoes or blow-up clowns.

Menu

Consider the "what you would find under the circus tent" menu.
- appetizers: popcorn, peanuts
- main course: hot dogs, corn dogs, hamburgers
- dessert: snow cones, funnel cakes, apple fries, cotton candy
- specialty drinks: blue raspberry lemonade

Entertainment

You'll need a few real clowns, of course! In addition, hire someone to create balloon animals when the clowns are not performing. Ask the person who will create the balloon animals to hold a demonstration and teach the crowd how to make a simple balloon animal.

Souvenirs/Party Favors

Give guests the colorful hats you used to decorate the tables.

Fund Raisers

If you need to raise funds, charge a small fee for balloon animals, face painting, hair braiding or carnival games.

Keywords

umbrella, big shoes, padded rear-end, tiny hat, bulbous red nose, mismatched clothing, funny hair, slapstick, Bozo, Charlie Chaplain, tramps, Red Skelton, Clem Kadiddlehopper, Freddie the Freeloader, Barnum & Bailey Clown College, honk honk, miniature cars, ric rac trim, big pom pon buttons, jester, ruffles, polka dots, big glasses, clown face, antics, acrobat, aerialist, Barnum and Bailey, calliope, Big Top, funambulist, grease paint, gag, jumbo, vehicle floats, zany, cutup, farceur, jokester, clodhopper, **www.celebration-solutions.com/clowns.html**

Decoration Themes

Introduction

Cryptography is the science of creating secret communications, intelligible only to the person possessing the key. Codes use words, phrases, syllables, numbers, and letters opposite their secret equivalents. Each end of the communication has to have a copy of the codebook. Unlike codes, ciphers utilize variables when they convert plaintext into ciphertext, so the receiver must have a key with the variables and a key that decodes the text. Codes and ciphers are the tools of spies, so engage your guests by letting them in on a "secret."

Ambiance

Think of mystery and intrigue … a meeting in a back alley … a puzzle to be solved. Keep the lighting low and uneven, like a classic Hitchcock film. Play spooky or mysterious music in the background. The soundtracks of mystery movies or sci-fi flicks might be a place to start looking.

Colors

Use dark, mysterious "spook" colors of deep green and charcoal grey.

Suggested Attire

The suggested attire is "cloak and dagger." Let your guests decide whether they will come dressed as James Bond or an undercover G-man.

Invitations

"Unlock the key to a great time." Create a crossword puzzle with the details and directions or print the invitation backwards so that it must be read in a mirror. Send a ransom note or a cyphertext with a codekey.

Decorations

Set the tables with deep green tablecloths and black china. Give each guest a "Top Secret" envelope at his or her place setting with a printed menu inside. Use a puzzle for your centerpiece. Print puzzles that have a cipher to be decoded once the puzzle is put together. Let your guests know what the menu or the evening's entertainment is in the deciphered code.

Keywords

puzzles, codes, code breakers, decoder rings, riddles, clues, Riddler, Sherlock Holmes, master spy, cryptogram, hidden meaning, enciphering, encoding, invisible ink, Scotland Yard, FBI, forensics, morse code, sign language, invisible ink, codebook, encryption, steganography, scrambler, secrecy, microfilm, lookup table, ciphertext, cryptographer, cryptograph, anagram, acrostic, compute, decode, decipher, crack the code, translate, interpret, render, explain, construe, solve, figure out, unravel, disentangle, mission, high-tech wizardry, surveillance, fool

```
100101
1110101
00100101
1110100
```

Codes & Ciphers

To create a spooky back alley look, create murals of old brick walls with graffiti on it. Against the walls, every so often place an old-fashioned lamppost. Don't forget some of the tools of spies — the cone of silence or the shoe telephone (for you Maxwell Smart fans), a jet pack, a Rolex blade-magnet-bullet deflector watch, or an underwater rebreather (for you James Bond fans).

Menu

Consider this "old adversary of the Cold War (Czechoslovakian)" menu. All dishes should be served "under cover" — of course!
- appetizers: Chlebicky (canapes — thin slices of smoked meat on bread)
- main course: Goulas (goulash — meat, vegetable soup), potato dumplings
- dessert: plum jam strudel with ice cream
- specialty drinks: East Wings (vodka, cherry brandy, Campari and lemon twist)

Entertainment

See how well your guests can decipher codes. Keep your guests working on one riddle after another and make each code to solve a contest between tables. Give a prize to the table that finishes each code first. When you create the codes, make the answer something familiar to the people in the group.

Souvenirs/Party Favors

As guests depart, give each guest a box wrapped all in black. Inside place some "stuff of spies" like a magnifying glass, a puzzle or riddle book, a DVD of a spy movie or a paperback of a spy story.

Fund Raisers

If you need to raise funds, conduct a "blind" auction. Auction Chinese boxes (boxes with hidden compartments). Tell guests what it's possible to win by bidding, but not what's actually in each box. For example, if you would auction 20 boxes, you would list all 20 items available, but not list which item goes in which box. Or, let guests solve riddles to figure out which box holds what prize.

Keywords

the enemy, box of tricks, secret, under wraps, covert, confidential, stealth, furtive, clandestine, subterfuge, evasion, ensconced, buried, shrouded, cloaked, veiled, masked, incognito, camouflaged, unrevealed, undisclosed, secluded, secretive, isolated, obscure, abstruse, mysterious, arcane, cryptic, mystical, enigmatic, puzzling, anagram, deductive reasoning, game, garble, flip-flop, filter, secrecy, hidden, underhanded, covert, riddle, conundrum, crossword, clandestine, furtive, hole-and-corner, **www.celebration-solutions.com/codes.html**

Decoration Themes

Introduction

As early as the 11th Century, the Chinese were making rockets and explosives. Gunpowder used during battle was also used for celebrations of victory or peace. Fireworks displays became popular in resorts and public gardens in the 19th Century and are used for many celebrations today. There's something magical about fireworks. They're here and then they're gone. Imagine your guests looking up into the night sky with anticipation of the next illuminated burst and the wonderment as the splendor fades away.

Ambiance

Think ooooh, ahhhhh — awe and wonder. Keep the lighting low to highlight the light show and play audio files of firework bursts and crowds ooohing and aaahing occasionally in the background. Fireworks bursts have an unmistakable smell. It's too dangerous to keep unexploded fireworks indoors, but the spent shells will give you the smell you're after.

Colors

Use "eye-popping" colors of cobalt blue, metallic silver and gold, and violet.

Suggested Attire

The suggested attire is "4th of July" casual.

Invitations

"Come to an ooooooh … no … ahhhhhh-some celebration." Find a star burst or use a photocard of a firework burst for your invitation. Or, send a fiber-optic light wand with the invitation.

Decorations

Set the tables with cobalt blue tablecloths and white china. For centerpieces, use fiber-optic or laser lights that continuously change color. Cover small paper mache stars with gold, silver or violet glitter glue and pile different sizes and colors around the base of the laser light. Fill decorative star tins with candy for each place setting.

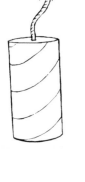

Keywords

sulfur, charcoal, festivities, red, white, blue, firecrackers, aerial shells, aerial display, pyrotechnics, patriotic, sparklers, bottle rockets, roman candles, CABOOM, flares, illuminated, smoke, explosion, explosive, incendiary, illumination, gunpowder, potassium chlorate, saltpeter, charcoal, sulfur, pinwheels, smoke screen, flare, flash powder, sparkler, aluminum, iron, zinc or magnesium dust, stars, bursting charge, fuse, shell, mortar, shower of sparks, multibreak shells, palm, round, ring, roundel, serpentine, blast, discharge, detonation, bang, boom,

Fireworks

Create a fireworks show on the ceiling. Cover the ceiling with midnight blue balloons that have small dots of glitter paint on them to look like a starry sky. Create starbursts by bundling wire together like a bouquet, bending the individual wires out like a starburst and attaching large metallic confetti stars to the ends of the wires. Hang them from the ceiling high enough so that even the tallest guest will not bump into them.

For the walls, use good poster-sized photographs of firework bursts around famous monuments like the Statue of Liberty or Washington Monument.

Menu

Consider this "typical 4th of July" menu.
- appetizers: pasta salad with feta cheese and cherry tomatoes
- main course: chicken salad sandwiches with BBQ beans
- dessert: watermelon quarters and peanut butter-chocolate pralines
- specialty drinks: lemonade or Strawberry-Banana Kefir (banana, strawberries, honey, vanilla yogurt and apple juice)

Entertainment

Hire a pyrotechnics company to put on a fireworks show out of doors. Pyrotechnics are also possible indoors, but they can be very dangerous if not done properly. If you want to conduct an indoor pyrotechnics show, you'll need a venue that will allow for such a show and a professional pyrotechnics firm to set up and run the fireworks.

Souvenirs/Party Favors

Send each guest home with a black T-shirt with a colorful firework burst design on it.

Fund Raisers

If you need to raise funds, sell tickets for your fireworks show to members of the public, or auction off the fireworks prints you used for decorations.

Keywords

burst, eruption, crash, thunder, shot, crack, report, salvo, volley, fusillade, outburst, burst, flare-up, eruption, flammable, percussion, bangers, burn, thermodynamics, rocket plumes, plume flicker, glitter, sparkle, twinkle, flicker, wink, shimmer, bedazzle, gleam, glare, illuminate, radiant, gloss, shine, luster, iridescence, splendor, radiance, bombette, ball stars, comet, shell, firefly, glitter, burst charge, strobe-pot, rocket, Roman candle, aerial salute, whizzer, shoot, plummet, beaming, brilliant, incandescent, **www.celebration-solutions.com/firework.html**

Celebration Solutions

Decoration Themes

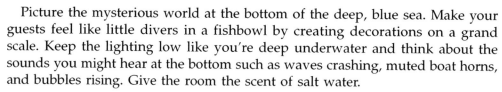

Introduction

There is a magical world under the sea. Sea serpents have long inspired fascination and terror of the possibility of fire-breathing, mariner-eating monsters. Picture an animal whose head can reach the top of a mast, with a body as broad as a ship covered with shellwork or scales, paddlelike paws and a pointed snout that spouts like a whale. Imagine a world where not only are there fantastical sea serpents, but colorful forests of seaweed, carpets of starfish, and clams so large that their shells can be used as bath tubs. Take your guests on a deep sea dive down to the wild home of the sea creatures.

Ambiance

Picture the mysterious world at the bottom of the deep, blue sea. Make your guests feel like little divers in a fishbowl by creating decorations on a grand scale. Keep the lighting low like you're deep underwater and think about the sounds you might hear at the bottom such as waves crashing, muted boat horns, and bubbles rising. Give the room the scent of salt water.

Colors

Use "bottom-of-the-deep-blue-sea" colors of bright blue, green and yellow.

Suggested Attire

The suggested attire is "deep in the brine" casual.

Invitations

"Come to a party 'Under the Boardwalk' … *way under*." Use a cartoon character with its head underwater, or a photograph of brightly-colored fish. Or, fill a small jar or glass bowl with glass beads or the colored rocks used for fish tanks along with a small plastic diver to hold your message.

Decorations

Set the tables with deep blue tablecloths and bright yellow place settings. Make placemats using photographs of brightly-colored fish or other underwater scenes. Create a sea of "bubbles" at the top of the room using blue balloons in different shades and different sizes. Allow a few strings of bubbles to look like they're

Keywords

legendary sea creatures, Loch Ness Monster, mermaid, submersibles, early underwater gear, bubbles, aquariums, underwater, divers, shipwrecks, coral reefs, killer whale, scuba, gills, fins, scales, sharks, eels, stingray, sea serpent, ocean, lakes, rivers, star fish, fishnet, fish hooks, lobster, crab, shark, guppy, tuna, sailfish, marlin, halibut, puffers, swordfish, herring, minnows, sunfish, perch, seaweed, catfish, tropical, sea bass, sea horse, anglers, cod, trout, guppies, tank, marine museum, lanternfish, starfish, skeleton, shells, schools of fish,

Sea Creatures

rising up to the surface by anchoring them on different lengths of string from the floor. Build a seaweed forest from green, see-through gauze material anchored at the top and bottom by dowels. Give the walls portholes with the faces of giant creatures looking in or cover an entire wall with a design that look like the scales of a large sea creature. To make the design look more real, give it one large flipper made of gauze or tissue paper on a wire frame that will move with the movement of the air. As a finishing touch, create a life-sized, old-fashioned underwater diver with an old, metal, bubble helmet. Surround the diver with oversized, colorful styrofoam rocks … just like the diver would look at the bottom of a fish tank.

Menu

Consider this "drawn from the deep" menu.
- appetizers: seafood bisque with mini crab cakes
- main course: hearty paella with a medley of "sea" foods
- dessert: mint ice cream with deep green "sea weed" frosting topped with gold (chocolate) coins
- specialty drinks: Blue champagne (vodka, curacao, Cointreau, lemon juice and champagne)

Entertainment

Hire a storyteller to do a reading from the *Rime of the Ancient Mariner* or *20,000 Leagues under the Sea*. Teach your guests to play *Squid*. This is a game based upon the 12th Century game *Gluckshaus*. To win the game, you must navigate the ocean depths without encountering the giant squid. You'll find a board and game rules on the web page for this theme.

Souvenirs/Party Favors

Send guests home with a screen saver of underwater scenes.

Fund Raisers

If you need to raise funds, sell seafood cookbooks, dinners for two at a seafood restaurant, or annual passes to a local aquarium.

Keywords

snorkel, scuba gear, breathing apparatus, giant squid, giant octopus, Captain Nemo, mermaid, 20,000 Leagues Under the Sea, Jules Verne, nautilus, serpent, shrimp, crawfish, anemone, angelfish, scorpionfish, ocean depths, flying fish, ammonites, fossils, mollusk, clams, plankton, saber-toothed salmon, sea stars, Tasmanian globster, Bermuda blob, megamouth shark, sea stars, blue-ringed octopus, cone shells, bristle worms, fire coral, stingrays, moray eels, pearl essence, mollusk, crustacean, spawn, **www.celebration-solutions.com/seacr.html**

Decoration Themes

Introduction

Stamps were first used in England in 1840 featuring a portrait of Queen Victoria on a black background called the Penny Black. Today, stamp collecting is one of the most popular hobbies in the world. Stamps come in all shapes and sizes and are issued by almost every nation in the world, one Continent (Antarctica) and the Vatican. Transport your guests back to romantic days gone by decorating with stamps from countries or empires that no longer exist.

Ambiance

Imagine a journey back in time to a gallery of lost empires. Keep the lighting bright to show off the decorations and use music from 19th Century to play in the background.

Colors

Use traditional "ink" colors of vermillion red, ultramarine blue and grey green.

Suggested Attire

The suggested attire is "travel around the world with a backpack" casual.

Invitations

"We're sure to get your 'stamp' of approval at our celebration." Go to a stamp dealer and buy a package of stamps from the British Empire and around the world to fix onto your invitations.

Decorations

Set the tables with ultramarine blue tablecloths, vermillion red place settings and grey green napkins. Any stamps you have left over from your invitations could be laminated into placemats or napkin rings. Purchase old-fashioned post-cards and create a ring of postcards in the center of the table using placard holders.

Blow up some of the more interesting stamps such as the triangle-shaped stamps to poster size. Consult a stamp guide for interesting stamps from places such as Bechuanaland, Burma, Cape of Good Hope, Ceylon, Christmas Island, Falkland

Keywords

Philatelic, travel, postage, destination, far away places, post mark, philatelic, blocks, singles, first day covers, plate blocks, mint sheets, plate numbers, magnifying glass, tongs, hinges, stamp mounts, catalogs, collector's books, the Penny Black, philately, pre-cancelled, cancelled, triangle, Inverted Jenny, misprints, commemoratives, pictorials, topicals, proofs, lithography, perforation, stock book, glassine envelopes, topicals, mint condition, aerogram, airmail, authentication, watermark, booklet, cancel, triangles, certified mail, revenue stamps, duck

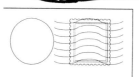

Stamps

Islands, Gibraltar, Hong Kong, Madagascar, Malawi, Malta, Montserrat, Niue, Penrhyn, Tanzania, or Tokelau.

Menu

Consider this "cuisine from around the British Empire" menu.

- appetizers: cockle and muscle chowder from Ireland
- main course: Seekh kababs (meat and vegetable kebabs) from India
- dessert: coconut and almond cookies with vanilla sherbet from Persia
- specialty drinks: Imperial Fizz (blended whiskey, light rum, fresh lemon juice, sugar, sparkling water) or Commonwealth Cocktails (Canadian whiskey, Grand Marnier, lemon juice, orange twist)

Entertainment

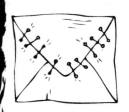

Match the entertainment to the feast. Change the music with the course being served — Celtic music with the appetizers, Indian music with the main course, and Persian music with the dessert. Play a game of *Where in the World?* The world is a very different place today than it was in the 19th Century when stamps were first used. Look through a stamp guide and pick out a list of countries that no longer exist. Give your guests an outline of each continent and see if they can place these countries in the correct place.

Souvenirs/Party Favors

Give each guest a small stamp collection from different countries that they can take home as a souvenir. Place a rare or valuable stamp in one set. At the appointed time, ask guests to look at their stamps and announce which one is the winning stamp.

Fund Raisers

If you need to raise funds, look at the stamp sets sold through the U.S. Postal Service (www.stampsonline.com) or other philatelic services (www.philatelic.com or www.philately.com). There are stamp collecting kits for all interests from Disney stamps to worldwide collections.

Keywords

stamps, coil, counterfeit, definitive, die cut, embossing, express, face value, fancy cancel, franking, gravure, imperforate, intaglio, inverts, engraving, miniature sheet, nondenominated, overprint, pair, parcel post, postage due, postcard, se-tenant, zeppelins, zip code, hobby, British Commonwealth, watermark, British colonial, Zanzibar, halfpenny, Transvaal, Stellaland, Straights Settlements, aerogramme, cancel mark, triangulars, coils, errors, forgery, mint, die proofs, dead letter, seal, seapost, airpost, **www.celebration-solutions.com/stamps.html**

Celebration Solutions

Destination Themes

Introduction

Antarctica is the fifth largest continent and the last to be discovered. Antarctica lies 600 miles from South America and 2,500 miles from Africa. Until the 1770s, Antarctica was a place of legend, a myth. It is surrounded by an often stormy, ice-dotted sea. It's the windiest place in the world where gales can hit 200 miles per hour (322 kph). Mean temperatures are generally about 20° F (11° C) making the Antarctic the coldest region in the world. The people who have ventured down to Antarctica are a hearty, brave, adventurous, if not quirky, bunch. Bundle up your guests for a trip to the bottom of the world.

Ambiance

Picture a cold, frozen, mysterious wasteland. Keep the lighting high to accentuate the white color. Backgrounds sounds are a must. Use sounds of the howling wind, the creak of the ice, the occasional sound of a barking dog or a voice calling out way off in the distance.

Colors

Use "frozen" colors of white, white, white, silver and light grey.

Suggested Attire

The suggested attire is "keep yourself warm and cozy" casual.

Invitations

"Join us for an adventure to the land *down under*, the land down under." Invite your guests to "Expedition Antarctica" by using photographs of the frozen continent, or sending a frozen treat. You don't have to send the real thing, a gift certificate to the local ice cream shop would do. Or, send the DVD of *Shackleton* to get your guests in the mood.

Decorations

Set the tables with white tablecloths and white china. Consult a chocolatier for your centerpieces. Antarctica is full of tall mountain peaks. How about a chocolate mountain with white chocolate capped peaks? The wait staff can play a role

Keywords

South Pole, iceberg, ice shelf, snow, below zero, glaciers, South Shetland islands, Mount Erebus, coldest temp - 128.6 F, aurora australis, geomagnetic pole, Captain James Cook (1773), Robert Falcon Scott (1901), Ernest Shackleton (1908), Roald Admundson reached the South Pole in 1911, seal hunters, extreme cold, scientific stations, Antarctic Treaty, gusty wind, beaches, jagged coastline, Antarctic Convergence, ice shelves, calving, icebergs, prevailing winds, circumpolar currents, Transantarctic Mountains, Ross Island, continuous darkness,

Antarctica

in your decorations, too. Ask them to dress all in white — white jackets, white shirts, white ties and white pants.

For the walls, use posters of polar expeditions, dog sleds, or explorers on skis. To make the room look like the remote antarctic, you'll need snow … movie prop snow, that is. Use the fake snow to sprinkle on the tables, create drifts or use a blower to make it "snow" over the entrance to the room.

Menu

Consider this "warm … warm … warm" menu. Put together a basket with a small thermos of each item in this menu.

- appetizers: tomato soup with fresh mozzarella
- main course: chicken corn chowder with hot corn bread
- dessert: steaming hot chocolate pudding cake with raspberry sauce
- specialty drinks: Hot Brick Toddy (whiskey, hot water, sugar, butter and cinnamon)

Entertainment

Show scenes from *Shackleton* with Kenneth Branagh, *Endurance* with Liam Neeson or one of the many documentaries about the coldest continent. Introduce your guests to the game *Antarctic Adventure*. It is loosely based on the 16th Century game *Goose*. To win the game, you'll need to make it to the South Pole and back without falling into a crevasse! You'll find a board and rules on the web page for this theme.

Souvenirs/Party Favors

Send your guests home with a snow globe, or mittens and fleece scarves, or a jacket with "Mission Antarctica" embroidered on a pocket flap.

Fund Raisers

If you need to raise funds, raffle a ski weekend complete with ski passes and a ride on a dog sled.

Keywords

snow pack, algae, lichen, moss, tundra, krill, jellyfish, squid, seals, whales, seabirds, penguins, albatross, elephant seals, copper, silver, gold, South Georgia Islands, South Sandwich Islands, Elephant Island, whalers, McMurdo Sound, Beardmore Glacier, Roosevelt Island, sled dogs, skidoo, meteorites, highest elevation - 16,066 feet, Weddell Sea, pack ice, windy polar desert, sea ice, ice floes, crystals, flakes, glacier bergs, ice breakers, bergy bits, growlers, sea smoke, ice blink, ice floe, katabatic winds, **www.celebration-solutions.com/antarc.html**

Destination Themes

AUSTRALIA

Introduction

The continent of Australia remained largely unknown to the outside world until the 17th Century when the first permanent settlement was established as a penal colony. The continent remained a colony of Britain until 1901 when the colonies became the Commonwealth of Australia. Today, Australia is a nation of 18 million people that hosts millions of tourists every year. Let your guests vicariously visit the Sydney Opera House, the Great Barrier Reef, beautiful beaches and the extensive outback.

Ambiance

Picture the hot, dusty, wild Australian outback. Keep the lighting high like the noonday sun and play Aboriginal music in the background. Give the room a dusty, desert or wild herb smell.

Colors

Use "outback" colors of brick red and deep, golden yellow.

Suggested Attire

The suggested attire is "relaxed and friendly" casual.

Invitations

"Come meet with us ... mate!" Find Australian travel posters to send your invitation on, or write a short travelogue. You could also send your message via boomerang (just be careful with your aim!).

Decorations

Set the tables with white china, deep golden yellow napkins and brick red tablecloths decorated with aboriginal designs. You can find good examples of Australian aboriginal art at www.aboriginalartonline.com. Use bush hats for your centerpieces.

Australia's a popular tourist destination, so it should be easy to cover the walls with travel posters of the highlights — Sydney, Ayers Rock, the outback or the Great Barrier Reef. Contact a travel agent who arranges trips to Australia

Keywords

"the big A," New South Wales, Queensland, South Australia, Tasmania, Victoria, Western Australia, Christmas Island, aborigines, Captain Cook, 1788 Botany Bay (British convicts first arrived), Aussie, Uluru (Ayers Rock), Great Barrier Reef, kangaroo, koala, wallaby, dingo, Sydney, Melbourne, Brisbane, Perth, Adelaide, Canberra, Union Jack, Great Barrier Reef, koala, kangaroo, Sydney Opera House, outback, aborigine, Maori, dingo, Perth, Adelaide, Canberra, Union Jack, Sydney Opera House, Outback, Maori, "Crickey," Crocodile, Digaree doo,

Australia

and ask for any extra posters they might have, or contact the Australia Tourist Commission for help. You'll find them online at www.australia.com.

Menu

Consider this "dinner down under" menu.
- appetizers: onion blossoms with ranch dressing
- main course: prawns and yellow pepper kabobs and sweet-tangy pork ribs
- dessert: soft serve ice cream in waffle cones with fresh fruit toppings
- specialty drinks: beer (Australia is the beer-drinking capital of the world)

Entertainment

Play the music of Australian rock groups. If you're not familiar with the latest and greatest in Australian rock, here are some of the recent winners of the Australian Music Awards: Alex Lloyd, Delta Goodrem, Powderfinger, The Waifs, Keith Urban and John Farnham.

Hold a "Beer Can Regatta." Every year, the citizens of Alice Springs hold a regatta. Undeterred by the fact that the river on which the race is held has *no* water, contestants sail their boats in the dry river bed on metal tracks.

Give each table a can of Foster's lager (Australian for beer 'mate!), the makings of a sail and rigging, and enough Lego™ to create a cart with wheels to hold the beer can. Set up a long track with a gentle slope and race four cars at a time. Each winner advances to the next round. Give the winning racing crew (table) a prize. If you have a large crowd, set up more than one race track.

Souvenirs/Party Favors

Send guests home with a bush hat and a boomerang.

Fund Raisers

If you need to raise funds, arrange for a sale of Australian aboriginal art, travel books or DVDs of the IMAX movie about Australia, or raffle a trip to the land down under.

Keywords

aboriginal art, boomerangs, Crocodile Dundee, 'down under,' giant lizards, dingo, Tasmania, great white sharks, boomerang, cave paintings, totems, eucalyptus, didjeridu (musical instrument), quartz peaks, limestone caves, rain forest, rock art, iconography, body painting, ochre, dot painting, monoliths, rock masses, desert, cricket, rugby, camel races, "avagoodweegend," "back o' beyond," "billabong," "dunny," "g'day or gidday," "knickers in a knot," "big bik-kies," "brumby," "cheerio," "have a natter," dinki-di," **www.celebration-solutions.com/aussie.html**

Celebration Solutions

Destination Themes

Introduction

Although China has more than 6,000 years of history, art, architecture, music and literature, for centuries it was a secluded place of mystery. Even though traders traveled along the silk road, not many Westerners explored the interior of China. Marco Polo traveled throughout China and when he returned to the west, he had tales of emperors and armies, a great wall, high mountains and plains that reached the end of the world. Take your guests on an exotic journey to ancient China.

Ambiance

Travel back to the grand dining hall in the Forbidden City — the traditional home of the Chinese emperors. Use traditional red Chinese lamps to provide light and play instrumental Chinese music in the background. Go to an Asian market and buy spices used for Chinese cooking to give the room an exotic smell.

Colors

Use "imperial" colors of red, black and golden yellow.

Suggested Attire

The suggested attire is a "night in the emperor's palace" cocktail.

Invitations

"To have friends from afar is happiness, is it not? — Confucius." Use the Chinese character for welcome or friendship on the front of your invitation. It is a tradition in China to send decorated red envelopes on special occasions, so send your invitation in a red envelope.

Decorations

Set the tables with red tablecloths. For centerpieces, on top of the tablecloths lay a black overcloth with the symbols for luck, prosperity and good fortune stamped or embroidered in yellow. Round, silk, red lanterns are a must for ceiling decorations. Lanterns of this type would have been found in every area of the Forbidden City.

Keywords

Great Wall, Forbidden City, Emperor, Empress, jades, bronzes, silks, chop, lantern, opera, acrobats, dragon, Yangtze, Terra Cotta Warriors, calligraphy, characters, dynasty, Qin, Beijing, Hong Kong, Shanghai, Chongqing, gunpowder, silk, rice, Tibetan plateau, Inner Mongolia, Gobi Desert, giant panda, Confucius, Cultural Revolution, Tiananmen Square, opium wars, Yuan, mah-jong, rickshaw, abacus, Middle Kingdom, Chang Jiang - Yangtze River, Huang He - Yellow River, Zhu Jiang - Pearl River, vast deserts, towering mountains, high plateaus, broad

China

To decorate the walls, find examples of the Guilin school of Chinese painting. These paintings are very distinctive for their tall, peaked mountains. To give the prints a more expensive look, add a brocade or silk border and hang them from a dowel at the top. To give the print weight and stability, use a dowel at the bottom edge, as well.

Menu

Consider serving this Chinese menu "family style."
- appetizers: hot and sour or rice wine soup
- main course: steamed duck with preserved plums, 5-spice beef, bok choy, bamboo shoots and mushrooms
- dessert: poached pears with honey, lemon and raisins
- specialty drinks: jasmine tea and Golden Dragon (brandy, yellow Chartreuse, lemon twist)

Entertainment

Mah Jong is a very popular game in China. Set up tables of four and teach guests how to play. Players occupy the points of the compass — north, south, east and west — and must put together hands of tiles somewhat like playing *Gin Rummy* with cards. If you have any experienced players, spread them out to different tables so that they can assist the newer players. You'll find instructions for the game at the web page for this theme.

Souvenirs/Party Favors

Send each guest home with a decorative Chinese knot wall hanging. Chinese knots first appeared in the Tang Dynasty (960-1229 A.D.). These decorations are made from a single rope and represent wishes such as happiness, luck, auspiciousness and longevity.

Fund Raisers

If you need to raise funds, sell *Mah Jong* sets. Guests who have just learned to play, may want to play again with their family or friends.

Keywords

plains, 1.6 billion people, inventors of paper, gunpowder, porcelain and silk, warlords, paper lanterns, dynasty, Confucius, jade carving, landscape paintings, sculpture, bronze bells, zither, gongs, drums, cymbals, swords, foot binding, palace, acrobats, bamboo, pagoda, barges, bicycles, bridges, Buddha, Qing Tombs, monasteries, cranes, dragon boat races, embroidery, folding fans, fireworks, Flying Tigers, Mongols, Peking Opera, Silk Road, tea, "Better to be deprived of food for three days, than tea for one," **www.celebration-solutions.com/china.html**

Destination Themes

Introduction

The Federal District of the United States, more commonly known as the District of Columbia, is situated on the Potomac and Anacostia rivers between Maryland and Virginia. Established by an Act of Congress in 1791, the District is well known for its cultural institutions, historic landmarks and parks, not to mention the heart of the nation's political scene. Washington is named after the country's first president, George Washington and is one of the country's most popular tourist destinations. Ask your guests to spend an evening in the seat of power during the most beautiful time of year — when the cherry trees are blooming.

Ambiance

Picture Washington, D.C. in the early spring. Keep the lighting bright like a beautiful spring day. Cherry blossoms are fragrant so use a light floral scented spray or potpourri pots to give the room a light scent.

Colors

Use "patriotic" colors of red, white and blue.

Suggested Attire

The suggested attire is "power-tie" business.

Invitations

"Join us for a march on the mall." Use a good photograph of Washington, D.C. with the cherry blossoms in full bloom for your invitation.

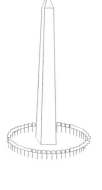

Decorations

Set the tables with white tablecloths with two red stripes and large red stars, like the District of Columbia flag. The diagonal streets in the city of Washington are all named after states, so create sign posts using different state names for your centerpieces. Use pink, silk cherry blossoms to twist around the sign post bases.

For the walls, use aerial maps of the capital. Enlarge them into poster or mural size. For the cherry trees, take some large (2" or larger) piping filler cord and

Keywords

politics, politicians, Washington monument, Lincoln memorial, Jefferson memorial, cherry blossoms, memorials, monuments, Capitol, Congress, House, Senate, Supreme Court, White House, national, flag, representatives, Dumbarton Oaks gardens, Iwo Jima, Korean, Vietnam, Smithsonian, Air and Space Museum, Potomac, Anacostia, Lafayette Square, independence, constitution, Bill of Rights, National Zoo, C&O Canal, Constitution Hall, Daughters of the American Revolution, Declaration of Independence, Frederick Douglass, Kennedy Center, embassy

District of Columbia

wind a thin wire around the length of the cord. This will let you shape and bend the cord. Cover the cords with dark brown material or ribbon and wind several strands together for the trunk. Allow the "branches" to creep out onto the ceiling and secure them to the ceiling tile framework. Add a generous amount of silk or tissue paper cherry blossoms to the limbs.

Menu

Consider this "Capitol Members-Only dining room" menu.
- appetizers: *Green Party* salad and *Senate* bean soup
- main course: *Tory* tortellini with red and yellow peppers, *Democratic* 'bray'sed new potatoes
- dessert: *GOP* elephant-ear vanilla-almond cookies with *Whig* amaretto whipped cream
- specialty drinks: *Reform Party* Rumfustian (ale, gin, fino sherry, sugar, egg yolks, lemon twist, cinnamon stick, cloves, allspice, nutmeg), *Libertarian* Loudspeaker (brandy, gin, triple sec, lemon juice), *Socialist* Scorpion (gold rum, brandy, almond syrup, lemon juice, orange juice and lemon slice)

Entertainment

If you're not up for rousing Sousa marches, the musical group The Capitol Steps have been spoofing life in Washington for decades. See how much your guests know about the nation's capital. Play a game of Washington trivia. See if your guests recognize the name of Charles L'Enfant the designer of the city, or the name of the state street on which the White House is located.

Souvenirs/Party Favors

Give each guest a bookmark of the famous Washington cherry blossoms or a nice coffee table book about Washington, D.C.

Fund Raisers

If you need to raise funds, arrange for a sight-seeing package to Washington, D.C. along with tickets for the popular attractions like the White House tour, the Holocaust museum and the Smithsonian.

Keywords

row, federal architecture, Federal Reserve, Foggy Bottom, Folger Shakespeare Library, Ford's Theatre, Georgetown, Pierre Charles L'Enfant, Library of Congress, Dolley Madison, The Mall, National Archives, Old Executive Office Building, White House, CIA, FBI, Department of State, Tidal Basin, National Cathedral, Union Station, International Spy Museum, Holocaust Museum, between Virginia and Maryland on the Potomac River, Willard Hotel, Anacostia River, Redskins football, Wizards basketball, Capitals, Senators, **www.celebration-solutions.com/washdc.html**

Destination Themes

Introduction

Known as the place where the Alps meet the sea, Monaco is a small, independent principality located on the Mediterranean. Monaco has been ruled by the Grimaldi family since Francois Grimaldi and his men, disguised as monks, captured Monaco in 1297. In 1856, when the Prince of Monaco was short of cash, he established the first casino. Today, Monaco is a tourist mecca that boasts one of the wealthiest guest lists in all of Europe. Let your guests feel like they have joined the rich and famous flocking to this tiny coastal nation to see and be seen in the fine hotels, restaurants, yachts and casinos.

Ambiance

Picture yourself in the Grande Casino in Monte Carlo. Imagine one of the old, elaborately decorated theaters of the past that's dripping with wealth — gold fixtures, luxurious velvet curtains and deep, plush carpets. Use lamplight to keep the lighting low, close and intimate. Think about the sounds you would hear in a casino such as clinking glasses, chips being stacked and unstacked, and dealers calling out hands.

Colors

Use "winning hand" colors of red, black and white.

Suggested Attire

The suggested attire is "high rollin' " black tie.

Invitations

"Join us for a grand time in the Grande Casino." Use one of the symbols of gambling for your invitations such as aces, dice showing sevens, a baccarat hand, a roulette wheel or a craps table.

Decorations

Set the tables with alternating red and black tablecloths, white china, gold utensils and gold-stemmed glasses. Seven is a lucky number in gambling, so create large 7s out of styrofoam for the centerpieces. Cover the numbers in white, satin ribbon and add red, white and black metallic confetti 7s to them. Surround the base of the 7s with face cards standing on end.

Hang red material like curtains from ceiling to floor. Draw the material back and tie it

Keywords

"The Rock," Princess Grace (Grace Kelly), Prince Ranier Grimaldi, Monegasque, heir apparent, Monte Carlo, principality, Mediterranean, gambling, yachts, Alps, Monaco Grand Prix, French cuisine, wines, harbor, money, mountains, sea, lifestyle, independent, principality, 700 year-long Grimaldi Dynasty, "One Square Mile," cathedral, ancient fortified town, medieval palace, changing of the guard, Gallery of Mirrors, oceanographical museum, Opera, baccarat, craps, blackjack, roulette, 7, nightlife, Hermitage Hotel, Jardin Exotique, gambling, good

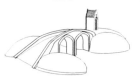

Monaco

together with a black, velvet ribbon for a curtain tie. Place a crest of Monaco between the curtains.

Menu

Consider this "sophisticated, strictly high-stakes" menu.
- appetizers: mushroom tarts
- main course: scallop and shrimp seviche, marinated roasted pork in chutney butter
- dessert: crepes with orange glaze
- specialty drinks: Sazerac (bourbon, pernod, sugar, bitters, lemon twist)

Entertainment

Entertain your guests with games of chance. Rent the tables and dealers from a company but make sure you're in compliance with local laws that regulate gambling. Leave ample room for the gaming tables so guests can make their way easily from table to table to visit, or from game to game to play.

Baccarat is a game popular in the casinos of Monaco. It's often played in a roped off area to attract the high rollers, or the more sophisticated, monied players. The name Baccarat comes from the Italian word Baccara meaning zero. In Baccarat, the cards are dealt in hands similar to Black Jack but the scoring is different. The only part of the combined card score that counts is the last number, so a 3, a Jack and a 3, or two Jacks and a 3, would all equal a score of 3. The player with the highest number wins.

Give a special prize to the big winner of the evening. This will give guests an incentive to play all night long.

Souvenirs/Party Favors

Send guests home with a deck of playing cards featuring scenes of Monaco and print gambling chips with the name and date of the party on them. Tie the cards with a gold ribbon and place a gambling chip under the bow.

Fund Raisers

If you need to raise funds, sell tickets for a trip to a local casino, or raffle off a weekend in Las Vegas or Monaco.

Keywords

luck, casino, cabaret, sporting clubs, spectacular coastline, Rolls Royces, yachts, jewels, splendor, magnificence, grandiosity, exquisite, splendid, spectacle, pomp, grandeur, pageantry, ceremony, elegance, beauty, lavish, rich, posh, plush, swanky, ritz, dazzling, stately, ornate, resplendent, fine, splash, glittering, glitz, glamour, cote d'azur, perched atop a craig, spectacular view, displays of Napoleon's personal effects, mountain and sea, an exceptional lifestyle, steep rocky coastline, celebrities, royalty, **www.celebration-solutions.com/monaco.html**

Destination Themes

Introduction

New Orleans — one of the most picturesque and interesting cities in the nation — has a character and personality all its own. New Orleans was founded in 1718 and is the birthplace of jazz. The city is really an island with the river on one side and Lake Ponchartrain and the marshes on the other. Although New Orleans is most well-known for its celebration of Mardi Gras, it is often said that "if you've seen New Orleans, you've seen the world." Treat your guests to an evening in the "Big Easy."

Ambiance

Wander the famous French Quarter of New Orleans at night. Keep the lighting low and use twinkle lights for a little sparkle in the scene. Dixieland jazz is a must, so if you're not planning to hire a live band for entertainment, play good jazz recordings in the background. New Orleans is also known for its spicy Cajun food. Use the smell of these spices to help set the scene.

Colors

Use "Mardi Gras" colors of violet, green and metallic gold.

Suggested Attire

The suggested attire is black. Ask your guests to come attired in black which will let the bright colors of the decorations stand out.

Invitations

"Laissez le bon temps roullet!" (Let the good times roll). Use a good photograph of revelers at Mardi Gras or one of the floats at a Mardi Gras parade for your invitations.

Decorations

Set the tables with violet tablecloths and green place settings. Pile the center of the tables high with gold bullion — gold coins, gold beads and gold masks.

Re-create the architectural style of the French Quarter with its white buildings, green shutters and wrought iron work. Since real shutters are heavy (and expensive), create shutters out of light, inexpensive balsa wood.

For the wrought iron, use round foam that can be bent and has a memory. This type of foam is often used in kids toys. Form your iron pattern and secure the pieces together with

Keywords

French quarter, jazz, Cajun, Acadian, Creole, French, saxophones, musicians, beignets, French Quarter, Mardi Gras, Fat Tuesday, Mardi Gras monarchy, the Rex parade, Mystick Krewe of Comus, Twelfth Night Revelers, beads, masks, mint julep, Café du Monde, jambalaya, gumbo, 'Po' Boys, swamp, Bourbon Street, Jazzland Theme Park, Voodoo Museum, plantation, House of Blues, paddle wheelers, Mississippi delta, Battle of New Orleans, Amistad, bayou, Garden District, Lake Ponchartrain, Carnival, parades, floats, pagents, costumes,

New Orleans

glue or ties. Spray paint the whole works shiny black.

Place old-fashioned street lamp occasionally along the walls and use posters from Mardi Gras celebrations of the past (check eBay). They're quite playful and will make a colorful addition to the decor.

Menu

Consider this "French Quarter in the Big Easy" menu.
- appetizers: crawfish salad
- main course: shrimp creole and crawfish-sausage jambalaya
- dessert: beignets, chocolate chess pie and chicory coffee drinks
- specialty drinks: Hurricanes (dark rum, light rum, passion fruit syrup, lime juice) or Planter's Punch (gold rum, bourbon, cognac, Pernod, bitters, sugar syrup, lemon juice, sparkling water and lemon slice)

Entertainment

As each guest enters, give him or her a colorful, feathered Mardi Gras mask. Hire actors to dress up in wild, colorful Mardi Gras costumes and throw beads and candy to the guests as they enter the room. The music of New Orleans is upbeat and energetic. Hire a dixieland jazz band to play traditional New Orleans-style stomps, rags, and marches. Or hire a zydeco band — an evolution of more traditional Cajun and Creole music found mostly in southwestern Louisiana.

Souvenirs/Party Favors

Send each guest home with a bag of gold and silver doubloons. These are the coins traditionally thrown to party-goers at Mardi Gras. Wrap the coins in purple or green gauze cloth tied with a gold ribbon.

Fund Raisers

If you need to raise funds, ask a baker to create a giant King Cake. King Cakes are a tradition at Mardi Gras. Make sure that each piece of cake holds a prize and that one piece of cake holds the grand prize. Tell guests what prizes are possible to win and sell pieces of the cake.

Keywords

masked balls, street dances, street music, Spring Fiesta, Le Petit Theatre du Vieux Carre, oysters Rockefeller, crayfish bisque, pompano en papillote, King cake, fancy wrought iron, St Charles trolley, masks, feathers, magnolia blossoms, palm trees, fancy balls, Jazz Festival, brass-band parades, Paul Prudhomme, blackened redfish, the Saints, Spanish moss, Dixie, miles of canals, Superdome, fiddles, trombones, bass, Huey P Long, streetcars, steamboat jazz cruise, riverboat, cities of the dead, **www.celebration-solutions.com/newo.html**

Destination Themes

Introduction

The Serengeti, a mostly flat, open grassland in Africa, has a few rocky hills and areas of bushy savannah where more than 200 species of animals live. In 1913, great stretches of Africa were still unknown in the west when Stewart Edward White, an American hunter, set out from Nairobi and found the Serengeti. He wrote: "We walked for miles over burnt out country... Then I saw the green trees of the river, walked two miles more and found myself in paradise." In the years since White's excursion, the Serengeti has come to symbolize paradise to many. Take your guests on a safari under "the high noble arc of the cloudless African sky — Stewart Edward White."

Ambiance

Imagine the great savannah plains of the Serengeti. Keep the lighting high as if you are on a photo safari and be sure to play sounds of exotic wildlife in the background. Use earth or fresh air scents to make the room smell like the great outdoors.

Colors

Use "safari" colors of soft red, light grey green and soft yellow.

Suggested Attire

The suggested attire is "hiking about" casual.

Invitations

"Let the drums of Africa beat in your heart ... when you join us for a celebration of the Serengeti." Use a closeup print of an animal hide like zebra or tiger stripes for your invitation, or use cards showing the wildlife of the area.

Decorations

Set the tables with soft grey green tablecloths, soft yellow place settings and animal hide-patterned fabric for napkins. Think about zebra stripes and leopard spots or more abstract patterns like wrinkled elephant skin or lion fur. If you can't find material that is pre-printed this way, you can take a photograph, transfer it to iron-on material and iron it on to a plain, white fabric napkin.

Use a picture of the grasslands to make a repeating mural for the longest, plainest wall. Find a silhouette of an acadia tree. Create trees of different sizes and place the trees in

Keywords

Serengeti meaning 'endless plains,' calm beauty, quick violence, grandeur, wildlife, Great Migration, leopards, lions, tigers, giraffes, gnus, gazelles, elephants, wildebeasts, savannah, safari, masks, spears, shields, tribesmen, endless miles across the wilds of East Africa, Lion King, monkeys, meercats, gorillas, baboons, elephants, leopards, giraffes, rhinos, wildebeests, gazelles, warthogs, birds, tall grass, Pride Rock, hyenas, Tree of Life, panthers, cheetahs, herds, zebras, cape buffalo, impala, hippos, butterflies, lizards, flamingos, yak, tusks, ivory,

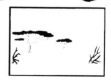

Serengeti

different parts of the mural, biggest in the foreground, smallest closest to the horizon to create a feeling of distance. On the other walls, use good wildlife photographs of elephants, lions, zebras or giraffes.

Menu

Consider this "safari" menu.
- appetizers: lion's mane salad (use sprouts to create the mane, cucumber slices for the ears, black olives for the eyes radish florets for the nose and shredded carrots for the mouth)
- main course: tiger sandwiches (get loaves of sandwich bread made from alternating stripes of dark and light rye and load them with shaved roast beef and horseradish sauce)
- dessert: zebra cheesecake (light and dark chocolate cheesecake)
- specialty drinks: West African fruit punch

Entertainment

Play the music of southern Africa while you show scenes about the wildlife of the Serengeti. The Zulu and Xhosa people of southern Africa share a musical style. Both enjoy a strong tradition of singing to celebrate special events in a call-and-response choral style. Instrumental music featuring mouth harps, clapping and rattles is also popular.

While you listen to the music, watch a slideshow of still photographs, or arrange for a showing of one of the many documentaries made about the area.

Show your guests how to play the game of *Safari*. It is based on the 16th Century game *Goose*. To win the game, you'll have to make your way through the Serengeti without encountering a hungry lion. You'll find a board and rules on the web page for this theme.

Souvenirs/Party Favors

Send guests home with a souvenir canvas backpack stamped with an animal logo.

Fund Raisers

If you need to raise funds, raffle a photo safari to the Serengeti, sell photographs of Serengeti wildlife, or photography classes with a wildlife photographer.

Keywords

survival of the fittest, circle of life, predator, mahogany, diamonds, acacia trees, kopjes (rock formations), woodlands, plains, rivers, volcanoes, game preserve, poachers, Cradle of Mankind, Leakeys' discovery of Lucy at Olduvai Gorge, Ngorongoro crater, Lake Victoria, Mara River, endangered black rhino, conservation, Masai people, endless plains, Tanzania, billowing clouds carrying the promise of rain, daily thunderstorms, wildlife viewing, prides of lions, columns of wildebeasts, unspoiled wonder, **www.celebration-solutions.com/sereng.html**

Celebration Solutions

Destination Themes

Introduction

In 1291, Schwyz became the first member of the confederation which is now Switzerland. The Swiss flag, a red square with a centered white cross, is a variation of the traditional flag of the Schwyz region. Switzerland has a rich and diverse cultural heritage including influences from the German, French, Italian and Rhaeto-Roman cultures. Switzerland is best known for banking, watchmaking, chocolates, beautiful villages and striking Alpine scenery. Take your guests on a trek through the Alps of Switzerland.

Ambiance

Imagine the spectacular beauty surrounding an Alpine chalet. Use floor spots to light up the wall decorations but otherwise keep the lighting low. Use table lamps to provide the ambient lighting. Play audio files of snow coming down the mountain, Swiss music and Alpine yodeling in the background. The Swiss are famous for their chocolates, so give the room a scent of chocolate.

Colors

Use "high-mountain" colors of red, white and cornflower blue.

Suggested Attire

The suggested attire is "mountaineering" casual.

Invitations

"By all accounts … you're the tops!" Create a passbook invitation that looks like a bank book issued for a secret Swiss account, or send famous Swiss chocolates.

Decorations

Set the tables with white tablecloths. The craft of embroidery is popular in Switzerland. Use an oversized cross stitch pattern to "stitch" the edges of the tablecloths. You don't have to actually stitch the material. You can transfer the pattern onto the fabric using iron-on material and then use colorful fabric paint to simulate the stitches. For centerpieces, ask a baker to create Matterhorn cakes. Decorate the base of the cakes with white edelweiss and cornflower-blue icing flowers.

On the walls, create "windows" looking out over the Alps. Use large posters of Alpine scenery and give them a simple window frame. You can use a simple picture frame just

Keywords

Zurich, Alps, watches, chocolates, alpenhorn, Geneva, United Nations, neutrality, Heidi, Romansch, cantons, Bern, Basel, Lausanne, yodeling, cheese, Swiss Bank Account, edelweiss, white cross, neutrality, Swiss Army Knife, goats, Matterhorn, Zermatt, St. Moritz, Jura, village, diversity, herding cows, Montreaux, Lake Geneva, Raclette cheese, fondue, bratwurst, horse-drawn carriages, Matterhorn, Interlaken, Luzern, glaciers, Bern, Nordic, Alpine, clap dancing, Carolingian, Romanesque architecture, poetry of the minnesingers, cathedrals,

Switzerland

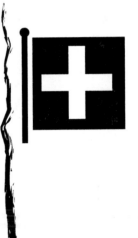

add the crossbars like real windows. Between the windows, use pine wreaths with home-made paper or silk roses. Wreaths are common wall decorations in Switzerland. Real pine wreaths are not only beautiful, they will add a nice fragrance to the room.

Giant chess boards are common in Switzerland. If you have room, create a checker-board on the floor with foam squares and create the playing pieces out of wire forms or paper maché.

Menu

Consider this "traditional Swiss" menu.

- appetizers: marinated mushroom spinach salad
- main course: Fondue — the basic ingredients are cheese, garlic, flour, white wine and kirsch liqueur. Rub the pot with a garlic clove and melt the cheese slowly over a stone. Add the wine and keep the mix at a bubbling temperature over a flame. Give diners a plate of chunks of white bread that they can spear with a long, two-pronged fork and dunk into the sauce. As the sauce boils away, it gets stronger and better. Tradition holds that the person who lets bread fall into the pot has to buy a bottle of white wine for the table.
- dessert: Kirschtorte (cherry tart) and Toblerone chocolates
- specialty drinks: Macaroon (vodka, chocolate liqueur, amaretto, orange twist)

Entertainment

Hire clap dancers or Swiss folk musicians to entertain your guests. Marionette shows are popular in the Alps as well. Show your guests how to play the 12th Century game *Gluckshaus* (meaning lucky house). It was popular in central Europe then and today. You will find a board and rules on the web page for this theme.

Souvenirs/Party Favors

Send each guest home with a Swiss army knife or a Swatch watch.

Fund Raisers

If you need to raise funds, sell prints of the beautiful scenery in Switzerland or tickets to a luxury train trip through the Alps.

Keywords

castles, avalanches, chalets, folk music, alphorn, cow bells, cantons, William Tell, Swiss bank accounts, Swiss francs, Eiger, Monch, Jungfrau, ice palace, Interlaken, Lake Lucern, alpine, waterfalls, cobblestones, fountains, clock towers, cable cars, hiking, backpacking, mountaineering, skiing, snowshoeing, view trains, mountain passes, valleys, medieval castles, funicular, glaciers, Alpine villages, Swiss Army knives, skiing, sledding, tobogganing, ice-skating, medieval, cuckoo clock, neutrality, tower, **www.celebration-solutions.com/switz.html**

Destination Themes

Introduction

Transylvania, meaning "beyond the forest," is a region in central Romania. Although the area is known for its agriculture and gold mining, Transylvania is most popularly known for its folklore … most notably vampires — beings that rise from the grave during the night, often in the form of a bat, and suck the blood of sleeping humans for nourishment. Various talismans and herbs supposedly avert vampires, but they can only be destroyed by stakes driven through the heart. The most well known, of course, is Count Dracula or Vlad Tepes the impaler who was a member of the Order of Dracul (the dragon). Invite your guests for a night in the creepy underworld of vampires.

Ambiance

Imagine the dark, damp atmosphere of Dracula's Castle. Keep the lighting very low. Create blinking "eyes" in the dark, string blinking lights behind a cloth or sheet of butcher paper with eye shapes cut out of it. To make the effect more dramatic, use yellow or red mylar to cover the cut-outs. Play a good CD of creepy Halloween sounds in the background. Give the room a musty smell, like an old castle keep.

Colors

Use "spooky" colors of midnight black, blood red and cat's eye yellow.

Suggested Attire

The suggested attire is "vampire" chic. If your guests are unlikely to want to dress up as vampires, ask the wait staff to don the fangs and cloaks.

Invitations

"Count Dracula would be pleased if you would join him *as his* … rather … *for* dinner." Cut construction paper into coffin-shapes that open or send the invitation written in red food color gel or puff paint on a wooden stake.

Decorations

Set the tables with black tablecloths, black china and red-stemmed glasses. Create a bouquet of daggers for your centerpieces. Surround the bottom of the dagger bouquets with blood red rose buds.

For the walls, you'll need cob webs, strings of garlic, wooden stakes and crosses to ward off any potential ill effects of the "vampires."

Keywords

Carpathian Mountains, Vlad the Impaler, vampire, pale skin, wooden steak through the heart, bat, coffin, cape, fangs, Borsa, Sighetul Marmatrel, Baia Mar, castles, Dark Shadows, Anne Rice, Gothic architecture, Moldavia, Valachia, Banat, Romania, Gypsy, Crisara, Monasteries, Michael the Brave tomb, Iron Gates Museum, Tirgoviste, Bran Castle - the castle of Count Dracula (Vlad the Impaler), Order of the Dragon, green cape representing dragon scales, red cape representing the blood of the martyrs, undead, grave-diggers, morgue, gravestones,

Transylvania

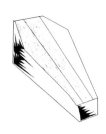

Create tall, narrow, Gothic windows using tissue paper or colored mylar for the window panes. If you want to light the windows. Create the window as a 4" deep window box and add Christmas tree lighting. If you'll put the windows on a slightly larger base, the windows can be freestanding, up against the walls.

To give guests a place to have their pictures made, create a tall, standing coffin with a swing-open door. This prop will require a steady and sturdy base, so it cannot tip over.

Menu

Consider this menu from "Count Dracula's" part of Romania.
- appetizers: Tocana (a soup made with chicken onions and garlic)
- main course: Mititei (small spicy meatballs made from pork mixed with beef often served with mustard) and Sarmale (cabbage or grape leaves stuffed with rice, meat and herbs)
- dessert: Placinte (pancakes or thick crepes with vanilla syrup and whipped cream)
- specialty drinks: Tuica (brandy made from plums and is common at almost any celebration in Romania)

Entertainment

Hire a DJ or band and hold a "Vampire's Ball." Hold a contest and let the guests vote for the best vampire costume. Arrange to have a few episodes of the 1960s cult series *Dark Shadows* playing on screens around the room.

Souvenirs/Party Favors

Take a group picture of everyone in costume early in the evening. Use a digital camera and make prints at the site. Use clear photo corners to attach the prints to a simple stand up board covered with black taffeta. Use a blood red ribbon to attach a copy of Bram Stoker's *Dracula* to the picture. Give the packages to guests as they leave.

Fund Raisers

If you need to raise funds, auction professionally made costumes. Show the guests examples of the costumer's work, but let them know that the highest bidder will be able to design a costume of their choosing.

Keywords

bats, buried face down, crucifix, garlic will ward off vampires, no reflection in mirrors, wolves, weakened by sunlight, Bram Stoker, a corpse during the day but comes to life at night, lives by sucking the blood from living persons who then become vampires, stake driven through the heart, superstition, hexes, undead, werewolves, biting the neck, living dead, dense, dark forests, fangs dripping with blood, black cape flapping in the wind, yellow eyes staring, frightened, ghoul, ghost, prince of darkness, **www.celebration-solutions.com/transylv.html**

Destination Themes

Introduction

Yellowstone is known for its spectacular geysers, hot springs, canyons and fossil forests. The first explorer to visit the Yellowstone area was John Colter in 1807 who left the Lewis and Clark expedition to explore the region. Future explorations helped to publicize the beauty of the area as a national park. Photographs by William Henry Jackson and the paintings of artist Thomas Moran convinced President Ulysses S. Grant to sign a bill creating the park in 1872. Visitors have been amazed by its awesome beauty ever since. Give your guests an enjoyable evening in America's best loved park.

Ambiance

Picture a comfy log cabin in the middle of Yellowstone. Use lamplight to make the room feel cozy and warm. Play the sounds of a crackling fireplace in the background and give the room a pine scent.

Colors

Use "great outdoors" colors of leather brown, sky blue and forest green.

Suggested Attire

The suggested attire is "flannel shirts and jeans" casual.

Invitations

"Oh come all ye old faithful … to a party in Yellowstone." Use a good photograph of Old Faithful for your invitations or wrap your invitation in a bolo tie that guests can wear to the party.

Decorations

Set the tables with forest green flannel tablecloths, sky-blue china and use leather ties for napkin rings. Use real pine boughs, oversized pine cones, and rust sculptures of different animals in silhouette for your centerpieces.

For the walls, create "log cabin" windows. Pick a season and use large posters of Yellowstone during that season to show in the windows. Use a photograph or graphic of hewn logs for the area around the outside of the window. Leave the edges of the logs ragged and irregular.

Keywords

geyser, forest, wildlife, animals, mountain, lake, Old Faithful, landmarks, lodges, wolves, buffalo, bison, fire, first National Park, Teddy Roosevelt, mud pots, Rangers, moose, Rocky Mountains, volcanic plateau, Gallatin Range, Washburn Range, Absaroka Range, Yellowstone River, Grand Canyon of the Yellowstone, waterfalls, Inspiration Point, Tower Falls, Obsidian Cliff, geysers, hot springs, mud volcanoes, paint pots, fumaroles, gas, steam, bugling elk, fossil forests, white-out snowstorms, trout on the line, mountain peaks, polychrome canyons,

Yellowstone

Every good log cabin has a fireplace. Use a small fan to blow nylon "flames" from between fake logs to give the fire movement. Use marbled matte board to create the rest of the fireplace and the mantel.

Menu

Consider this menu fit for a "rucksack." Give away the rucksack to each guest as a souvenir of the celebration.

- appetizers: Firehole Favorites (curried potato salad)
- main course: Buffalo Bill's (roast beef on baguettes with herbed mayonnaise)
- dessert: Paint Pots (ice cream with lots of topping choices)
- specialty drinks: Grand Geysers (Brandy Swizzle - brandy, lemon juice, cherry brandy, ginger ale, lemon wheel)

Entertainment

Entertain your guests with bluegrass music. Bluegrass is a style of southern string band music that became popular in the 1930s and '40s. The records of the Blue Grass Boys were so popular on the radio that announcers began using the term "bluegrass music." Bluegrass comes from mountain, gospel, and blues music, and generally involves a traditional, often melancholy, subject. It is played by an acoustic string band of fiddles, banjos, mandolins, guitars, dobros and basses, which may be augmented by the harmonica, mouth harp, accordion, jug, and spoons.

If you have an appropriate place to do so, hold a Paul Bunyan (lumberjack) contest. Hold contests in wood splitting or two-man crosscut sawing. You can find out more information about lumberjack contests at www.usaxemen.com.

Souvenirs/Party Favors

Give your guests a leather-bound personal journal and a leather bookmark stamped with a bison picture.

Fund Raisers

If you need to raise funds, sell pictures or nice coffee table books about the famous park, or raffle off trips to Yellowstone at different times of the year.

Keywords

boiling cauldrons, cliffs of black obsidian, heat of the thermal waters, campfires, national treasure, beaver, trappers, howling wolves, stagecoaches, frigid winters and short summers, Theodore Roosevelt, John Muir, snowshoes, toboggan, lodgepole pine forests, spirit of adventure, Indian paintbrush, waterfowl, grizzly bears, conservation, outdoor recreation, antelope, eagle, wolf, cottonwoods, aspen, spruce, fir, clean, crisp air, snow falling in the quiet, snowmobiles, beautiful mountain meadows, **www.celebration-solutions.com/yellowst.html**

Entertainment Themes

Introduction

In 1851, the schooner *America* of the New York Yacht Club received a "hundred guinea cup" from the Royal Yacht Squadron for winning a race around the Isle of Wight against fifteen British yachts. Renamed the America's Cup, it was offered as a challenge trophy by the New York Yacht Cub, with the first challenge taking place in 1870. Some of the winning yachts include the *Mischief*, the *Mayflower*, the *Resolute*, the *Intrepid*, the *Courageous* and the *Stars and Stripes*. Today the America's Cup Race is a pride contest matching the fastest, sleekest, fiberglass-hulled, 12-meter, racing schooners. Bring your guests down to the water's edge for an afternoon of sailing and fun.

Ambiance

Visit a yacht club filled with race-day excitement. Keep the lighting sunshine bright like a cloudless sky at noon. Use the audio from an old broadcast to get the feel for the lingo of a yacht race and make up some competing ships of your own. Assign a "ship" to each table to give guests a stake in the audio race. Give the room the scent of salt sea air.

Colors

Use "high-seas" colors of bright sea blue and sun yellow.

Suggested Attire

The suggested attire is "yacht club" casual.

Invitations

"Anchors aweigh my friends … anchors aweigh." Write your invitation on a nautical flag or send the details written on the sail of a toy sailboat.

Decorations

Set the tables with bright, sea-blue tablecloths and white china. Fold bright yellow napkins like boat sails and lay out a line of nautical flags in a circle around the center of each table. In the center of the flags, create a spinnaker from starched, cotton material so it will look like it is full. Give each table the name of a ship that will be sailing during the "race."

To decorate the walls, string lines of nautical flags near the ceiling and use oversized posters of the great 12-meter ships in action. Make these very big and very colorful. Boats

Keywords

sailing, watercraft, water, wind, sun, sea, sail, waves, crest, splash, mast, jib, spinnaker, rudder, captain, mate, helm, wheel, tiller, competition, nautical décor, anchors, crests, yuppie, skipper, dock siders, naval, swift, maneuverable, regatta, anchor, amidships, ballast, battens, beam, bilge, boat hook, bowsprit, cast off, centerboard, dock, draft, drift, fathom, fetch, float, fore, aft, foremast, grommet, ground tackle, gudgeon, halyard, headwind, headsail, headstay, heave ho, helm, jib, jibe, keel, knot, lanyard, leeward, lifeline, mainmast,

America's Cup

racing under a clear blue sky are beautiful but inclement weather can make for very dramatic sailing pictures, as well.

Menu

Consider this "yacht club" menu.
- appetizers: mussel pots and crab salad
- main course: lobster chowder and mahi mahi with apricot glaze
- dessert: ice cream in parfait glasses with colored cookies for sails
- specialty drinks: Regent's punch (sweet white wine, Madeira, triple sec, cognac, champagne, dark run, strong black iced tea, fresh lemon juice, orange juice, sugar, sparkling water)

Entertainment

Play scenes or audio of a real yacht race, then hold races of your own. As a warm up for the big race, ask guests to play a matching game, give them a list of sailing terms and see who can match the most, or let them guess the answers. The funniest answer wins.

When you're ready for the races, make each table a relay team. Use toy sail boats in a shallow tub of water. Racers using hand fans must blow their boat across the tub, and with the help of their teammate on the other side, maneuver the boat around a buoy and back. If there are eight members in the team, the race will end when the boat has made eight trips across the water and come to rest against the side of the tub (finish line).

Souvenirs/Party Favors

Give each guest a decorative beach bag filled with all the things they might need to be a spectator at a real yacht race — a sun visor, sunglasses, a beach ball, tanning lotion, a beach towel and zinc oxide.

Fund Raisers

If you need to raise funds, auction off prints of the America's Cup race, sailing lessons, or a day of fully-catered sailing. You will find John Mecray's celebrated collection of America's Cup limited edition collector prints at www.mecray.com. You can find more information at the America's Cup Official Website at www.americascup.com.

Keywords

mainsail, mizzen, moor, mooring, buoy, offshore, outboard, pennant, port, reef, rigging, scull, skeg, spinnaker, squall, starboard, staysail, stem, stern, tack, tiller, topside, trim, veer, waterline, weather, whip, winch, windward, yacht, yawl, staysail schooner, barquentine, cutter, sloop, brigantine, bark, brig, fully-rigged ship, aground, amidships, ballast, batten down the hatch, before the wind, bobstays, bowline, catamaran, clove hitch, come about, furling, blue water, coastal cruising, celestial navigation, **www.celebration-solutions.com/amercup.html**

Entertainment Themes

Introduction

Bad B Movies — they're so ridiculous that they're funny. The storyline is ridiculous, the dialog is ridiculous and the acting is more than ridiculous. Roger Ebert, the movie critic, has it exactly right about Bad B movies when he refers to them as "clichés, stereotypes, obligatory scenes, hackneyed formulas, shopworn conventions, and outdated archetypes." How could a movie be anything but bad with titles like *Rat Fink a Boo Boo*, *Zombies of the Stratosphere*, *Sorority Babes in the Slimeball Bowl-O-Rama* or *The Incredibly Strange Creatures Who Stopped Living and Became Mixed-up Zombies*. Your guests are bound to have a blast "playing a role" in a Bad B Movie.

Ambiance

This theme is Bad … B … cheesy. It's the capsule of a *Plan 9 from Outer Space* spacecraft or a city helpless before *Godzilla*. Keep the lighting low and use some of the more memorable lines or monster noises from these "infamous" films in the background.

Colors

Use "rundown movie theater" colors of brown, gold and velvet red.

Suggested Attire

The suggested attire is "nerd" casual. If you want to make this a costume party, ask your guests to come dressed as one of the characters in their favorite Bad B movie.

Invitations

"Come help us save Gotham from the 'Attack of the Killer Tomatoes'!" Send your invitations on monster-shaped foot prints, on an oversized insect, or on toy space ships hanging from fishing line.

Decorations

Set the tables with kitchy, red, crushed velvet tablecloths and gold, plastic place settings including the wine glasses. Fill the center of the tables with bowls full of "pure junk" finger food — Ho-Ho's, Ding Dongs, White Castles, licorice strings, mini doughnuts, Marshmallow Peeps, Moon Pies, Twinkies, etc.

On the walls, hang movie posters of the more famous "B" films or create "film strips" with pictures from those movies in them. Hang the film strips at random angles all over the walls.

Keywords

Godzilla, Plan 9 From Outer Space, monster movies, Attack of the Killer Tomatoes, Rocky Horror Picture Show, Golden turkey awards, Zombies of the Stratosphere, robots, big furry spiders, gadgets, blinking lights, visible string, aliens, Rat Fink a Boo Boo, The Fungus of Terror, Assault of the Killer Bimbos, Yog-Monster from Space, Zombies of the Stratosphere, Bloodsucking Nazi Zombies, Cannibal Woman in the Avocado Jungle of Death, They Saved Hitler's Brain, cliché, stereotype, hackneyed, shopworn, outdated, mad scientist, The Killer Shrews,

Bad B Movie Film Festival

Cover a couple of tables with "space ship" control panels full of blinking lights and gears covered with aluminum foil.

From the ceiling, hang blinking space ships and colorful planets from string or visible fishing line.

Use Lego™ to build a "mini-city" near the room entrance so that guests will feel like Godzilla walking through the streets of Gotham as they enter.

Menu

Consider this "bad … bad … and (no doubt) bad for you" menu.
- appetizers: cheese doodles and peanut butter and jelly finger sandwiches
- main course: beans and franks, macaroni and cheese, and chili-cheese fries
- dessert: hot popcorn in big movie theater tubs
- specialty drinks: generic beer (just to look at, though, not to drink!) or Zombies (anejo rum, dark rum, fresh lime juice, pineapple juice, apricot brandy, bitters, rum, pineapple spear, mint sprig)

Entertainment

You must, of course, arrange for a showing of a bad B movie. Give guests rubber-tipped darts that they can shoot at the screen during the cheesiest moments in the film. Some pretty famous actors today have appeared in very bad movies early in their careers. Check the lists of the Golden Turkey Awards and hold a contest to see who can name the actors who "starred" in some of these cinematic gems. (It's true … Leonard Nimoy made his film debut in the 1952 movie serial *Zombies of the Stratosphere*).

Souvenirs/Party Favors

Give guests all of the fixin's for a Bad B Home Movie Festival — a tub of microwave popcorn, cheese doodles, coupons for pizza, dart guns for four and a DVD of your favorite bad B film.

Fund Raisers

If you need to raise funds, sell T-shirts with cartoon characters as bad B actors, bad B movies collections on DVD, or movie posters from the best of the worst bad B films.

Keywords

Night of the Lepus, Blaxploitation movies, Scream, Blacula, Scream, Dawn of the Dead, Attack of the Mushroom People, Cottonpickin' Chickenpickers, Cat Woman on the Moon, Godzilla's Revenge, Devil Girl From Mars, Mesa of Lost Women, The Swarm, I Married a Monster From Outer Space, The Incredibly Strange Creatures Who Stopped Living and Became Mixed-up Zombies, The Twonky, cliches, stereotypes, hackneyed, outdated, so ridiculous that they're funny, darkly glamorous, Hellcats in High Heels, **www.celebration-solutions.com/badb.html**

Celebration Solutions

Entertainment Themes

Introduction

Formed in Liverpool, England from a group called the Quarry Men, the Beatles became the most popular musical group of the 1960s. The "British invasion" took place in on February 7, 1964 when the Beatles deplaned at JFK to a throng of screaming fans. Once they appeared on the Ed Sullivan show, Beatlemania consumed America, Americans consumed Beatlemania and the greatest act of the rock era was born. Crewcuts gave way to moptops, girls professed their love for John, Paul, George or Ringo, and boys bought guitars and Beatle boots. By 1970, they had called it quits, splintering a generation. Even if your guests didn't grow up in the heyday of the Beatles, they'll have a good time reliving the era of the Fab 4.

Ambiance

Attend a Beatles' concert at the Hollywood Bowl. Light the place up! The best concerts take place in perfect weather. You'll need tunes from the Fab 4, of course, and background sounds of screaming fans. We realize that a concert of this type probably would have had the smell of "ganja," but we don't recommend this!

Colors

Use "60s psychedelic" colors of pink, yellow, lime green and brilliant orange.

Suggested Attire

The suggested attire is "height of the 60s — nehru jackets, love beads, stove-pipe jeans, ankle boots and rose colored glasses" casual.

Invitations

"The British are Back!" Use a photograph of the Fab 4 performing or send a copy of the Beatles' *One* CD (a collection of their number one hits) with your invite.

Decorations

Set the tables with psychedelic tablecloths and place settings of all different colors. You'll need artifacts for the centerpieces. Look for late 60s-era personal transistor radios. They were very popular with the High School crowd during that time. Or, use miniature guitars and drum sets adorned with the Beatles logo.

On the walls, play up the "British" invasion. Hang Union Jack flags on the walls. Place them at a variety of different angles and let them overlap. Make a trip to the used record

Keywords

Fab Four, Beatlemania, Liverpool, the British Invasion of 1964, idols, Sgt Pepper's Lonely Heart's Club Band, White album, Quarry Men, George Harrison, John Lennon, Paul McCartney, Ringo Starr, original members Stuart Sutcliffe, Peter Best, rock-n-roll, first single - Love Me Do, I Want to Hold Your Hand, A Hard Day's Night, Abbey Road, Rock and Roll Hall of Fame, "beat" scene, moptops, Parlophon Records, stage, microphones, guitars, drums, Apple Records, 45 records, charging guitars, exuberant harmonies, top of the charts, She Loves You,

Beatles

store and pick up a few old Beatles albums. Add both the album jackets and the records to the mix on the walls.

Create a shrine to the mod fashions of the 1960s. Dress a few mannequins in Pocahontas head bands, wild curly hair, love beads, shirts with giant-gaudy-Goucho sleeves, suede vests with fringe, wide belts, mini-skirts or stove pipe jeans, and go-go or ankle boots.

Menu

Consider this "English pub" menu.
- appetizers: artichoke dip and bread
- main course: pasties (meat and potatoes in a pastry), braised new potatoes and green beans
- dessert: ambrosia salad
- specialty drinks: London Docks (dry red wine, dark rum, honey, lemon peel, cinnamon stick, nutmeg, and boiling water) or English ale

Entertainment

Beatles music, of course. Many of the Beatles performances are now out on DVD. Arrange to play scenes from one of their performances on screens around the room.

See how much your guests know (or remember) about the Beatles. Play Beatles trivia. Make up trivia cards for each table. Give each person a stack of five or six cards to read from. The first person reads a question and the person on their left answers and so on around the table. If you can answer correctly, you get one point. If you answer incorrectly and someone else at the table can answer correctly, they get the point. The person with the most points at each table wins a prize.

Souvenirs/Party Favors

As guests enter the party, give them love beads, peace sign medallions and rose-colored granny glasses to adorn their 60s attire.

Fund Raisers

If you need to raise funds, auction off mint condition Beatles albums, Beatles music CDs, Beatles performance DVDs, and other Beatles memorabilia.

Keywords

phenomenon, Ed Sullivan Show, 1970 breakup, Can't Buy Me Love, riotous tours, Help!, psychedelic imagery, worldwide chart-toppers, thousands of screaming fans, Penny Lane, Strawberry Fields Forever, Hey Jude, Yoko Ono, Let It Be, The Long and Winding Road, Nehru jackets, love beads, rose colored glasses, Yellow Submarine, Eleanor Rigby, Penny Lane, round glasses, beards, hippies, I Saw Her Standing There, Ticket to Ride, Magical Mystery Tour, Long and Winding Road, Zapple, Long Tall Sally, **www.celebration-solutions.com/beatles.html**

Entertainment Themes

Introduction

Although ancient and medieval artists produced comic art, it was the invention of printing in Europe in the 15th Century that made it possible for artists to distribute their drawings to the masses. Caricature drawing originated in the 16th Century and often poked fun at the monarch. Undertandably, these cartoonists mostly remained anonymous. In the 19th Century, magazines such as Punch, known for its satirical cartoons, became popular. Today, every daily newspaper runs pages and pages of cartoons, but it's the Sunday funnies — in all their big, full-color fun — that you and your guests will be celebrating in this theme.

Ambiance

Picture a lazy, leisurely, Sunday morning breakfast. Turn the room into a giant breakfast nook. Turn the lighting up high like a bright summer morning, and play soft music in the background. Occasionally, play the lead off from a recognizable cartoon television show. Fill the air with the smell of fresh coffee, maple syrup and bacon.

Colors

Use "Sunday Funnies" colors of blue green, light green and yellow.

Suggested Attire

The suggested attire is "come in your jammies" casual.

Invitations

"Join us in your jammies … for an evening of 'funnies' fun." Save up the Sunday papers for a few weeks or buy a few extra copies and cut blocks from the funnies to send as your invitations. Or, pick out a few of your favorites and send an anthology of those cartoons.

Decorations

Set the tables with yellow flannel tablecloths, light green plates, large blue coffee cups for lattes, and colorful plastic utensils. Use oversized, colorful, kids' alarm clocks or cartoon-character clocks for your centerpieces.

Paper the walls with the Sunday funnies and get a few lifesize cartoon character cutouts to place throughout the room.

Keywords

satire, political cartoons, funnies, balloons, comic strips, animation, Charles Schulz, William Hogarth, comic books, political satire, Punch, caricatures, balloons, gag panel, Little Orphan Annie, Katzenjamer Kids, Batman, Blondie, Superman, Sad Sack, Peanuts, Dilbert, Marmaduke, Tex Avery, Porky Pig, Disney, Hi & Lois, Hagar, Little Lulu, Nancy, Lil Abner, Garfield, Spiderman, Mutt & Jeff, Betty Boop, Yosemite Sam, Flintstones, Peanuts, Dennis the Menace, Marvel comics, Archie, Gasoline Alley, Doonsbury, Beetle Bailey, Calvin & Hobbes, Blondie, The

Cartoons

Pick your favorite cartoon characters and create giant balloon sculptures of them. If you need to get instructions or ideas for making a balloon sculpture, check out the resources at Balloon Headquarters at www.balloonhq.com.

Menu
Consider this "Sunday-morning" feast.
- appetizers: cartoon-character cereal
- main course: pancakes, stuffed french toast, eggs, bacon and hash browns
- dessert: mini-Belgian waffles with fresh fruit and whipped cream
- specialty drinks: Mimosas (champagne and orange juice) and Bloody Mary's

Entertainment
See how well your guests know their cartoons. Show cartoon characters, scenes from animated cartoons, or play audio clips from the theme songs and see if your guests can guess the correct answers. See if your guests can figure out the year that Blondie Boopadoop married Dagwood Bumstead (1933), the year that Flash Gordon and L'il Abner debuted (1934), that the first Woody Woodpecker cartoon was called Knock Knock, the year that Bugs Bunny and Elmer Fudd first met (1940), the year Doonesbury cartoonist Gary Trudeau was born (1948), the year Dick Tracy married Tess Truehart (1950), the year the Peanuts first debuted (1952), the year Pebbles Flintstone was born (1963), the year that Far Side first appeared (1980), the year the Simpsons became the longest running television cartoon (1996), and the year that the final Peanuts strip appeared in the Sunday paper (2000).

Souvenirs/Party Favors
Hire an artist to make caricatures of your guests that they can take with them as a souvenir of the event.

Fund Raisers
If you need to raise funds, sell original cartoon art. Original art is collectible and will continue to gain in value. Or, auction an appearance in a cartoon strip. The winning bidder will appear as a character in a newspaper cartoon. If you can make this arrangement with a nationally syndicated cartoonist, great, but don't forget about local cartoon artists who work for local daily, weekly, college or school newspapers as well.

Keywords

New Yorker, Popeye, Charles Schultz, superheroes, sketch, pencil, ink, etching, engraving, nibbed dip pen, crosshatching, stipple, grayscale, syndication, broadsheets, allusion, satire, Steamboat Willie, Mickey Mouse, Rocky and Bullwinkle, Caspar the friendly ghost, Deputy Dawg, The Jetsons, Kukla, Fran and Ollie, Popeye, Scooby-Doo, Underdog, Woody Woodpecker, cel, comix, Marvel Comics, Archie Comics, rotoscope, storyboard, splash panel, Sunday, superhero, Anime, frame, funny animal, **www.celebration-solutions.com/cartoons.html**

Celebration Solutions

Entertainment Themes

Introduction

Cary Grant (1904-1986), born as Archibald Alexander Leach, was a British-born American motion-picture actor known for his debonair manner. He worked in Vaudeville and became a leading musical-comedy actor in New York. In 1932, he went to Hollywood where he appeared in seven films that year. He is well known for his romantic and sophisticated comedies as well as his appearances in Alfred Hitchcock's classic films. Invite your guests back to the postwar '40s for a night of charm and elegance.

Ambiance

Picture a scene out of a Cary Grant romantic comedy. Play sound clips of his voice and great lines from his films in the background. Keep the lighting low and romantic. Use a light scent of honeysuckle like you might smell on an early summer evening.

Colors

Use "suave and debonair" colors of charcoal grey, light grey and white.

Suggested Attire

The suggested attire is "dashing and debonair" formal.

Invitations

"Be the 'Talk of the Town' … Join us for a dashing and debonair celebration of Cary Grant." Use a photograph of the actor for the invitation front or send a white bow tie attached to a formal invitation.

Decorations

Set the tables with deep charcoal grey tablecloths, white china and gold-stemmed glasses. Find photographs of Cary Grant in romantic poses with his leading ladies. For centerpieces, frame and stand the pictures on angel hair sprinkled with silver glitter.

Use plenty of tall plants like ficus trees to make the room feel like a garden patio and fill the trees with white twinkle lights. Don't skimp on the lights. The more lighting you put on the trees, the lower you can leave the ambient lighting, the more intimate and romantic the look of the room.

Arrange to show scenes from Cary Grant's romantic comedies on a giant screen at one end of the room. Look for his funny favorites — from the 1932 classic *This is the Night*, to

Keywords

top hat and tails, leading man, debonair, Oscar nominations, She Done Him Wrong with Mae West, The Philadelphia Story with Katherine Hepburn, Holiday, An Affair to Remember, Suspicion, Notorious, Arsenic and Old Lace, To Catch a Thief with Grace Kelly, North by Northwest, His Girl Friday, I was a Male War Bride, simple charm, disarmingly funny, ageless, heroic, comic, romantic, stylish, looks as if he belongs in top hat and tails, impeccably dressed, cleft in his chin, enigmatic, charming, elegant hero, genteel, wives Virginia Cherill, Barbara

Cary Grant

an appearance with Mae West in *I'm No Angel*, to the rare, but very funny *When You're in Love*, to a brilliant pairing with Katherine Hepburn in *Bringing Up Baby*, to the screwball comedy *His Girl Friday*, to the postwar *Bachelor and the Bobby Soxer*, to the fan-favorite *Operation Petticoat*.

Menu

Consider this "smart and sophisticated" menu.
- appetizers: baked ricotta with red pepper chutney
- main course: sirloin tips with chestnut puree and wild mushroom croquettes
- dessert: cranberry-filled pears
- specialty drinks: Tuxedo (gin, dry vermouth, maraschino liqueur, orange bitters, maraschino cherry)

Entertainment

It wouldn't be a night of romance without slow dancing. Hire a band that can do justice to romantic dance music or ask a DJ to put together a collection of the dance favorites of the 1930s and '40s.

Start off the dancing with a demonstration from a local dance troupe. Then give the crowd a few lessons in ballroom dancing. Formal dancing isn't as common today as it was in generations past, and your younger guests might like a chance to learn a few steps before they hit the dance floor with their favorite girl or guy.

Souvenirs/Party Favors

Give your guests a souvenir that they can wear to other formal events like cuff links for men and button covers or french shirt cuffs for women. Or give each guest a copy of a classic Cary Grant film on DVD.

Fund Raisers

If you need to raise funds, arrange for a Cary Grant film festival and sell tickets. Reserve a theater to show (two or three) movies in a row. Set aside an area of the theater especially for intermissions. Include snacks or meals during the first and second intermissions, and coffee and dessert after the last showing.

Keywords

Hutton, Betsy Drake, Dyan Cannon and Barbara Harris, socialites, mannerly, beefcake, desirable, Vaudeville, Broadway, a smashing wardrobe, immortal one-liners, superbly tailored English suits, unflappable sophistication, romantic comedies, western, war pictures, screwball comedies, dramas, Bringing Up Baby, "a little boy who ran away from home, joined the circus, and became a star," Archie Leach, British-born, leading ladies, attracted women like magnets, star of the silver screen, To Catch a Thief, **www.celebration-solutions.com/carygr.html**

Celebration Solutions

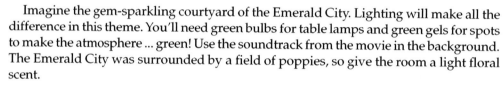

Entertainment Themes

Introduction

The Wizard of Oz is one of the most-loved films in motion picture history. Dorothy Gale is caught in a tornado after a run-in with a disagreeable neighbor Miss Gulch. The twister carries Dorothy and her house away to the land of Oz where she is met by Munchkins. After being given instructions to follow the yellow brick road, she meets up with a scarecrow, a tin woodsman and a cowardly lion who accompany her to the Emerald City, where she hopes to meet the famous Wizard of Oz. Take your guests on a journey to "meet the Wizard."

Ambiance

Imagine the gem-sparkling courtyard of the Emerald City. Lighting will make all the difference in this theme. You'll need green bulbs for table lamps and green gels for spots to make the atmosphere … green! Use the soundtrack from the movie in the background. The Emerald City was surrounded by a field of poppies, so give the room a light floral scent.

Colors

Use "dream-sequence" colors of emerald green, pretty pink and sparkling yellow.

Suggested Attire

The suggested attire is "anything you've got in emerald green" casual.

Invitations

"Follow the yellow brick road … and join us for an evening in the Emerald City." Write your invitations on yellow vinyl marked like the yellow brick road, or cover your invitation in a see-through emerald, green mylar sheet.

Decorations

Set the tables with emerald green tablecloths, white china and green-stemmed goblets. In the center of each table place a table lamp with an emerald green shade and a green light bulb. At the base of the lamps, place a pair of "ruby slippers." Buy pairs of women's shoes at a thrift store. Cover the exteriors with red glitters and sequins and the interiors with white satin or glitter.

At the entrance to the room, hire a couple of actors to dress up like the big Beefeater

Keywords

"We're not in Kansas anymore …," Oz, Tin Man, Dorothy, Auntie Em, Uncle Henry, Cowardly Lion, Scarecrow, wizard, wicked witch, "I'll get you, my pretty, and your little dog, too!", poppies, crystal ball, broom, fire, man behind the curtain, horse of a different color, good witch, Glenda the Good, ruby slippers, Professor Marvel, "Bell out of order, please knock," Beefeater guard with big handlebar mustache, fur hat and fuzzy gloves, "Nobody's ever seen the great Oz," ruby slippers, Wash & Brush Up Company, new straw, polished tin, haircut and perm,

Emerald City

guards Dorothy encountered at the gate of the Emerald city. Use a projector to shine a large image of the Emerald city on the farthest wall and use yellow vinyl material to create a "yellow brick road" leading up to it.

Create the booth where the Great and Wonderful Oz spun the dials and pushed on the controls. You can do this by hanging a curtain from a large diameter ring suspended from the ceiling or on a standing frame. Inside the booth on a small covered table, place a box with lever controls and a wheel with a handle to spin.

Menu

Consider this "off to see the wizard" menu. Put the whole meal in a basket along with a beanie baby Toto.
- appetizers: Scarecrow peppers (yellow peppers with pilaf stuffing)
- main course: Cowardly lion sandwiches (chicken breast and thinly sliced green apple on sourdough roles)
- dessert: Dorothy's coffee-toffee pie
- specialty drinks: Tin Man's Emerald Cocktail (gin, green crème de menthe, bitters and maraschino cherry)

Entertainment

See if your guests can fill in the blanks with the words from the songs from the *Wizard of Oz*. See how well they remember what comes after "Follow the yellow brick road ..." or "Somewhere, over the rainbow ..." or "Ha Ha Ha, Ho Ho Ho and a couple of tra la la's ..." or "Ding dong, the witch is dead ... " or see if they know who sang the line: "I could while away the hours, conferrin' with the flowers, consulting with the rain." After they guess, play the song from the soundtrack.

Souvenirs/Party Favors

As guests leave with their baskets and Toto, add goodies to the basket. Give each guest a DVD of the Wizard of Oz movie, a red heart, "liquid" courage, an Emerald City University diploma.

Fund Raisers

If you need to raise funds, auction off Wizard of Oz memorabilia.

Keywords

"It's how we laugh the day away in the merry old land of Oz," skywriting witch, "Surrender Dorothy," "If I only had a brain," Toto, basket, "I am Oz, the great and powerful," smoke and fire, wizard's control panel, Doctor of Thinkology, medal for meritorious conduct against wicked witches, testimonial for a great heart, Miracle Wonderland Carnival Company, "If I ever go looking for my heart's desire again, I won't look any farther than my own back yard," "Close your eyes, tap your heels together 3 times," **www.celebration-solutions.com/emercity.html**

Celebration Solutions

Entertainment Themes

Introduction

The *Flintstones* was prime-time's first animated series. It burst onto the screen in 1960, and has been there in one form or another ever since! The *Flintstones* is presently seen in 22 languages in more than 80 countries around the world, and is on somewhere every minute of the day. "Yabba-dabba-doo!" for the modern stone-aged family! One of the reasons we like this theme is that the *Flintstones* was so clever at taking hot actors and well-known places and incorporating them into the show. Do the same thing for people and places your audience will recognize. Crank up the cable TV and watch a few episodes to get ideas.

Ambiance

Visit the Flintstone home in the beautiful, prehistoric metropolis of Bedrock. Use lamps to provide soft light and, of course, you'll want to hear a few "Yabba-dabba-doo's" in the background. Use peat to give the room a slightly dusty, earthy smell.

Colors

Use "quarry" colors of stone tan, slate grey and light blue.

Suggested Attire

The suggested attire is "yabba dabba do" casual.

Invitations

"Gather up your modern, stone-aged family and join us for an evening in Bedrock." Send invitations on paper that looks like granite or slate, or cut funny Fred Flintstone ties.

Decorations

Set the tables with stone tan tablecloths, stoneware instead of china, and ceramic cups instead of glasses. One of the most enduring images of the Flintstones is the giant rack of brontosaurus ribs that topples the car at the Drive-In in the show's opening sequence. Create racks of giant ribs from covered wire frames for your centerpieces.

Keywords

Fred, Barney, Wilma, Betty, Bam Bam, Pebbles, Cobblestone Lane, quarry, rocks, dinosaurs, Dino, bones, bird whistle, rock wheels, peddle car, elephant dishwasher, dinosaur ribs, horn phone, Bedrock, Hanna-Barbera, Mr Slate, quarry, brontosaurus burgers, pterodactyl eggs, bird telephone, Bed Rock, horn phone, peddle car, saber tooth tiger, pearl necklace, big stitches, Pebbles, Bam Bam, Hoppy, Fred's tie, palm trees, stone buildings, turtle foot stool, canopy on the car, bare feet, sundial watches, Drive-In, bird beak knife, chisel pencil, stone-tablet

Flintstones

Take a cue from television to set the stage for this theme with large styrofoam or floral foam boulders. Spray paint them a light tan and use a sponge to add darker colors for texture.

Create stone "windows" for the walls and hang fabric animal skin curtains in them — just like those in the Flintstone's living room.

Menu

Consider this "Bedrock Café" menu.

- appetizers: Pterodactyl eggs (deviled eggs), Dinosaur ribs (honey glazed pork ribs)
- main course: Brontosaurus burgers (1/2 pound hamburgers) with all the fixin's
- dessert: Granite pie (key lime with toasted coconut topping)
- specialty drinks: Sledgehammer (apple brandy, brandy, gold rum, Pernod)

Entertainment

Arrange for a bank of televisions or a large screen to show episodes of the *Flintstones*. Play a game of *Make it Bedrock*. See if your guests can take the names of cities, actors, bands or movies and see if they can make them fit into the Bedrock of the Flintstones. For example, the nation's capital might be named Washingstone. Give prizes for the most inventive answers.

Souvenirs/Party Favors

As guests enter, give them a "costume." Give the women big pearl necklaces like Wilma and Betty wore, and big, goofy (clip-on) ties to clip on like Fred wore.

Fund Raisers

If you need to raise funds, create a cutout of Fred's car with Dino's head sticking out of the roof. Allow guests to have their pictures taken with the cutout and sell the pictures.

Keywords

books, the Lodge, Celebrities who made appearances include: Rock Quarry, Gary Granite, Stony Curtis, Ann-Margrock, and Jimmy Darrock; TV celebs Ed Sullystone, Jimmy O'Neill-stone, Rocky Genial, Perry Masonry, Alvin Brickrock, Larry Lava, the Cartrocks, the Great Mesmo, Superstone, the Gruesomes, Samantha and Darrin Stephens, and Sassie; musical artists Hoagy Carmichael, the Way Outs, Hot Lips Hannigan, Scat Von Rocktoven, and Rock Roll; boxer Sonny Dempstone, slapstick, Chip Rockefeller, **www.celebration-solutions.com/flintst.html**

Entertainment Themes

Introduction

Frank Sinatra (1915-1998) was one of the most famous singers of his generation. He sang with the big bands of Harry James and Tommy Dorsey in the 1930s but branched out to a solo career during the 1940s. His light baritone has been described as "subtle, yet sublime, penetrating and sophisticated, part jazz and pure sound." He became the idol of the bobby-soxers, a headliner in the nightclubs and lounges of Las Vegas, and a star of the big screen. Use Sinatra's music to inspire a romantic evening of dining and dancing.

Ambiance

Picture a Las Vegas nightclub in the late 1940s when the troops were back home and the country was "swinging." Use table lamps for lighting and keep the music hoppin'.

Colors

Use "wingtips and double breasted suit" colors of khaki brown, sand tan and light orange.

Suggested Attire

The suggested attire is "night out on the town in the 1940s" cocktail.

Invitations

"Come fly with me … come fly, come fly away … for a night of '40s magic." Send your invitations on an old vinyl album. Redecorate the cover and write the invitation details on the album in white ink. If you can't bear to destroy a piece of Americana no matter how scratched and worn, buy stiff, black, plastic sheets and cut album shapes instead.

Decorations

Set the tables with khaki tablecloths, white china and light orange napkins for a splash of color. Use a fancy napkin fold to give the table height and depth. For the centerpieces, create "cathedral" radios, popular in the late 1930s and early '40s. If you like, make these centerpieces of cake, big enough to feed the entire table.

Keywords

Francis Albert Sinatra, My Way, the kid from Hoboken, Tommy Dorsey's band, nightclubs, singer, actor, saloon singer, torch songs, swing era, lead singer on the Lucky Strike Hit Parade, Columbia Records, wide-shouldered, bow-tied crooner, "Swoonlight Sinatra," "Prince Charming of the Juke Box," Ol' Blue Eyes, Chairman of the Board, Swoonatra, autograph-seeker mobs, Bob Hope, Bing Crosby, the Swooners (his baseball team), Billboard charts, Hollywood Bowl, dancing with Gene Kelly, snap-brim hat, loose tie, and coat thrown casually over his

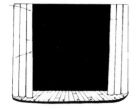

Frank Sinatra

Create facades that look like old-fashioned juke boxes to place throughout the room and place oversized, old-fashioned microphones on steady microphone stands against the walls.

Menu

Consider this "celebration of Frank Sinatra's movies" menu.

- appetizers: *Anchors Aweigh* (shrimp cocktail), *On the Waterfront* (oysters on the half shell)
- main course: *Manchurian Candidate* (a variety of Chinese dishes)
- dessert: *Guys and Dolls* (white chocolate and macadamia nut cheesecake with chocolate sauce)
- specialty drinks: *High Society* martinis

Entertainment

If you can, find a soloist who can do Frank Sinatra justice and a pianist to back him up Las Vegas lounge style. If not, play Frank Sinatra music from his early records during the 1930s and 1940s. Think about the songs he was most famous for such as *My Way, You Go to My Head, Fly Me to the Moon, Someone to Watch Over Me, My Blue Heaven, Fools Rush In, My Kind of Town, That Old Black Magic,* or *Embraceable You.*

Frank Sinatra

Souvenirs/Party Favors

Give each guest a name badge with their initials in the style of an old radio call sign (i.e. John James Smith would be WJJS) and have fancy martini glasses etched with the name Sinatra on them. You can put the *Anchors Aweigh* shrimp cocktail in the martini glasses, or pass them out to guests from the bar.

Fund Raisers

If you need to raise funds, sell Frank Sinatra album collections on CD or his most popular films or performances on DVD. Some of his best performances are available on a 2-DVD set entitled, *A Man and His Music (Parts I and II).*

Keywords

shoulder, wives Nancy Barbato, Ava Gardner, Mia Farrow and Barbara Blakely, Academy Award, dangerous allure, punch and swagger, jazzy, bluesy piano solos, Rat Pack - Sinatra, Sammy Davis Jr, Dean Martin, Joey Bishop and Peter Lawford, Las Vegas, balladeer, Hoboken, New Jersey, Manchurian Candidate, From Here to Eternity, Young at Heart, High Society, Pal Joey, odd-ball parts in off-beat movies, rhythmic, tense, instinctive, Ocean's 11, Anchors Aweigh, Guys-Dolls, 'Hoboken Horn Blower,' **www.celebration-solutions.com/sinatra.html**

Entertainment Themes

Introduction

Impressionism was a painting style that originated in France in the late 19th Century. Impressionist painters broke most of the former rules of painting by capturing what they saw rather than a stylized vision of beauty that was popular in earlier art. Impressionists used broken brushtrokes of bright, unmixed colors on rough surfaces to give their paintings texture and often simplified compositions, without detail, for a striking overall effect. Give your guests a tour of an Impressionist's studio.

Ambiance

Picture a working art studio filled with supplies and both finished art and works in progress. Keep the lighting high to show off the artwork and play soft music that won't distract your guests while they "play." Open up some paint so that the room smells like an artist is hard at work.

Colors

Use "Van Gogh" colors theme of sunflower yellow, pumpkin orange and deep leaf green.

Suggested Attire

The suggested attire is "don't wear anything you wouldn't want to get paint on" casual.

Invitations

"Life is a big canvas, throw all the paint on it you can" — Danny Kaye (1913-1987). There are plenty of impressionist cards available out there or take a familiar photo and use image editing program to make it look like a painting.

Decorations

Set the tables with sunflower yellow tablecloths, deep green place settings and pumpkin orange napkins. Create paintbrush bouquets for centerpieces. Dip clean brushes in acrylic or oil paints so that the paint will stay on the brush. Allow the

Keywords

Manet, Matisse, Seurat, Renoir, Degas, Pissarro, Monet, Cassatt, Pissarro, Caillebotte, Braque, Bonnard, Dufy, Renoir, Morisot, pure color that make an impression, broken color painting, sketchy, loose, inexact, landscapes, dabs, realistic subjects, Barbizon school, seascapes, vibrant color, lively brushtrokes, themes from everyday life, high contrast, French influence, Societe Snonyme, Paris Salon - the official showplace for French art, an impression of the observed scene, heyday from 1860 to 1880, bright, primary colors - red, blue, yellow, no attempt to

Impressionists

brushes to dry and repeat the coating until the brush is well saturated with paint. Place the brushes in a tall, clear vase.

For wall decorations, use pictures of sites familiar to your guest. Use an image editing program to apply a brush filter to make the picture look like it's been painted. Blow these pictures up into poster size and wrap them onto light balsa wood frames as if they were stretched canvases. Place them on easels throughout the room.

Menu

This menu will leave an "impression" on your guests.
- appetizers: sweet violet salad (yes, the flowers are edible)
- main course: turkey tetrazini with warm herb bread and butter
- dessert: fruit boats with lemon sherbet
- specialty drinks: Fuzzy Martini (vanilla-flavored vodka, coffee-flavored vodka, peach schnapps) or Champs d'Elysses (cognac, yellow Chartreuse, lemon juice, bitters, sugar)

Entertainment

Hire an artist to give a painting demonstration and to give guests a painting lesson. Then let your guests help decorate the room. Either give guests blank canvases on easels or hang blank butcher paper on the walls and let them paint with brushes or sponges.

Souvenirs/Party Favors

Give your guests a calendar, note cards, or a print of famous paintings done by one of the impressionists.

Fund Raisers

If you need to raise funds, sell learn to pain packages. In the packages, include a how-to watercolor book, watercolor paper, watercolor paints and lessons with a watercolor instructor.

Keywords

disguise brush strokes, rarely used black, study of light and color, studio, open-air painting, Monet's The Luncheon, Monet's Lily Pond, Monet's Haystacks at Sunset, Renoir's The Swing, Van Gogh's Sunflowers, Toulouse-Latrec's Woman with Gloves, Surrat's Sunday Afternoon, Renoir's La Loge, Degas's Dance Foyer at the Opera, Monet in his Studio Boat, candid glimpses, fleeting effects of sunlight, expression, structure, form, Van Gogh's Flower Beds in Holland, optical color mix, warm red, yellow and red, **www.celebration-solutions.com/impress.html**

Entertainment Themes

Introduction

James Bond is the hero of a series of popular spy adventure novels by the English writer Ian Fleming. As a member of MI6, the counter-intelligence wing of the British Secret Service, Bond is an enigma. He's handsome and debonair — a man born to be a spy. He has superb fighting skills, a singular commitment to dangerous missions and he always gets the girl. He's irresistible, self-confident, has a typically British sense of humor and, always, a secret agenda. Bring your guests along on a secret mission, James Bond style.

Ambiance

Visit the inimitable Q's lab. Keep the lighting high to show off the works in progress in the lab. Of course, you'll need Bond theme music and audio files of Bond's best exchanges with the master of gadgets — the cantankerous Q.

Colors

Use "dashingly-handsome" colors of black-tie black and white-tie white.

Suggested Attire

The suggested attire is "James Bone" black tie ... what else!

Invitations

"Top Secret ... For Your Eyes Only." "You've been chosen to fulfill a mission for her Majesty's Secret Service." Send your invitation in an envelope within an envelope marked Top Secret. Or, send the invitation details on a CD that guests can read on a computer. You can be really creative with a multimedia invitation.

Decorations

Set the tables with white linens, black china and black-stemmed martini glasses. Fill the center of the table with gadgets — lots and lots of gadgets. Find hand-held games, toys that beep, flip phones, ray guns — anything that feels like a good spy gadget.

Dress mannequins or dress forms with uniforms you can find at a military

Keywords ——

007, intrigue, Bond girls, M, Q, Ian Fleming, British Intelligence, MI6, Moneypenny, Double-0, enigma, loner, counter-intelligence, Her Majesty's Secret Service, British Secret Service, code of honor, spy, superb fighting skills, unwavering commitment, danger, self-confident, sardonic humor, secret agenda, Commander Bond, licensed to kill, ultimate evil, deadly aim, commando, Walther PPK, shoulder holster, crack shot, martial arts, stealth, tailored clothes, tuxedo, battle dress, homing device, gadgets, watch laser, champagne, martini, shaken not

James Bond

surplus store — cammo, field or dress uniforms. Fill the pockets of the uniforms with gadgets and label the gadgets. Be creative. Let the gadgets perform fantastic feats — sunglasses with satellite uplinks, or watches with lasers, or pagers with fingerprint readers, etc.

Menu

Consider this "European chic" menu.

- appetizers: sauteed scallops on green salad
- main course: couscous with lamb and chicken, and cherry tomatoes with white bean puree
- dessert: caramelized pear tartlets
- specialty drinks: James Bond Martini (gin, vodka, Lillet blanc - shaken not stirred) and champagne

Entertainment

Play the theme song from the Bond movies as guests enter the party. Show the best action clips from the Bond movies on screens around the room. Play a game of *Assassin*. Each guest at the table gets a card face down. The player with the X will be the assassin. Everyone looks at each other around the table. If the Assassin winks at you, you must call out "I've been hit" and drop out. If the Assassin "hits" everyone at the table without someone at the table catching on to who the assassin, he wins.

Souvenirs/Party Favors

Give your guests a fun, but practical gadget such as a pen with a personal voice recorder in it.

Fund Raisers

If you need to raise funds, give your guests a chance to bid on activities that are "spy-like." For example, you might want to auction tickets for fighter pilot for a day, a flight simulator, a tour of a military installation, or a ride in a race car.

Keywords —

stirred, criminal's lair, world domination, top-secret, decoder, throwing knife, remote control car, Aston Martin, BMW, laser, bombs, underwater guns, Little Nellie (personal helicopter), safecracker, wave walker, steel teeth, the Lover's card, speed boats, Wet Nellie (underwater car - Lotus Esprit), limpet mines, space station, Acrostar (personal jet), the Q Boat (submarine), parahawks, diplomatic pouch, Sean Connery, George Lazenby, Roger Moore, Timothy Dalton, Pierce Brosnan, villains, action, gadgets, **www.celebration-solutions.com/jbond.html**

Entertainment Themes

Introduction

Born in 1909 in Connecticut, Katharine Hepburn grew up in a large family and was known as Kit. As a young girl, Katharine Hepburn was an athlete who fantasized about becoming a movie star. She attended Bryn Mawr college where she strengthened her love for the theater. She married once, briefly, but never took to the married life. Her love for Spencer Tracy was legendary, and that's what this theme is all about … legendary lovers. Invite your favorite couples for a night of "amour."

Ambiance

Celebrate history's legendary lovers like Spencer Tracy and Katherine Hepburn — perfect for Valentine's day or anniversary parties. Keep the lighting low, close and intimate, and the music must, of course, be romantic. Use light perfume to give the air the scent of romance.

Colors

Use warm "New England fall" colors of deep rich greens and auburn reds.

Suggested Attire

The suggested attire is "I'm in the mood for love" cocktail.

Invitations

"True love is eternal" — Honore de Balzac (1799-1850). Send a separate invitation to each guest. "Bring your leading lady (or leading man) with you for a night filled with love and romance, like Katherine Hepburn and Spencer Tracy." On the outside of the invitation place a picture of either Tracy or Hepburn. On the inside, use a picture of them embracing.

Decorations

Set the tables with deep green tablecloths with lighter green napkins, deep crimson china and silver flatware. If possible, set the tables for two. Place small candle lamps or lanterns in the center of the tables. Place a single, red rose at the place setting of each of your women guests.

Keywords

Katharine Houghton Hepburn, actress, 4 Academy Awards, 11 Academy Award nominations, spunky, Spencer Tracy, The Philadelphia Story, Morning Glory, Little Women, Bringing up Baby, Adam's Rib, African Queen, Guess Who's Coming to Diner, Lion in Winter, Rooster Cogburn, On Golden Pond, The Corn if Green, vibrant personality, 1942's Woman of the Year, theater, critical acclaim, film studio, screen test, strong-willed, high-pitched voice, New England accent, performance, critics, reviews, co-star, Douglas Fairbanks, Jr., Henry Fonda, sweet yet

Katherine Hepburn

Use posters of famous kisses for your wall decorations. Use a lot of them. Make the walls look like a gallery of romance.

Menu

Consider this "perfect in pairs" menu.
- appetizers: Anthony and Cleopatra (Roman anti pasto salad)
- main course: Napoleon and Josephine (split grill of chicken cordon bleu and pork loin stuffed with apples)
- dessert: Bogart and Bacall (white and dark chocolate mousse)
- specialty drinks: Velvet Kisses (gin, crème de bananes, pineapple juice or passion fruit juice, half and half, and grenadine) and Love Cocktails (sloe gin, lemon juice, raspberry syrup, egg white)

Entertainment

You can hardly have a "greatest lovers" party without slow dancing. Hire a band that can play the romantic tunes from the '30s, '40s and '50s when Katharine Hepburn was at her movie-making best. Play a game of *Categories*. Have each guest write their significant other's full first name in a column down a sheet of paper. During each round, guests will write down an object that begins with the first letter of each letter of their partner's name. Choose categories for the women like sports cars and categories for the men like flowers. The first pair to come up with an object for each letter wins.

Souvenirs/Party Favors

As guests leave, give them gifts to give their significant others. Wrap the gifts for the women in red tied with a white ribbon and put a note on it that reads, "A gift to give to her." Wrap the men's gifts in green tied with darker green ribbon and attach a note that reads, "A gift to give to him." Choose something romantic like chocolates, scented candles or bath salts.

Fund Raisers

If you need to raise funds, auction romantic carriage rides, a night in the honeymoon suite, or a weekend at a get-away bed and breakfast.

Keywords

tough, biographer, melodramatic roles, tailored clothes, candid, Yankee, willful, heroine, Cary Grant, Jimmy Stewart, Humphrey Bogart, strong, confident, "one of the boys," private, Hollywood Women's Press Club's Sour Apple Award, red hair, freckles, grande dame, feisty, resilient, prominent cheekbones, tall, slender, perfectionist, professional, mania for privacy, beauty, grace, talent, devotion, Rooster Cogburn and the Lady, the Queen of Hollywood, screwball comedies, Best Actress Oscars, box office, **www.celebration-solutions.com/hepburn.html**

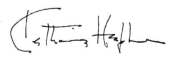

Entertainment Themes

Introduction

The Kentucky Derby — a famous horse race held at Churchill Downs racetrack in Louisville, Kentucky on the first Saturday in May — is a great American tradition. The race brings together the top three-year-old horses in the world. The track and race were founded in 1875 by Meriwether Lewis Clark, grandson of the explorer William Clark, who wanted to replicate England's Epsom Derby. The race is one and a quarter miles long and the first of three races that make up the Triple Crown. Invite your guests to join in the spectacle that is the Kentucky Derby.

Ambiance

Imagine race day in the owner's clubhouse. Keep the lighting high like sunshine streaming through the windows looking out over the racetrack. Play recordings of horse races and crowd noise in the background. Give the room the smell of freshly cut grass, like the rolling hills of Kentucky.

Colors

Use "race day" colors of grass green, rose red and white.

Suggested Attire

The suggested attire is "race day" afternoon formal.

Invitations

"Come join us ... in a run for the roses." With the popularity of the movie *Seabiscuit*, you shouldn't have trouble finding good ol' horse racing photographs, or you could send an audio file of the bugler's race call followed by your invitation message.

Decorations

Set the tables with rose red tablecloths, white china and green napkins. Fill the center of the tables with bouquets of red roses. Put a racing form at each place setting to give guests a chance to look over the entrants before the races begin.

Keywords ——————————

Kentucky, horses, riding crops, saddles, colors, jockey's silks, winner's wreath, mint juleps, top hats and tails, sport of kings, betting, stables, bookmaking, Triple Crown, handicap, winner's circle, paddock, photo-finish, thoroughbreds, escorted by lead ponies, trumpeter blows the battle call, positioned in individual stalls at the starting gate, starting line, come from behind, homestretch, lengths, 1 minute 32 second mile is the record for a horse on a dirt course, the chance of a lifetime, run for the roses, jockey's colors, Churchill Downs, crop,

Kentucky Derby

For wall decorations, use portraits of famous Kentucky Derby winners such as War Admiral, Whirlaway, Citation, Tim Tam, Secretariat, Seattle Slew, Affirmed, Alysheba, Unbridled, Charismatic and Funny Cide. Create a horseshoe-shaped bouquet of miniature roses to hang around the pictures. The winner of the Derby is presented with a similar bouquet.

In a corner of the room create a "tack" area with a hay bale or two, saddles, jockey silks, helmets, crops and boots.

Menu

Consider this "race day at Churchill Downs" menu.
- appetizers: Benedictine sandwiches (cucumber and cream cheese)
- main course: goose with chestnut stuffing
- dessert: strawberry tartlets with pink frosting rose petals
- specialty drinks: Mint Juleps (what else!) or Jockey Club Cocktails (gin, white crème de cacao, fresh lemon juice, bitters)

Entertainment

Hire an announcer from a local race track to help you create audio of fictional races. Play the audio and give every guest a racing form. Set up "betting" windows for guests to place their wagers. Allow guests to place bets on win, place or show, but otherwise it should be straight 1-1 odds betting since the winners are pre-determined. If you gave odds, you might give away the winning horse. Give away trip to the real Kentucky Derby to the big winner for the evening.

Souvenirs/Party Favors

Give guests a copy of the popular movie *Seabiscuit* in paperback or on DVD.

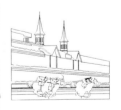

Fund Raisers

If you need to raise funds, allow guests to wager real money. If you do, make certain that you comply with any local laws regarding gambling or games of chance.

Keywords

jodphurs, born to run, foals, yearling, 3-year-olds, stables, trainer, pasture, paddock, soft rolling hills of Kentucky, stallions, fillies, withers, hoof, fetlock, breeding, snaffle bit, blinker, shadow roll, up in the irons, hands on the reins, stop watch, talk-of-the-town parties, starting lineup, the field is drawn, post position, high rollers, grandstand, clubhouse, racegoers, countdown, They're Off!, winning tradition, timeless beauty, farrier, horseshoes, win, place, show, hoofbeats, quarter, finish line, back of the pack, **www.celebration-solutions.com/kderby.html**

Kentucky

Entertainment Themes

Introduction

Lon Chaney (1883-1930) was an American motion-picture actor best known for his horror films first appearing in 1913. He often appeared in gruesome and grotesque makeup of characters warped by deformities. He is most well known for his roles in the titles roles of *The Hunchback of Notre Dame* and the *Phantom of the Opera*. He is often known as the man of a thousand faces because of his makeup techniques. Take your guests to a place where monsters — and the imagination — run wild.

Ambiance

This theme is creepy ... like Halloween on steroids. Keep the lighting as low as a castle dungeon and you'll need background sounds of howling wolves, creaking stairs, rattling chains, thunder and flashes of lightning. Give the room a musty, dusty smell like you would find in an old castle.

Colors

Use "creepy, crawly" colors of black, charcoal grey and light grey.

Suggested Attire

The suggested attire is "monsters and ghouls" costume. This party is all about the costumes. Encourage guests to come dressed as the creepiest, gruesomest monster they can imagine.

Invitations

"Help us to have a Good E-e-e-vning ... with your presence at our party." Find fuzzy tarantulas and glue their feet to your invitation. Dot the invitation with red (blood) ink blobs or include Halloween props in the invitation.

Decorations

Set the tables with black tablecloths, charcoal grey place settings and light grey napkins. For centerpieces, use standard Halloween fare — bowls of eyeballs, bloody hands coming out of the table, wax fingers, etc.

Coble together windows of old plywood and half-hanging shutters. String

Keywords

horror, monsters, Hunchback of Notre Dame, Phantom of the Opera, pantomime, gruesome, gory, Man of a Thousand Faces, Oliver Twist, Treasure Island, grotesque makeup, disguises, The Unholy Three, While the City Sleeps, wolf man, Dracula, Frankenstein, mummy, gouged, blood, Vincent Price, Boris Karloff, Bela Lugosi, Peter Lorre, Bride of Frankenstein, costume, changed appearance, conceal, strange, weird, bizarre, distorted, gnarled, monstrous, hideous, horrible, horrendous, frightening, Body Snatcher, "Good E-e-e-vning," grave robbers,

Lon Chaney

around "faux" spider webs and a few spiders. Search the second-hand stores for old trunks and cover them with a light talcum dust.

Menu

This celebration needs some "Halloween" fare.

- appetizers: jello and whipped cream salad
- main course: turkey with cornbread stuffing and green beans
- dessert: apple tarts and pumpkin cheesecake
- specialty drinks: Corpse Revivers (apple brandy, brandy, sweet vermouth) and hot apple cider

Entertainment

Hire a DJ to put together a collection of "Monster Mash" and other songs about ghouls that guests can dance to. Stick to lively, energetic tunes for your "Monster's Ball." Give away prizes for the best costume and the costumes that look most like a character Lon Chaney played in a movie, such as the *Hunchback of Notre Dame* or the *Phantom of the Opera*.

Souvenirs/Party Favors

Create a black and white flip book showing every guest in costume. As guests enter the party, ask photographers to get shots of each guest in costume. During the party, layout the pictures six (6) to a page, one page for each guest, so that each stack will create six flip books. Ask the printer to photocopy, cut and bind the books together. This can be done quickly and delivered back to the party before the guests leave.

Fund Raisers

If you need to raise funds, sell copies of the classic monster movies on DVD such as *Shadows*, *A Thousand Faces*, *The Ace of Hearts*, *The Wolfman*, *Nomads from the North*, *Werewolf of London*, *Frankenstein Meets the Wolf Man*, *The Devil's Messenger*, *Nosferatu*, *The Phantom of the Opera* or *The Hunchback of Notre Dame*.

Keywords

zombie, vampire, glowing red eyes, dripping fangs, pronounced limp, spooky house, curse, Prince of Darkness, mad monk, mad scientist, gloomy castle, "stark, raving mad," abominable, sinister, werewolf, villain, scream, tomb, coffin, ghost, hairy hand, giant, corpse, evil, specimen, menace, psycho, occult, howl, beast, Dr Jekyl, Mr Hyde, sneer, hypnotist, creepy, bogeyman, hobgoblin, ogre, gorgon, phantom, nightmare, creepy, horrifying, hair stand on end, Creature from the Black Lagoon, Monster Mash, **www.celebration-solutions.com/lcheney.html**

Celebration Solutions

Entertainment Themes

Introduction

The Louvre, properly known as the Musee du Louvre, is the national art museum of France and the palace in which it is housed is located on the banks of the Seine River. The palace was a residence of the Kings of France until 1862. It is one of the largest palaces in the world and occupies the site of a 13th Century fortress. In 1793, the Louvre was opened as a public museum. The nucleus of the museum's collection includes many Italian Renaissance paintings including many by Leonardo da Vinci, but it's most well known as the place where the Mona Lisa resides. Let your guests walk the halls the world's most renowned museum.

Ambiance

Picture the stately, grand museum of the masters. Look at the lighting in an art museum. Highlight your "artworks" but keep the lighting low throughout the rest of the room.

Colors

Use "Dutch Masters" colors of deep blue green, light blue green and dark mauve.

Suggested Attire

The suggested attire is "walking through the halls of art history" cocktail.

Invitations

"Join us for a Special Exhibition." Use art cards of the I.M. Pei pyramid in front of the Louvre or prints of the Mona Lisa. Frame them using a paper print that looks like an antique frame and place your invitation below the frame like an identification placard you would see below a painting in a museum.

Decorations

Set the tables with deep blue-green table cloths, light blue-green place settings and mauve napkins. Give each table a different centerpiece. Think about using art palettes, small statues, replicas of the David, sculptures or miniature portraits on little easels.

Keywords

Venus de Milo, Mona Lisa, Raphael, Titian, Leonardo da Vinci, Michaelangelo, Rubens, Rembrandt, Vermeer, Durer, Pissaro, Renoir, Degas, Toulouse-Lautrec, Cezanne, Egyptian antiquities, Oriental antiquities, Crown jewels of France, impressionists, post-impressionists, I.M. Pei glass pyramid, ancient Egyptian mummies, Roman statues, Etruscan pottery, bronze Apollo, Greek friezes, Byzantian silver, Coptic figures, relief figures in gold, ivory altars, intricate mosaics, early Christian art, funerary art, cherubs, marble sculptures, self-portraits, Italian

Louvre

For the wall art, arrange of a show of local artists or students. Invite the artists to join the party to talk about their work. If a guest wants to purchase a piece, the artist and guest can make arrangements to meet later for the sale. To give the room a little more visual substance, place small statues on shoulder-high plaster pedestals against the walls between every couple of works of art.

Menu
Consider this "French bistro" menu.
- appetizers: pear and walnut salad
- main course: Cornish game hens with lime spice marinade, herbed zucchini
- dessert: chocolate torts
- specialty drinks: Parisians (gin, dry vermouth, crème de cassis)

Entertainment
Hire a string quartet to play for guests as they wander the halls of your Louvre. If you need help finding a string quartet for your event, look at the listings at GigMasters, www. gigmasters.com. They list more than 15,000 musicians and musical groups.

Hire a photographer to take pictures of the guests during the party. Then use an image editing program to allow guests to choose an artistic filter to apply to their picture so that the print will look like something that's been painted or created in colored pencil. The effects can be really interesting. Give each individual or couple a copy of their print as they leave.

Souvenirs/Party Favors
Give each guest a museum-type souvenir such as a paperweight of the famous I.M. Pei pyramid or a desk calendar featuring the art of the Louvre.

Fund Raisers
If you need to raise funds, sell copies of the "Great Museum" tours available on CDs for viewing on a computer.

Keywords

renaissance paintings, portraits, scenes of life at court, battle scenes, Dutch masters, learned and sophisticated, collection of works, gardens, still-lifes, preservation, display, grand galleries, Hall Napoleon, Richelieu Wing, Department of Prints and Drawing, objects d'art, famous artists, Dutch masters, Art Deco style, realists, aboriginal art, surrealism, romanticism, Dada, cubism, baroque, classicism, Rembrandt's Christ at Emmaus, salon exhibits, decorative ceilings, acquisitions, unveiling, musee, **www.celebration-solutions.com/louvre.html**

Entertainment Themes

Introduction

M*A*S*H, which stands for mobile army surgical hospital, was originally a motion-picture comedy about combat surgeons during the Korean War which became a hit television series. Surgeons Trapper John McIntyre and Hawkeye Pierce provide the backbone for the story as they try to forget the war. Major Burns and his not-so-secret lover Major Houlihan are often fodder for the surgeon's fun. Ask your guests to play a role in the much-loved series.

Ambiance

Visit the "Swamp" — the tent where the doctors made their home. You'll need background sounds like helicopters coming and going, and jeeps entering and exiting the camp. Keep the lighting low like you would find inside a tent. The real Swamp probably smelled of a still and old socks. A better alternative might be the smell of oiled canvas.

Colors

Use "combat" colors of army green and khaki tan.

Suggested Attire

The suggested attire is anything you would see on M*A*S*H — army greens, hospital scrubs, one of Clinger's crazy outfits or Hawkeye's bathrobe.

Invitations

"Know this. You can cut me off from the civilized world. You can incarcerate me with two moronic cellmates. You can torture me with your thrice daily swill, but you cannot break the spirit of a Winchester. My voice shall be heard from this wilderness and I shall be delivered from this fetid and festering sewer" — Charles Emerson Winchester III, U.S. Army, MD. Use the logo for M*A*S*H and a memorable quote from one of the characters or find something at the Army Surplus store to send your invitation on.

Decorations

Set the tables mess hall style. Use khaki tablecloths, cammo napkins, mess kits and metal trays. In one of character Frank Burns' more famous scenes, he ar-

Keywords

8063rd, Hawkeye, BJ, Ferret face, Hot Lips, Klinger, Capt Benjamin Franklin Pierce, Capt BJ Honeycut, Colonel Henry Blake, Colonel Sherman T Potter, Corporal Radar O'Reilly, Major Margaret Hoolihan, Father John Francis Mulcahy, Sgt Maxwell Q Klinger, Major Frank Burns, Major Charles Emerson Winchester III, Nurse Kelley, Sidney Freedman, Major Flagg, Radar's teddy bear, the Swamp, tents, OR, triage, choppers, Rosie's Bar, Officer's Club, Korean War, 38th Parallel, hospital, Army, operating room, surgery, bandages, blood, music, radio, tents,

M*A*S*H

ranged the condiments precisely by height and color in the center of the table. You should too.

For the walls, create "tent" windows with roll-up khaki curtains. Hang army green socks from a clothesline and, of course, you will need a still (a fake one, naturally).

Place signs posts outside the entrance and around any open spaces in the room. Are your guests coming from different home towns? Put their towns and the mileages on the signs.

Menu

Consider this "Army mess hall" menu.
- appetisers: corn rissoto
- main course: SOS (aka *#@ on a shingle, but we've substituted meatloaf, drop biscuits and green beans)
- dessert: peach cobbler
- specialty drinks: Artillery Punch (bourbon, red wine, dark rum, appricot brandy, gin, strong black tea, orange juice, lemon juice, lime juice, and sugar)

Entertainment

Hire a DJ to play music from 1950-1953, the time of the Korean War. Hold M*A*S*H-style goofy races that can be held indoors — a gurney race, a Father Mulcahy marathon, or a Sister Teresa's Orphanage spoon race. Watch a few episodes to get ideas.

Souvenirs/Party Favors

Give guests a season of M*A*S*H episodes on DVD, or an army green, M*A*S*H 4077 T-shirt.

Fund Raisers

If you need to raise funds, ask guests to "buy their rank." Sell stick-on versions of lapel insignia such as Captain's bars, Major's oak clusters and Colonel's eagles. The higher the rank the greater the cost.

Keywords ——————————————

irreverent, MPs, still, Klinger's outrageous outfits, red cross, Hawaiian shirts, pink bathrobe, moose, black market, Chief Surgeon, aide station, five o'clock Charlie, sniper, mail call, chow line, Officer of the Day, Private Charles Lamb, VIP tent, regular army, bug-out, Sophie, Ottumwa, Iowa, Mill Valley, Maine, Toledo Mudhens, sign post, post-op, "You've been dipping into the sacramental wine," "Jocularity," Babette the guinea pig, Edna the cow, Radar's Uncle Ed, Daisy and Sluggo, grape Nehi, Peg and Erin, **www.celebration-solutions.com/mash.html**

Entertainment Themes

Introduction

Modern magic has its roots in ancient pagan temples where doors were rigged to open with a sound like a peal of thunder, statues that poured wine when a fire was kindled on an altar, and magic lanterns that could project images of demons on clouds of smoke. In the Middle Ages, such devices were improved by "sorcerers" who claimed to have powers. Today, magic is the art of entertaining with tricks that defy the eye and the laws of physics using misdirection, suggestion, imitation and concealment to trick the viewer into believing they're seeing what should be impossible. Give your guests a night of enchantment.

Ambiance

This theme is all about mystery and magic. Keep the lighting low and use a fog machine or dry ice to create misty atmosphere. Play mystical celtic music in the background.

Colors

Use "card-trick" colors of black, white and red.

Suggested Attire

The suggested attire is "magic show" cocktail.

Invitations

"We'd like to 'make you appear' at a celebration of mystery and wonder." Send a mystery message that appears when wiped with water or print the message so it must be read in a mirror. Or, send a kit with a simple magic trick along with your invitation.

Decorations

Set the tables with white tablecloths, white china and red napkins. For your centerpieces, turn top hats upside down and fill them with white beanie baby bunnies. Add a magic wand and a pair of white gloves to each place setting.

For wall decorations, create giant aces in each of the different suits. Use patterned wrapping paper to create the hearts, diamonds, clubs and spades to give

Keywords

cape, wand, top hat, bow tie, wizard, sleight of hand, black magic, white magic, scorceror, witches, druids, faeries, David Copperfield, Harry Potter, Merlin, Harry Houdini, magician, trick, wand, hat, cape, gloves, hidden, casting spells, mind reader, illusion, pulled a rabbit from a hat, levitation, hypnotism, fire-eater, wand, disappear, David Copperfield, Siegfried and Roy, conjuring, manual dexterity, stage tricks, floating on air, clairvoyance, telepathy, saw a woman in half, levitation, Indian rope trick, hocus pocus, "now you see it ... now you don't,"

Magic

the cards some texture. Arrange them in "hands" and place a hand every so often down the walls.

Build a "disappearing" box that guests can step into, close the curtain, exit through the back and pull the curtain open to show anyone watching that they have disappeared. Place crystal balls and magic lanterns on the serving tables. Encourage guests to pick up the lanterns and rub them to make a wish.

Menu

Consider this "simply magical" menu.
- appetisers: roast tomato soup
- main course: spicy pork roast with asparagus and mini bleu cheese soufflets
- dessert: Baked Alaska
- specialty drinks: Blue Blazers (scotch, boiling water, confectioners' sugar. Light — carefully!) or Black Magic (vodka, coffee liqueur, fresh lemon juice)

Entertainment

Hire a magician to perform magic tricks. Use the fog machine to create a dramatic entrance for the performer. At the end of the show, ask the magician to teach the audience a slight of hand trick. Pass out any materials that might be necessary for the trick and give guests plenty of time to practice the trick before the magician leaves.

In addition to the magician, hire fortune tellers to divine the future, read tea leaves, palms or predict guests' fortunes through the cards.

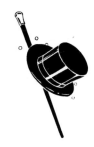

Souvenirs/Party Favors

Give each guest a top hat full of easy-to-perform magic tricks — card tricks, coin tricks, slight of hand tricks or a book of tricks.

Fund Raisers

If you need to raise funds, sell private lessons with a magician or tickets to a popular magic show.

Keywords

illusionist, escape artist, telekinesis, parlor tricks, palming the card, gimmick, props, spellbound, Doug Henning, coin tricks, grifters, cups and balls, "before your very eyes," Uri Geller, gags, stunts, brain teasers, silk handkerchiefs, knot tricks, setup, vanish, black arts, smoke and mirrors, "look into my eyes," mind reader, Kreskin, hypnotic, The Amazing …, three-card Monte, Penn and Teller, magnetism, "Abracadabra," conjurer, Hocus Pocus, prestidigitation, "Sim Sala Bim," spells, tokens, bewitchment, **www.celebration-solutions.com/magic.html**

Celebration Solutions

Entertainment Themes

Introduction

In its first year, 1935, the MONOPOLY™ game was the best-selling game in America. Today, it's the best-selling board game in the world, sold in 80 countries and produced in 26 languages. Over its 65-year history, an estimated 500 million people have played! The object of the game is to become the richest player on the board by buying, selling, renting, and trading properties. A set consists of the board, play money, models of hotels and houses, dice, special cards, and tokens. The streets on the board were named after those in Atlantic City, N.J., where the inventor, Charles Darrow, vacationed. Invite your guests to come and play the world's most popular game.

Ambiance

This theme is "game-playing" happy. Keep the lighting high and use the bright, cheerful colors of the game to give the room a fun, playful atmosphere. Play music in the background but keep the volume low, so guests can talk to each other while they play.

Colors

Use "Boardwalk" colors of Park Place blue, Baltic Avenue purple and Marvin Gardens yellow.

Suggested Attire

The suggested attire is "play clothes" casual.

Invitations

"Our celebration will be greatly *enriched* by your presence." Attach the cards and the play money for the game to your invitation.

Decorations

Set the tables with alternating Park Place blue, Baltic Avenue purple and Marvin Gardens yellow tablecloths with napkins to match. Use white china and oversized playing cards for placemats. For centerpieces, create big playing pieces and spray paint them silver. Garden statuary works well for this.

Keywords

Parker Brothers, game, Park Place, Do Not Pass Go, play money, playing pieces, Community Chest, Chance, Go to Jail, Get out of Jail free, houses, hotels, railroad, Electric Company, property deals, financial bargaining, estate, public utilities, Short Line Railroad, buy, sell, rents, mortgages, taxes, fines, trips to jail, evade bankruptcy, wooden houses, wooden hotels, rules, As you Pass GO, Collect $200, B&O Railroad, Boardwalk, Park Place, Marvin Gardens, Baltic Avenue, Reading Railroad, banker, Electric Company, paying rent, collect $100, Free

Monopoly™

For wall decorations, create poster-sized Community Chest and Chance cards. Make the inscriptions about something familiar (tax day) or about your local community. Get "community" chests and fill them with prizes. Create balloon boquets using the colors from the streets and put a "prize" inside each balloon. Visit local businesses and to get discount coupons for ice cream or gourmet cookies to put inside the balloons. Toward the end of the party, ask each guest to take a balloon and pop it to see what their prize is.

Menu

Consider this " … only if you're game!" menu.
- appetisers: Marvin Gardens salad
- main course: Boardwalk Basket (fish and chips)
- dessert: Electric Company (lemon sherbet in parfait glasses)
- specialty drinks: Park Place (aka Swamp water — dark rum, blue Curacao, fresh orange juice, fresh lemon juice)

Entertainment

Give each table a Monopoly™ board. There are more than 30 different versions of Monopoly, so you could give every table a different one. Change the rules slightly so that the game will play really fast. Give each player a generous amount of play money. If a player lands on a property they have to buy it. If they already own it they have to build something on it. And if they land on someone else's property they must pay up. If a player runs out of cash, they're out of the game.

Souvenirs/Party Favors

Give each guest a copy of a make-your-own Monopoly or a version that features the place where you'll be holding your celebration.

Fund Raisers

If you need to raise funds, hire actors in black and white striped "jail" suits to come and present a few guests at a time with "Go directly to jail" cards. Implore the other guests to make a donation to get set the "jailbird" free.

Keywords

Parking, boot, racing car, iron, cannon, battleship, rocking horse, hat, purse, Water Works, thimble, lantern, dice, Grand Hotel, Title Deed, St James Place, Pennsylvania R.R., Christmas Fund matures, Collect $50 from every player, Bank Error in your favor collect $200, Pay Poor Tax $15, Advance to nearest Railroad, Advance to Go, Take a Ride on the Reading, pewter tokens, Short line, luxury tax, Do not pass Go, Do not collect $200, Take a walk on the Boardwalk, Go directly to Jail, Monopoly money, tokens, **www.celebration-solutions.com/monopoly.html**

Entertainment Themes

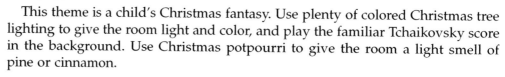

Introduction

The Nutcracker is best known as a ballet that was first performed in the Maryinsky Theater in St. Petersburg, Russia in 1892. Set to a Tchaikovsky score, it's a rich fantasy of color and elaborate costumes. The ballet opens with a Christmas party. A magician brings clockwork toys for the children, including a nutcracker for Clara. Late that night, after the guests have gone, Clara returns to look for her gift, which comes to life. After she helps him lead the toy soldiers to victory against invading mice, he turns into a handsome prince, who whisks her away through dancing snowflakes to the Kingdom of Sweets. There the Sugar Plum Fairy entertains Clara, and she and her cavalier dance a beautiful pas de deux. Invite your guests for a "dreamy" celebration.

Ambiance

This theme is a child's Christmas fantasy. Use plenty of colored Christmas tree lighting to give the room light and color, and play the familiar Tchaikovsky score in the background. Use Christmas potpourri to give the room a light smell of pine or cinnamon.

Colors

Use Christmas "fantasy" colors of pink, purple, teal, red and white.

Suggested Attire

The suggested attire is "a night out at the ballet" formal.

Invitations

" 'Twas the night before Christmas, and all through the night, the guests were all gathered, their joy a delight." Use a good picture of a nutcracker or send your invitation attached to a string of miniature Christmas lights.

Decorations

Set the tables with white tablecloths, white china, dark pink napkins and light pink napkin rings. Use miniature, decorated christmas trees with for your centerpieces. Place very small wrapped packages at the base of the trees.

Keywords

wooden soldiers, ballet, swan princess, dream, night, twinkle snow, children, cookies, sweet smells of hot chocolate and gingerbread, peppermint and Christmas pudding, snow-covered pine woods, white wig spun out of glass threads, twinkle in the eye, tiny dolls that dance on the palm of a hand, flowing capes and fur muffs, new-fallen snow, white candles, bounty of presents, delirious with excitement, apple-red cheeks, life-sized dolls named Harlequin and Columbine, an invisible key brought them to life, hobby horse, tug of war, petticoats and

Nutcracker

For the walls, create colorful, mural-sized nutcrackers. Place them every few feet down opposing walls, so they look like the nutcracker army. Either make all of the nutcrackers different, or use just two patterns, one for each side of the room.

Throughout the room place piles of oversized Christmas packages. Cover big moving boxes with bright, shimery Christmas paper and wide, shiny ribbon.

Fill any empty spaces in the room with full-sized Christmas trees covered in colored lights. Choose an ornament you think your guests will like as a party souvenir and cover the trees with them.

Menu

Consider this "delightful" holiday menu.
- appetisers: ambrosia salad
- main course: prime rib with green beans
- dessert: bread pudding with brandy syrup
- specialty drinks: Nutcracker (crème de noisette, coconut amaretto, and half and half, over ice)

Entertainment

Play the music from the Nutcracker Suite. After the meal, bring out a gift for each guest. Make sure that no two gifts are wrapped alike, but the gifts could all be the same. Give each guest a decorative nutcracker or a CD of the Nutcracker Suite music.

Souvenirs/Party Favors

As guests leave, encourage them to take home an ornament off the trees.

Fund Raisers

If you need to raise funds, sell tickets to a local performance of the Nutcracker ballet, or auction off fully-decorated trees for the holidays.

Keywords

patent leather shoes, squealing mice with long tails, garlands of tinsel, toy sentry in a guard box, Mouse King, little drummer bunny, a Prince emerges from the form of the nutcracker, lightly falling snow, guided by the Christmas star, the Land of Sweets, Sugar Plum fairy on the arm of her Cavalier, Dewdrop and her garlands of long-stemmed flowers, Spanish Gypsies, reindeer sleigh flies away from the enchanted palace, "The Nutcracker and the King of Mice" the most beautiful tree imaginable. **www.celebration-solutions.com/nutcrakr.html**

Entertainment Themes

Introduction

Oliver! Is a motion-picture musical based upon the novel *Oliver Twist* by Charles Dickens. Young Oliver Twist lives in a horrible orphanage. One day, he dares to ask for more food and gets thrown out into the street for his trouble. Oliver meets a pickpocket named the Artful Dodger, who takes him under his wing and helps adopt him into Fagin's criminal family. Oliver is not very adept as a pick-pocket. Soon he is caught and sent to court where a wealthy gentleman takes pity upon him, and takes him home to live in luxury. Unfortunately, a dangerous criminal, Bill Sikes, sets his sights on Oliver as a source of ransom. All's well that ends well, though, as Oliver is rescued from Sikes. Let your guests have a taste of Oliver's "hard knock" life.

Ambiance

Picture a tenement in Victorian-era London. Keep the lights low and use a fog machine to give the room the feel and smell of old London. Use the soundtrack from the movie for the background sound.

Colors

Use "grungy, London back-alley" colors of dark and light khaki green, and dark and light brown.

Suggested Attire

The suggested attire is "Artful Dodger grunge" casual.

Invitations

"The Artful Dodger slipped away from the 'coppers', but we hope you won't dodge our celebration!" Use a photograph of fancy jewels or send your invitation inside a 'filched' mini purse.

Decorations

Set the tables with dark khaki green tablecloths and napkins of different colors of tan and brown. Visit some flea markets so you can mix and match the place setting and flatware. While you're at the flea market buy old wallets, pocket

Keywords

London, orphanage, orphans, gruel, grimy, dirty, ragged clothes, pitiful, Artful Dodger, Fagin, Nancy, Bill Sykes, pickpockets, rogue, street urchin, "food, glorious food," "please, sir, I want some more," Boy for Sale, Victorian England, Dickens, Mr Bumble, "consider yourself one of the family," top hat, gloves without fingers, floppy bow ties, ragged pants, shoes with holes, bar maids, hideaway, tavern, "I'd do anything for you, dear, anything …," jewels from the tower, cheerio, pip pip, alleys, rooftops, thieves, get 'pinched,' lockup, flower market, wealthy

Oliver

watches and costume jewelry. Create a pile of "loot" in the middle of the table for centerpieces. To help give the room the feel of a grungy, back alley, create murals of exposed brick and stone. Place Victorian-era-looking gas street lamps every so often against the walls.

Menu

Consider this "early Victorian" menu.

- appetisers: crisp toast with mozarella and bruschetta topped with spiced beets or onion marmelade
- main course: Gruel (thick crab-corn chowder)
- dessert: coffee truffel pudding
- specialty drinks: London Fog (white crème de menthe, Pernod, vanilla ice cream)

Entertainment

Hire actors to come dressed in costume and scamper through the crowd making believe they're picking pockets and avoiding the cops. Or, hire musicians to perform the songs from the musical.

Play a game of *Pickpocket*. To win the game, you'll have to gather the most loot while avoiding entanglements with the law. You'll find a board and rules on the web page for this theme.

Souvenirs/Party Favors

Give each guest a "pickpocketed" wallet. Visit popular local businesses and fill the wallets full of coupons for products and services. Visit the new businesses first. They may be eager to offer your guests a coupon or free merchandise to get customers in the door.

Fund Raisers

If you need to raise funds, hold a "One Boy, Boy for Sale" sale. Ask a few guests to play along as the "Olivers" to be auctioned off. Implore their spouses and friends to make a contribution to get them back.

Keywords

patron, "Who will buy my sweet red, roses? Two blooms for a penny," gallows, worn and torn clothes, bob, pound, pence, shilling, bawdy house, oom pah pah, waif, denizens of an underworld, villains of various descriptions, underworld figures, picaresque novel, English Classics, wastrel, incorrigible, cur, cad, scoundrel, dastardly, blighter, rotter, louse, guttersnipe, nipper, ragamuffin, tatterdemalian, the bells of St Mary le Bow, Hackney Road, Whitechapel High Street, Bethnal Green, Mr Bumble, **www.celebration-solutions.com/oliver.html**

Entertainment Themes

Introduction

The *Phantom of the Opera* is a story of love and fear based on the 1911 novel by Gaston Leroux. In 1925, it was released as a silent motion picture starring Lon Chaney. In the 1980s, it became a hit in theaters around the world. In the story, a young opera singer named Christine catches the eye of the masked Phantom, a hideously deformed man living in the cellars of the opera house, who falls in love with her. He terrifies the opera company and scares away the lead soprano. Christine and Raoul, a nobleman, escape the Phantom and pledge their love to one another. Enraged at Christine's betrayal, the Phantom kidnaps her and forces her to choose between a life with him in the catacombs, or the death of Raoul. Invite your guests for a night in the Phantom's lair.

Ambiance

Imagine the place where the beautifully-clad opera-goers go to see and be seen — the Paris Opera House. To maintain the illusion that something scary is happening behind the scenes, you'll need background sounds of creatures moving through the catacombs and a few strange and creepy sounds. Keep the lighting low like the lamplight you would find in the real opera house.

Colors

Use "Paris Opera" colors of blood red, black and metallic gold.

Suggested Attire

The suggested attire is "bejeweled Paris opera" formal.

Invitations

"Don't be a Phantom at our celebration!" Create an opera program for your invitation or send the invitation along with long, white opera gloves.

Decorations

Set the tables with black tablecloths, gold-edged china, and red-stemmed wine glasses. Use floral centerpieces using red roses, babies breath and metallic gold accents in obsidian black vases.

Keywords

la Fantome de l'Opera, mask, cape, black hat, tuxedo, opera house, red rose, lavish, opulent surroundings, candleabras, chandeliers, grand staircases, carved ceiling, grand foyer, loggia, opera-goers in silks and jewels, honeycomb of passages behind the stage, the phantom seated at his organ, swinging from the chandelier, mysterious figure, a heroine placed in danger, sighting of the legend, a figure lingering near the dressing room door, the Phantom, Christine and Raoul, Box 5, Madame Giry, masked ball, a silhouette glimpsed for a second,

Phantom of the Opera

From the ceiling, hang beaded chandeliers. Create simple wire forms from gold rings and gold wire. String clear crystal beads from fishing line attached to the frame to create a pretty pattern.

Menu

Consider this "Paris opera-house gourmet" menu. Ask the wait staff to dress as the Phantom in black pants, white tuxedo shirts, black satin capes and white masks.

- appetisers: crab tartlets with zucchini puree
- main course: roasted duck with mango chutney and leak salad
- dessert: strawberry tarts with crème fraiche
- specialty drinks: Opera (gin, Dubonnet rouge, maraschino liqueur)

Entertainment

Arrange to play the music from the *Phantom of the Opera* score while your guests play tabletop Baccarat. Baccarat is a casino game popular in Europe, played with eight decks of cards without Jokers. Face cards count 0, Aces count 1, and numbered cards have their face value. When the value of the cards are added up, only the last number counts, so it's impossible to overdraw in Baccarat. For example, a nine and a two would equal eleven, but will count as 1. The hand closest to 9 wins. You'll find a tabletop Baccarat board and rules on the web page for this theme.

Souvenirs/Party Favors

Send each guest home with a copy of the *Phantom of the Opera* music CD performed by the original London cast or a paperback copy of the *Phantom of the Opera* by Gaston Leroux.

Fund Raisers

If you need to raise funds, auction a trip to a city where the *Phantom of the Opera* is playing, or a trip to Paris to see a performance at the Paris Opera House.

Keywords

wearing velvet breeches, a cloak and a feathered, broad-brimmed hat, backstage sightings, an understudy murdered in her dressing room, a chandelier falls into the audience, the Phantom's lair, mausoleum scene, through the mirror into the lair, Masquerade, disguise, costume, cloak, pretense, mummer, veiled, obscure, shadowy, mystical, enigmatic, ineffable, mystifying, shattered looking glass, cast, "Think of my fondly when this night has ended," "Look at your face in the mirror, you'll find me," **www.celebration-solutions.com/phantom.html**

Entertainment Themes

Introduction

William Shakespeare (1564-1616), an English playwright and poet, is recognized as the greatest playwright of all time and the most widely quoted author in history. His works continue to flow from the press 350 years after the first publication. His characters Hamlet, Lear and Othello are tragic heroes of magnificent stature and nobility. His clowns, Falstaff, Touchstone and Launce with his dog, are funny and irresistible. And his women, Juliet, Cleopatra and Lady Macbeth are idealized and unforgetable. Treat your guests to a "witty" look at the works of the Bard.

Ambiance

Picture a performance of *A Midsummer Night's Dream* in the Bard's Tudor-style Globe Theater. Keep the lights low and use plenty of twinkle lights to set the scene. Think about the sounds you would hear on a lazy summer evening at dusk — insects buzzing, birds chirping, or a breeze blowing.

Colors

Use "regal" colors of purple, white, sage green and metallic gold.

Suggested Attire

The suggested attire is "a night out at the theater" cocktail.

Invitations

"All the world is a stage … and we request your presence in our 'company.' " Make your invitations look like a volume of Cliff Notes. Depict *Measure for Measure* with rulers, weights or balances, and *MacBeth* with daggers.

Decorations

Set the tables with purple tablecloths, sage green napkins, pewter ale mugs, pewter plates. Place hurricane lamps on the tables as centerpieces, representing *The Tempest*. Around the bases of the lamps, place lightly flocked pine boughs, representing *A Winter's Tale*. In the pine boughs, place exactly 12 metallic confetti stars, representing *Twelfth Night*.

Keywords

The Bard, protagonist, antagonist, comedies, folly, farces, foibles slapstick, As You Like It, All's Well That Ends Well, Measure for Measure, Comedy of Errors, Two Gentlemen of Verona, Taming of the Shrew, Love's Labour's Lost, mistaken identity, A Midsummer Night's Dream, Merchant of Venice, romantic comedy, Much Ado about Nothing, Merry Wives of Windsor, Twelfth Night, histories, chronicles, English monarchs, Henry IV, Henry V, Richard II, King John, Henry VIII, tradgedies, revenge, murder, Macbeth, Othello, Romeo and Juliet, King Lear,

Shakespeare

Fill any empty spaces in the room with wreaths of grapevines and live potted plants filled with twinkle lights for *A Midsummer Night's* dreamy feel.

To create the feel of the Globe Theater, hang Tudor-style "rafters" made from 6" wide, deep brown ribbon. You only have to create a framework from the ribbons. You don't have to fill in the gaps. Look at pictures of an English castle's grand hall to get ideas.

Menu

Consider this "typically English" menu. Start off the meal with dessert and coffee to represent — *A Comedy of Errors.*
- appetisers: *Merry Wives of Windsor* — mixed green salad
- main course: *Much Ado about Nothing* — Shepherd's pie
- dessert: *As you Like It* — fix-it-yourself sundae bar
- specialty drinks: Poison punch — in loving memory of *Romeo and Juliet.*

Entertainment

Hold a contest between the Capulets and the Montagues. Split each table into a Capulet side and a Montague side. See if guests are able to guess which plays have been represented by what during the celebration. (You may have to provide a few cheat sheets with the names of Shakespeare's plays to guide them along.) Whichever side of the table with the most correct answers wins.

Souvenirs/Party Favors

Give each guest a paperback copy of Shakespeare's sonnets. Cover the books in romantic, Valentine's wrapping paper and tie them with a pink or red velvet ribbon.

Fund Raisers

If you need to raise funds, organize a *Merchant of Venice* sale or sell photographs taken at an *Anthony and Cleopatra* picture cutout.

Keywords

Hamlet, sonnets, seduction, devotion, Stratford-upon-Avon, plague, glove maker, Anne Hathaway, London, playwright, Queen Elizabeth I, Globe Theatre, The King's Men, King James I, Montagu, Capulet, Portia, Puck, Shylock, "To be or not to be," Ophelia, Prospero, King Lear, Cordelia, Desdemona, Stratford-upon-Avon, Blackfriars Theater, drama, stage show, theatricals, spectacle, extravaganza, farce, pageant, Merchant of Venice, "I could a tale unfold whose lightest word would harrow up thy soul," **www.celebration-solutions.com/thebard.html**

Entertainment Themes

Introduction

It all began in 1916, when D. W. Griffith changed the film industry forever by introducing the full-length masterpiece silent film *Intolerance*. Whether it was the westerns of Tom Mix or the melodramas of Mary Pickford, audiences loved the situational comedy, action scenes, massive sets, huge mobs, battles, chases, fights and last-minute rescues of the earliest motion pictures. Silent films made melodrama a household word. It was all drama and spectacle, and audiences ate it up! So will yours.

Ambiance

Picture an old-fashioned movie theater. Keep the lighting low to focus on the film clips and play early 20th Century music in the background, like what would have been heard while a silent movie played. And movie theaters always smell like popcorn.

Colors

Use "before-the talkies" colors of black and white.

Suggested Attire

The suggested attire is "kissing in the balcony" cocktail.

Invitations

"Our melodrama wouldn't be complete without you … please join us." Send your invitation in a black and white flip book. They're easy and inexpensive to make and will be fun for your guests to flip and read.

Decorations

Set the tables with black tablecloths, white napkins and white china. For centerpieces, create a few black, white and silver "movie" reels. Buy 3" shiny, black or silver ribbon on spools. Decorate the spools to look like film reels and glue 2" pictures of your guests or silent film stars to the last foot or so of the ribbon so that they look like the pictures on a film reel.

Keywords

cinemas, chase scenes, Keystone Kops, nickelodeon, melodramas, screen stars, studios, slapstick, feature films, shorts, newsreels, Charlie Chaplin, W C Fields, Douglas Fairbanks, Mary Pickford, flappers, Cecil B DeMille, Lillian Gish, Clara Bow, Gloria Swanson, Buster Keaton, Rudolph Valentino, Tom Mix, exaggerated makeup, one-reelers, American Mutoscope and Biograph Company, close-ups, towering sets, MGM, Paramount Pictures, Universal City, Fox Film Corporation, 24 frames per second made for less than smooth viewing, single cameras

Celebration Solutions

48

Silent Films

Use projectors throughout the room to show silent films on the walls like a multi-screen theater in the round. If the walls aren't white or smooth, you may have to hang white fabric or butcher paper to make the films look good. Hang mural-sized posters in any blank spaces on the walls

Find cutouts of silent film stars to stand up throughout the room.

Menu

Consider this "as glamorous as the stars who made silent films" menu.
- appetisers: spiced crabcakes with papaya chutney
- main course: stuffed pork filets with wild rice and scallions
- dessert: gourmet popcorn with parmesan, cheddar or caramel toppings
- specialty drinks: Charlie Chaplains (sloe gin, apricot brandy, lemon juice)

Entertainment

As guests enter, give them the opportunity to get "made up" as silent film stars. Hire a few makeup artists to put fake eyelashes and eye liner on the women, and create slicked-back, Brill cream hairdos for the men. Make sure a few of the party's organizers are already made up when guests arrive so that they can see what they'll look like after the makeup.

Watch a few silent films during dinner. The early films only lasted a few minutes each. Give guests a chance to step in front of a camera and perform a short scene in a melodrama. If you use a digital camera, these clips can be easily transferred to a CD that guests can take home with them.

Souvenirs/Party Favors

Give each guest or couple a picture of themselves made up as silent film stars and a CD of their silent film performance.

Fund Raisers

If you need to raise funds, sell the accessories that guests might like to add to their attire to make them look more like movie stars — long gloves, cigarette holders, rhinestone jewelry for the women; spats and fedora hats for the men.

Keywords

operating from fixed positions, comic, sentimental, melodramatic, box-office standing, directors, slapstick, staged, vamp, sight-gag, love story, satire, animated cartoons, spectacle, horror, gangster films, westerns, documentary, screwball comedy, costumes, décor, studio, extreme close ups, cliffhanger, sensational, emotional, sappy, maudlin, schmaltzy, tear-jerker, The Great Train Robbery, The Perils of Pauline, The Shiek, Pollyana, Birth of a Nation, The Mark of Zorro, producer, director, leading lady, **www.celebration-solutions.com/silents.html**

Entertainment Themes

Introduction

The pastime of journeying from home to some other place, near or far, has been popular since ancient times. Pleasure travel — summer excursions to Newport, R.I. or taking to the waters at a luxury spa — was largely only the pastime of the rich. With the development of the steam engine and comfortable oceangoing ships, traveling abroad became more comfortable. Today, with relatively cheap means of travel, tacky tourists can be found in every corner of the world, and at every imaginable bump in the road where you might find a tacky tourist attraction. Ask your guests to come along to a less "well known" tourist trap.

Ambiance

Create a tacky, roadside tourist attraction. Keep the lighting high like you're in the middle of a summer vacation. You'll need background sounds like you might hear at a typical tourist trap … conversations, people purchasing souvenirs, carnival rides and the like. Add fresh popcorn or cotton candy to your menu for the smell ... and the taste!

Colors

Use a "blizzard" of colors — orange, yellow, red, blue and green.

Suggested Attire

The suggested attire is "ticky tacky" casual.

Invitations

"Greetings from beautiful …(your party location)." Send your invitation on a postcard of a local tourist attraction, or make your invitation look like a plane or train ticket in a ticket wallet.

Decorations

Set the tables with whatever you have left over from other celebrations throughout the year. Nothing should match. Create a picture bouquet of travel brochures from local attractions and surround these attractive centerpieces with other tourist souvenirs.

Keywords

exotic locales, far away places, camera, sunglasses, Hawaiian shirts, tour companies, cruise ship, black socks, Bermuda shorts, camera around the neck, big floppy hats, ugly sunglasses, knee socks, bad tans, sunburns, flip flops, some 'interesting' tourist attractions: Guinness Book of Records, Ripley's Believe it or Not, Mercedez Benz tombstone, critter crossings, alien museums, the painting elephant, odd collections, prehistoric zoo, 50 foot woman with visible organs, a number of old-west Boot Hills, toilet seat museum, mysterious cursed tombs,

Tacky Tourists

Let your wall decorations become a cacophany of bumper stickers, postcards, travel posters, tourist placemats … anything that reminds you of "a day on the road." On the drive or lawn leading up to the facility, place lawn signs that look like tourist-stop billboards welcoming your guests to the celebration.

Menu

Consider this "beach-side boardwalk" menu.
- appetisers: soft, hot pretzels with spicy mustard
- main course: pizza, hot dogs, pita salad sandwiches, chicken fajita wraps
- dessert: cotton candy, salt water taffy
- specialty drinks: Floradora (gin, lime juice, grenadine, sugar, and sparkling water)

Entertainment

Put together a collection of "road trip" tunes. Besides song, include things you might hear if you were on the road crossing the country such as farm and weather reports, and traffic updates. Help the "tourists" get to know each other. Give each guest an envelope with six pieces from different postcards. Tell guests they must trade pieces with other guests until they have a complete card. The first person to complete a whole card, wins. Hold a contest for the guest with the best "tacky tourist" outfit and the best (or worst) tan.

Souvenirs/Party Favors

Give each guest a tourist "survival" kit with a bright orange or yellow luggage tag, a disposable camera, a postcard souvenir of the party, and a tourist souvenir from the area such as a stuffed animal, snowglobe or commemorative plate. Put the kit into a brightly colored gift bag with handles so they're easy to carry.

Fund Raisers

If you need to raise funds, ask guests to come prepared to go on an overnight mystery trip. Auction the trip off to the highest bidder. Near the end of the celebration, announce the winner and give them a big send off from the crowd. Hire a limosine to drive them to the airport or their destination.

Keywords

World's Largest … (flag, donut, chicken, kaleidoscope, ball of string, etc.), parking lot shipwreck, Cadillac Ranch, lightning portraits - ghostly images etched into glass, casino laundromat, official birthplaces, museums of the stars, quirky, miniature villages, odd mausoleums, odd modes of transportation, Souvenir Hut, Cyanide Hall of Fame, Ghost walk tours, Tour of the Stars' Homes, garish, gaudy, flashy, frumpy, shameless, obtrusive, crude, tawdry, tackiness is in the eye of the beholder, Gloria Gogetter, **www.celebration-solutions.com/tacky.html**

Entertainment Themes

Introduction

Tom Clancy is the unsurpassed King of the techno-military thriller. Intrigued by a news story about a mutiny aboard a frigate from the USSR, Clancy re-worked the incident to produce his first novel *The Hunt for Red October* in 1984. The book became an instant best-seller. Clancy has established himself as the undisputed master at technical detail, authenticity, intricate plotting, and razor-sharp suspense. Give your guests a little of taste of Tom Clancy-style intrigue.

Ambiance

Picture a "situation" room during a mission briefing. Keep the lighting low to create suspense or use colored light bulbs to give the room a greenish glow. Play sounds of buzzers, alarms and ringing telephones in the background.

Colors

Use "cammo" colors of khaki tan, khaki brown and khaki green.

Suggested Attire

The suggested attire is cammoflage. Encourage your guests to make a trip to the military surplus store in your area and get themselves some BDUs.

Invitations

"Your mission … should you choose to accept it … is to join us on …" Use a cammoflage pattern or send one of those pens that has a voice recording and a playback chip in it with your invitation message.

Decorations

Set the tables with khaki tan tablecloths, desert cammoflage napkins and metal place settings. For centerpieces, make a trip to the military surplus store and get some old equipment like field radios, helmets, jump boots or canvas rucksacks. Stuff the rucksacks to give them height and dimension.

To simulate a "situation room" feel, create table and wall panels with flashing lights, buttons and levers. Hang world-wide maps on the walls. Use a large map on a table to create a strategy display. Purchase lead or game-piece soldiers,

Keywords

techno-military thriller, Jack Ryan, Hunt for Red October, Red Storm Rising, Patriot Games, Sum of All Fears, Without Remorse, Cardinal of the Kremlin, Clear and Present Danger, Debt of Honor, naval history, realism, authenticity, intricate plotting, razor-sharp suspense, US-Soviet tension, terrorism, spies, secrets, strategic defense initiative, cutting-edge, commander, soldiers, military formations, mobile warfare, armored vehicles, combat power, mass, mobility, firepower, combat, mission, balance of forces, tanks, striking power, tactical

Tom Clancy

ships, tanks and planes to place in groups on the map.

In any open spaces in the room, place cutouts of combat figures.

Menu

Consider this "traveling the world after the bad guys" menu.

- appetisers: sour cream cucumbers from Poland
- main course: Kheyma Kebabs (lamb and onions) from Armenia and beef borscht from Russia
- dessert: beignets with vanilla syrup and Turkish coffee from Turkey
- specialty drinks: St. Petersburg (vodka, orange bitters, orange slice), Yorsh (vodka, beer), and Soviets (vodka, Manzanilla sherry, dry vermouth, lemon twist)

Entertainment

Play the soundtrack from one of Clancy's novels that has been made into a movie (e.g. *The Sum of All Fears*, *Net Force*, *Patriot Games*, or *Clear and Present Danger*). Set up areas where guests can play laser tag, darts, nerf tech targets, bullseye ball or any other game that requires throwing skills.

Souvenirs/Party Favors

Give each guest an audio or paperback book of one of Tom Clancy's novels such as *Shadow Warriors*, *The Teeth of the Tiger*, *Without Remorse*, *Rainbow Six*, *The Cardinal of the Kremlin*, *Executive Orders*, *The Hunt for Red October* or one of the *Op Center* or *Net Force* series. Wrap the books in a cammoflage bandana and use a military insignia pin to tie the bandana together.

Fund Raisers

If you need to raise funds, sell tickets to play paintball at a local paintball field. Sell full packages that include tickets to play with the group and rentals of any safety equipment or products a new player might need to try out the game.

Keywords

mobility, battlefield, infantry, weapons, mechanized infantry, artillery, self-propelled weapons, reconnaissance, reconnoiter, amphibious, helicopters, field fortifications, minefields, armored, brigade, division, regiment, strategic, logistics, sensors, electronics, night vision, guided missiles, sophisticated, gun, bomb, warheads, rockets, accuracy, range, destructive power, targets, strategist, schemer, intriguer, conspirer, conspirator, maneuverer, orchestrator, strategems, moves, operations, logistics, mission brief, **www.celebration-solutions.com/clancy.html**

Ethnic Themes

Introduction

The Dutch are known for their beautiful flowers, windmills and wooden clogs. They're also known for some of the great artists of all time such as Rembrandt, Vermeer and van Gogh. The Netherlands, as its name suggests, is a low-lying country with about half of the country's landmass lying below sea level. Holland's easily navigable rivers made the Dutch good traders who were able to open markets across the world. Take your guests on visit to the "glass city" as Holland is often called because of the many greenhouses there.

Ambiance

Visit a Dutch village in the spring when the tulips are in full bloom. Keep the lighting high like a perfect spring day. Add a light fragrance to the room of spring flowers such as hyacinth, peonies or lilacs.

Colors

Use "tulip and ceramic" colors theme of red, yellow and Delft blue.

Suggested Attire

The suggested attire is "traveling through the tulip festival" casual.

Invitations

"Welkom" (Welcome in Dutch). Use a good closeup photograph of a tulip or a print of a Dutch windmill. Or, send tulip bulbs that guests can plant in their own gardens along with your party invitation.

Decorations

Set the tables with Delft blue tablecloths, white china and fabric napkins that look like the patterns on Delft china. The peak season for tulips in Holland is the last week of April and the first week of May. If you're holding your party in the spring, use red and yellow tulip bouquets for your centerpieces.

If tulips are out of season, use silk tulips or create small windmills using pinwheels. Surround the base of the vase or windmill with small, plain, wooden "klompen" (shoes).

Keywords

Netherlands, Benelux, tulips, Rembrandt, Vermeer, Dutch masters, van Gogh, Amsterdam, Haarlem, den Haag, windmills, dikes, dams, wooden clogs, land reclaimed from the sea, low-lying green meadows, clean-wide waterways, canals, swing bridges, masts of fishing boats in ancient harbors, below sea level, Zuyder Zee, blond beaches, tulip fields, skyline of tall church steeples, unbroken farmlands of wheat and barley, acres of market garden produce, hills and castles, orchards in blossom, great shipbuilders, Delft pottery, narrow tall row houses,

Sabot

Dutch

On the walls, create a tribute to the tulip. Hang poster-sized, closeup photographs of tulips. Tulips come in a great variety of styles and colors, from white to black. At the base of the posters, place a vase full of the type of tulips in the picture.

Menu

Consider this "traditional Dutch" menu.

- appetizers: Speculaas (spicy, dark brown Christmas biscuits made in molds that look like ships)
- main course: Uismitjer (open-faced sandwich of buttered bread topped with thinly sliced roast beef or ham and two fried eggs)
- dessert: Ontbijkoek (spiced bread flavored with dark brown sugar, molasses, ground cloves, cinnamon, ginger and nutmeg) or Poffertjes (small, round doughnuts without a hole or filling, sprinkled with icing or sugar)
- specialty drinks: Tulips (apple brandy, sweet vermouth, apricot brandy, lemon juice)

Entertainment

Play Dutch folk music. You can find collections of Dutch folk music in the international section of your local music store or check out the collection of downloadable folk music online at www.laurasmidiheaven.com.

Set up games of *Quilles* or garden bowling. These games are easy to construct. You'll find a picture and instructions for constructing a set and rules of play on the web page for this theme.

Souvenirs/Party Favors

Give each guest a planted tulip bulb in a Delft blue decorative pot along with instructions for growing the tulip indoors.

Fund Raisers

If you need to raise funds, auction a spring garden redesign. Hire a landscape architect to plant spring flowers for the winner.

Keywords

colorful window boxes, Dutch masters paintings, Rembrandt, Vermeer, Anne Frank house, Gothic-style churches, van Gogh, pewter, the center of the diamond industry, Hans Brinker, skating over frozen canals, Gouda cheese, swans on the water, flower-embroidered skirts, klompen, maze of tiny streets, canal rides in glass-topped boats, narrow leaning houses, gabled windows, houseboats on canals, mills and few hills, bikes, proud and friendly people, dikes, blazing flower fields, mud flats, mussels, fried fish, **www.celebration-solutions.com/dutch.html**

Ethnic Themes

Introduction

Greece is the oldest civilization in Europe and laid the foundation for classic architecture, art and philosophy. Greece is famous for its landscape dominated by mountains, islands and the sea. At the crossroads of Europe, Asia and Africa, there are many cultural influences at work in Greece since ancient times. Ancient Greeks could hear the poems of Homer, watch the plays of Sophocles, learn philosophy from such men as Socrates or Plato, and hear the many mythological tales of the Gods. Let your guests feel the spirit of the ages with a trip back to ancient Greece.

Ambiance

Spend an evening in the temple of the Gods. Use soft lighting like you would find in a massive marble temple. Flutes and lyres are the instruments of Greek mythology, so use these sounds in the background. Greece, with all its islands, has an incredible coastline so give the room a seaside scent.

Colors

Use "Mediterranean" colors of white, deep sea blue and metallic gold.

Suggested Attire

The suggested attire is "Greek God or Goddess" cocktail.

Invitations

"By the command of Zeus … join us for a celebration." Use a photograph of an ancient Greek temple or a closeup of temple adornments such as arches, columns or marble statues for your invitation graphics.

Decorations

Set the tables with deep sea blue table cloths, white china and gold-stemmed glassware. For centerpieces, contact a baker who specializes in wedding cakes to create miniature cake temples. Give the temple a small round base, white colonnades (often used on wedding cakes) and a rounded, dome roof.

To make the room feel like a temple, buy white plaster columns that are about shoulder high and place a "gold" Greek or classic-looking sculpture on the ped-

Keywords

mythology, gladiator, acropolis, sword, soldiers, chariot, column, temples, classical, Mount Olympus, Olympia, Olympic games, drachma, Greek tragedy, centurion, Trojan War, Odysseus, Zeus, Athena, Poseidon, Hera, Hercules, Athens, Aegean, Mediterranean, Ionian, ouzo, amphitheater, Ulysses, olives, grapes, wine, seafarers, archaeology, Crete, King Minos, Thebes, Sparta, Athens, Troy, dorian columns, Pericles, philosophy, history, medicine, art, Greek alphabet, Homer, Illiad, Odyssey, Ovid, Sophocles, oracles at Delphi, pantheon, cyclops,

Greek

estal. You may find these made of paper maché, plaster or plastic. Either spray paint them gold, or cover them with gold foil. Place a pedestal every five feet or so along the walls.

Menu

Consider this "traditional Greek" menu.
- appetizers: Tzatkiki (a dip made from cucumbers and garlic mixed with yogurt, served with bread or vegetables)
- main course: Souvlaki (barbecued lamb kebabs), Moussaka (minced meat, eggplant and cheese pie), and Dolmades (vine leaves stuffed with minced meat and rice)
- dessert: Baklava (honey and date dessert in pastry layers)
- specialty drinks: Adonis (dry sherry, sweet vermouth, orange bitters and orange peel) or Ouzo (distilled from grapes after the wine is made and packs a punch!)

Entertainment

As guests enter, make them honorary citizens of Greece. Give the men crowns of silk leaves and give the women a long, white gauze wrap. Have a greeter attach the short end to the woman's right shoulder with a decorative gold pin. Then loosely drape the wrap across the front and over the left shoulder. Let the long end hang down in back.

The amphitheater was the place the Greeks gathered to watch plays. In a separate area, set up an amphitheater and arrange for a short play of a Greek classic.

Souvenirs/Party Favors

Give your guests replica coins from ancient Greece as souvenirs. Place the coins in a small box with a black velvet liner.

Fund Raisers

If you need to raise funds, auction a trip to Greece, or sell tickets to a Greek art exhibit, or dinners at a local Greek restaurant.

Keywords

Titans, Aegean Sea, Prometheus, Atlas, immortal, Pandora, gold-threaded clothes, shiny jewelry, Persephone, ambrosia, River Styx, flowers in the hair, marble, Narcissus, nymph, trident, sickle, omen, Perseus, cliff-top monasteries, white-washed walls, Parthenon, ouzo, boats, fishing villages, Mykonos, ruins, Ios, Temple of Apollo, Tomb of the Kings, stone walls, harbors, sea caves, beaches, beautiful sunsets, olives, archaeological sites, Byzantine churches, archaeological sites, landscape in time, **www.celebration-solutions.com/greek.html**

Introduction

Italy is a place where history seems to live on forever amid timeless style and sophistication. Italy has an incredibly varied landscape from the heights of the Alps in the north to volcanic islands in the south — a place of rare beauty and warmth. It's also a Mediterranean wonderland of warm beaches, ancient castles and beautifully-scented orchards that bask in nearly year-round sunshine. Italy is a stunningly diverse destination that captures the hearts and minds of people worldwide. We're sure you'll capture the hearts (and stomachs) of your guests with this theme.

Ambiance

Relax in an outdoor café in Tuscany. Keep the lighting bright like a perfect summer day, and play background sounds of things you would hear out of doors, like birds chirping and insects buzzing. Give the room the scent of olive oil, oregano and red wine.

Colors

Use "vineyard" colors of soft shades of terra-cotta tan and a deep grape purple.

Suggested Attire

The suggested attire is "late lunch on a warm and sunny terrace" casual.

Invitations

"Sei tu il festeggiato!" (It's your party! - in Italian). Use closeup photographs of grapes and grape leaves or of a wine bottle and glasses. Or, send along a bottle of Italian wine with two glasses etched with the time and date of the party.

Decorations

Set the tables with a grapes and grape leaf patterned fabric for tablecloths, deep purple napkins, and terra-cotta-colored stoneware place settings.

Make your centerpieces edible. Use a large square vase to hold different colored (and flavored) bread sticks. Surround the vase with table-sized servings of different anti-pasto choices.

Keywords

Venice, Rome, Vatican City, gondola, gondolier, leaning tower of Pisa, coliseum, bridge of sighs, Sicily, Florence, Leonardo da Vinci, Michelangelo, Boticelli, de Medici, leaning Tower of Piza, colorful boats, villa, bays, gulfs, coastline, Alps, stunning mountains, volcanoes, painting, sculpture, music, Gorgonzola, Parmesan, leather, textiles, red, white and green, il Duce, Mount Etna, stained glass, Catholic Church, cardinals, the Pope, Swiss Guards, Roman villas, ruins of Pompeii, baroque splendor, frescoes, accordion music, chianti, checkered

Italian

Line your walls with grape vines. Vineyard-grown grapes are grown on line strung between posts. Create these from woven vine material that you can find at a craft store. Attach silk grape leaves and wax grapes across the lines.

Menu

Consider this "traditional Italian" menu.

- appetizers: antipasto salad (provolone, artichoke hearts, celery, carrots, hard boiled eggs and olives)
- main course: minestrone soup and linguine with pesto
- dessert: biscuit tortoni (almond macaroon cookies with whipped cream and chopped maraschino cherries and almonds)
- specialty drinks: Italian Stallion (bourbon, Campari, sweet vermouth, bitters, lemon twist) or Italian Soda (Italian syrup of your choice, sparkling water, lime slice)

Entertainment

Play Italian folk music. You can find Italian folk music in the international section of your local music store, or online at www.cdnow.com.

Teach your guests how to play the royal game of *Ur*. *Ur* is one of the oldest known board games in the world and was popular in ancient Rome. One of the oldest known *Ur* boards in existence is nearly 4,500 years old. *Ur* is a race game that uses unusual pyramid-shaped dice. The winner is the first player to move all seven of his men on and off the board along a route of 20 squares. You'll find a board and instructions on the web page for this theme.

Souvenirs/Party Favors

Give each guest a cookbook featuring Tuscan cuisine.

Fund Raisers

If you need to raise funds, sell watercolor prints of the Tuscan scenery or coffee table books featuring the art of Florence.

Keywords

tablecloths, olive orchards, icon souvenirs, tapestries, mosaics, the Pieta, Sistine Chapel, ivy covered stone buildings, beautiful flower pots, clay roof tiles, green shutters, peaceful villages, variegated foliage of gentle woods, freshly baked bread, seasoned with salt and garlic, moistened with olive oil, spicy tomato sauce, cinnamon and honey flavored cakes, almonds, hazelnuts, candied fruits, ruby-red wine, volcanic hills, Etruscan tombs, fifteenth-century aqueducts, romance, dolce, Roman Empire, **www.celebration-solutions.com/italian.html**

Ethnic Themes

Introduction

The history of the peoples of North America is long and rich in tradition. In the Northeast, Native Americans used wood from the forests to build houses, canoes and tools. In the Pacific Northwest, they hunted the sea mammals and fished along the coast. Around the plains, Native Americans moved from place to place hunting buffalo. In the Southwest, they grew corn and built multilevel, apartment-style dwellings from adobe. In the Arctic, native inhabitants adapted to the harsh environment. Today, there are more than 500 recognized tribes, each with a different and distinct culture. Help your guests celebrate the rich and diverse cultures of America's native peoples.

Ambiance

Visit the desert southwest in the fall. Keep the lighting high like a crisp, cool day in the desert and play nature sounds in the background, such as birds chirping and wind rustling through the leaves. Give your desert scene the scent of sage or pinion pine.

Colors

Use "natural dye" colors of brick red and soft tan.

Suggested Attire

The suggested attire is "camping in the desert" casual.

Invitations

"And the wind said: May you be as strong as the oak, yet flexible as the birch; may you stand as tall as the redwood, live gracefully as the willow; and may you always bear fruit all your days on this earth" — Native American prayer. Use a closeup photograph of Native American beadwork or a scenic picture of the Monument Valley in Arizona for your invitations.

Decorations

Set the tables with brick red tablecloths, stoneware place settings and tan napkins. For centerpieces, use hand-woven baskets or place good photographs of the desert southwest in clear plastic stands. You can find stands that will hold

Keywords

Tribes, ties to the land, spirituality, oral histories, flatbread, blankets, turquoise, silver, spirits, nature, Sitting Bull, Crazy Horse, Geronimo, tomahawk, bow and arrow, buffalo, Lakota, Eskimo, Cherokee, Navajo, Choctaw, Sioux, Anasazi, strong corn, pumpkins, beans, acorns, grinding stones, arrow heads, atlatl, wampum, pottery, weaving, loom, basketry, carved masks, festivals, powwow, ceremonies, dancing, drums, flute, whistles, rattles, clapping sticks, totem pole, rawhide, pemmican, lodge, tipi, longhouse, wigwam, hogan, wickiup, sweat lodge,

Native American

two photographs back to back, three photographs in a triangle, or four photographs in a square.

Make the room a gallery of Native American weaving. Arrange for a showing of hand-crafted weaving. Use stands to hang and display the woven pieces. If possible, invite the artists to attend and talk about their work.

Menu

Consider this "southwestern" menu.

- appetizers: fry bread with plum, pear and cherry chutney
- main course: pumpkin soup with sage, marinated chicken on a bed of wild rice
- dessert: cinnamon apple pie with vanilla nut ice cream
- specialty drinks: Indian River (blended whiskey, raspberry liqueur, sweet vermouth, grapefruit juice), Indian Summer (apple brandy, hot apple cider, ground cinnamon)

Entertainment

Play traditional Native American music. You can find a great variety of contemporary and traditional Native American music at www.cdnow.com.

Introduce your guests to *Awithlaknannai*, a board game played by the Zuni Indians of New Mexico similar to *Nine Men's Morris* played in medieval Europe. Players who are familiar with the game of checkers will like this game of jumping and capturing the pieces of your opponent. You'll find a board and instructions on the web page for this theme.

Souvenirs/Party Favors

Give each guest a small piece of Native American pottery or a woven basket.

Fund Raisers

If you need to raise funds, auction off a trip to the desert southwest along with a guided trek through Canyon de Chelly or Monument Valley.

Keywords

kiva, pueblo, igloo, chickee, breechcloth, ceremonial headdress, body painting, hides, horses, deer, elk, caribou, bison, moccasins, beads, yucca, claws, teeth, shells, feathers, shaman, chief, medicine man, vision quest, hunting, trapping, trading, kayak, canoe, lacrosse, smoke signals, storytelling, petroglyphs, kachina dolls, bone, antlers, horn, totem, thunderbird, beaded clothes, maize, peace pipes, fetishes, arrow quiver, dream catcher, kachina dolls, weaving, arrowheads, canyon dwellings, riding quirt, **www.celebration-solutions.com/indian.html**

Ethnic Themes

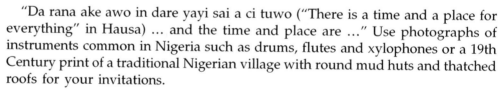

Introduction

The countryside of Nigeria is highly diverse ranging from lowlands along the coast and in the lower Niger Valley, to high plateaus and dry savannah in the north, mountains along the eastern border, tropical forest in the south all teeming with exotic wildlife. Nigerian art reflects African, Islamic and European influences. Nigeria is very well known for its textile trade born from traditional dress of colorful turbans and flowing robes with decorated sleeves as well as its beautiful bronze statuary. Nigeria also has a vast and rich musical heritage unequalled anywhere in West Africa. Bring your guests along for an amazing trip to Nigeria.

Ambiance

Travel to a rural village in the high plateaus of Nigeria. Keep the lighting high like a beautiful summer day and play traditional Nigerian music in the background. Use spices common to Nigerian cooking to scent the room.

Colors

Use "traditional textile" colors of gold yellow, deep green and bright orange.

Suggested Attire

The suggested attire is "visiting a Hausa village" casual.

Invitations

"Da rana ake awo in dare yayi sai a ci tuwo ("There is a time and a place for everything" in Hausa) ... and the time and place are ..." Use photographs of instruments common in Nigeria such as drums, flutes and xylophones or a 19th Century print of a traditional Nigerian village with round mud huts and thatched roofs for your invitations.

Decorations

Set the tables with traditional Nigerian cloth if you can find it, or use deep green tablecloths, bright orange or yellow place settings and napkins of the opposite color. Nigerian artists are famous for their wood carving and distinctive

Keywords

Lagos, Abuja, green and white flag, coastal, swamp, rain forest, savannah, smi-desert, Abuja, oil, coal, cocoa, Biafra, Lagos, storytelling, oral traditions, praise-singers, terra-cotta sculptures, bronze statues, ivory carvings, wooden masks, fetishes, Hausa, Yoruba, elaborately carved doors and veranda posts, drums, flutes, trumpets, xylophones, thumb pianos, juju music, masquerades, festivals, storytelling, costumed dance, puppet theater, acrobatics, high plains of Hausaland, Sokoto lowland, Yoruba highlands, mangroves, Niger Delta where the

Nigerian

black pottery. Use some of these pieces to fill the center of your tables.

Hang mural-sized posters of the high-plateau area of Nigeria or of the traditional village architecture of the area.

Menu

Consider this menu made with "typical Nigerian" ingredients.
- appetizers: apple coleslaw
- main course: chicken and shrimp with spiced Jollof rice and corn bread
- dessert: banana ice cream or pineapple milk sherbet
- specialty drinks: Xanadu (guava nectar, fresh lime juice, falernum, half and half)

Entertainment

Arrange for a performance of Nigerian masquerade dancers or play traditional Nigerian music. While we only found a few listings for Nigerian music at www.cdnow.com, there were many listings for Yoruba music, native to Africa but performed in the Caribbean, and hundreds of west African music titles.

Teach your guests to play one of the *Mancala* games. These board games have been popular in Africa for about 3,000 years. The board has six cups or spaces on each player's side to hold playing pieces. The object is to "sew" the pieces one at a time around the board so that the last piece played lands in a cup with the opponent's pieces in it, thereby capturing the pieces. Playing pieces are traditionally made with anything from stones to rare gems, although dried beans are inexpensive and work just as well. You'll find a board and instructions on the web page for this theme.

Souvenirs/Party Favors

Give each guest a small bronze statue typical of those made in Nigeria.

Fund Raisers

If you need to raise funds, sell the artwork that you used for centerpieces.

Keywords

rainy season is year-round, dry savanna regions, tropical hardwoods, including mahogany, iroko, and obeche, antelope, monkeys, jackals, hyenas, colorful turbans, flowing robes with highly decorated sleeves, Juju music, drums, flutes, trumpets, stringed instruments, xylophones, and thumb pianos, round mud huts with woven thatch roofs that reach a peak in the middle, cocoa beans, terra-cotta sculptures, bronze plaques, bronze statues, ivory, Ogbukele drums, obu ngusu ada (meeting house), **www.celebration-solutions.com/nigeria.html**

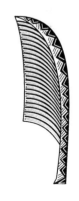

Celebration Solutions

Introduction

At the edge of the vast Mongolian steppes, is a spot along the historic Silk Road where nomadic peoples live. This is a land where emperors, princes, great warriors, explorers and spies came through at one time or another. It's also the area where caravans made their way carrying jade, coral, linens, lapis lazuli, glass, gold, iron, garlic, cinnamon, tea, cotton, and every other product merchants could sell. At one time or another the road was called the Fur Road, the Jade Road, the Emperor's Road and finally it became known for its most important commodity, the Silk Road. Take your guests to the place of endless sky and land — the home of the nomads.

Ambiance

Imagine a nomad's tent in the vast, treeless steppes. Keep the lighting low, like you would find in a traditional nomadic yurt (tent). For background sounds, play traditional Mongolian music as well as the sound of the wind blowing across the plains and cattle (or more likely yaks) being moved from place to place. Use peat to give the room an outdoor smell.

Colors

Use "wide-open-spaces" colors of brown, blue and green.

Suggested Attire

The suggested attire is "trekking" casual.

Invitations

"Come along with us." Use a picture of a caravan of animals or landscape pictures showing the vastness of the great plains for you invitations..

Decorations

In a traditional setting, meals would be served to guests sitting on pillows on the floor. If you think your guests would enjoy this, by all means. If not, set the tables with deep green tablecloths, blue or brown napkins, and stoneware place settings. Create a centerpiece sculpture of dried fruit. Not only will it look nice, but your guests can eat the pieces along with the appetizers.

Keywords

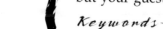

tents, skins, Yaks, hides, embroidery, caravans, bejeweled oasis, Marco Polo, transport back and forth, jade, tea, spices, gold, Silk Road, camel-stops, cargo, edge of the known world, seldom-visited oasis, trek, caravan trail, desert routes, outpost, on horseback, brilliantly patterned dresses with pants or thick bright stockings underneath, hair in glistening black braids, gypsy earrings, red, green or blue scarves interwoven with slivers of golden thread, merchants, carts, braying mules, two-wheeled carts, tall, bearded men wearing long robes with

Nomads

To make the room look like a nomadic yurt, hang earth-toned colored material from the ceiling and down the walls. Gather one end of the material strip together using a shower curtain ring and secure this end to the framework of the ceiling tiles. Hang a dowel from the ceiling to a spot about 5' high along the walls. Place the fabric around the outside of the dowel so that it hangs straight down like the side of a tent. You don't need to completely cover the walls. The shape of the hanging fabric will give the room the illusion of having a sloped roof. Place pillows on the floor along the walls at the edges of the fabric.

Menu

Consider this "made on the move" menu.
- appetizers: sweet flat bread with raising
- main course: stewed beef with mushrooms and stuffed cabbage leaves
- dessert: apple cobbler
- specialty drinks: Seventh Heaven (gin, maraschino liqueur, grapefruit juice, mint sprig)

Entertainment

Hire storytellers to tell some of the legends of the nomadic peoples and conduct your own version of the Naadam Festival. Traditionally this is called "the festival of the three manly games" — horse racing, archery and wrestling. Since these games are a little difficult to perform indoors, we've constructed a tabletop boardgame variety. To win the game, you must race your horse through obstacles, hit the mark with your arrows, and wrestle a host of fierce warriors before you get to the finish line. You'll find a board and instructions on the web page for this theme.

Souvenirs/Party Favors

Give each guest a nice coffee table book with photographs of the nomadic people of the Mongolian steppes.

Fund Raisers

If you need to raise funds, auction an adventure trek in Mongolia.

Keywords

silver-hilted daggers swinging from their belts, giggling children, cold noodles, grilled lamb, spices, potatoes, traders, middlemen, merchants, tambourines, strummed violins, long-necked guitars, herdsmen, vassals, fighting men, frontier stallions, yurt, felt tents, hurricanes of sand, ancient highway, powerful sun, gobi, a series of ancient gates and towers, snow-capped mountains in the distance, herders, signs of nature, stone stellas, ornament-like script, pasture, steppes, bow shooters, milk vodka, **www.celebration-solutions.com/nomad.html**

Mongolia

Ethnic Themes

Introduction

Russia is a land of great contrast, from the opulence of the Czars to the austerity of the Soviets. It's the world's largest country covering nearly half the globe, stretching across 11 time zones and two continents. The land climbs the high mountains of the Urals and crosses the great plains. It stretches from the frozen tundra of Siberia to the warm waters of the Crimea. Russia has a rich history of the arts including an easily recognized style of architecture that includes onion-domed cathedrals and luxurious palaces. Treat your guests to a "imperial" Russian celebration.

Ambiance

Dance the night away in the grand ballroom in the Winter Palace in St. Petersburg. Use candles to light up the room and mirrors to reflect the light and make the room look bigger.

Colors

Use "Winter Palace" colors of sage green, metallic gold and white.

Suggested Attire

The suggested attire is "visiting the Czar" formal.

Invitations

"Your presence is requested for an audience with the Czar." Use a picture of the imperial double eagle or the Fabergé eggs that were so popular with the Romanovs. Or, buy Matreshka (nesting dolls) and send a part of the invitation in each part of the doll.

Decorations

Set the tables with sage green tablecloths, white china, gold utensils and gold-stemmed glassware. Build Fabergé eggs for your centerpieces out of egg-shaped ornaments. You can find these ornaments made of styrofoam, glass or paper maché. Cover the eggs with satin ribbon, beads, faux jewels or anything else that will make the centerpiece look like the jewel-encrusted real thing.

Keywords

Czar, Romanov, matroishkas (nesting dolls), Siberia, Moscow, Saint Petersburg, Kiev, Cossack, Winter Palace, Hermitage, icons, ballet, opera, onion domes, orthodox, ruble, cyrillic alphabet, Pushkin, Dostoyevsky, Tchaikovsky, Chekhov, Stravinsky, Tolstoy, walls and towers, snow-swept streets, arched doorways, onion domes, slender narrow windows, icons, ornate stonework, intricate ironwork, red flags, double eagles, traditional costumes, wide-open steppes, an unending world of wheat and cattle, steppe country, forests so dense that you need a

Russian

Create a Romanov portrait gallery on the walls using pictures of the royal family in gilded frames. You don't have to use real frames that would be heavy to hang. You can create the effect using a image editing program. Print the portraits at poster size or larger.

Borrow or rent glamorous costumes like items that would have been worn at the Russian court. Use dress stands to give the costumes form and place them along the walls between the pictures in the portrait gallery.

Menu

Consider this "typical Russian" menu.

- appetizers: cabbage salad with black currants
- main course: beef Stroganoff and Pel-meni (a Siberian meat-filled ravioli covered with sour cream and pepper)
- dessert: Vareniki's vishnyama (Ukranian cherry dumplings) or bliny (crepes)
- specialty drinks: Cossacks (vodka, cognac, fresh lime juice and sugar) or cranberry vodka

Entertainment

Play Russian music and hire a dance troupe to demonstrate traditional Russian folk dancing.

Hire a band to play the kind of music that would have been used for ballroom dancing during a turn-of-the-century grand state dinner. The most popular ballroom dances are the Waltz, the Foxtrot (also called the two-step), the Quickstep, the Viennese Waltz and the Tango. Ask the dance troupe to help instruct your guests in these steps if they are unfamiliar with them.

Souvenirs/Party Favors

Give your guests a replica Fabergé egg, a travel guide to St. Petersburg, or a copy of *Nicholas and Alexandra* on DVD.

Fund Raisers

If you need to raise funds, auction a Russian river cruise.

Keywords

lantern at noon, science, philosophy, education, the arts, great space, vast silences, marshes of the Don, herdsmen moving great flocks, circus in every town, red clothing, black fur hats, traditional white robes to the knees, soft high boots, capes flung back, 185 ethnic groups, black fertile earth, miles and miles of railroad track, stern, rugged beauty, precious jems, red velvet hats with gold embroidery, green malachite urns, amber decorations, diamonds, gold, mysticism, occult, Lake Baikal, Siberia, **www.celebration-solutions.com/russian.html**

Ethnic Themes

Introduction

Among the instantly recognizable symbols of Scotland are kilts, tartans, golf, Scotch whisky and, of course, bagpipes. Scotland has some the world's finest highland scenery — white snowy peaks, deep blue lochs, purple heather covered hills, and the steel grey of the north sea. The islands of Scotland are some of the most remote places on earth, but the friendliness of the people will make you feel welcome and at home. Whisk your guests away to the misty, wild and rugged lands of Scotland.

Ambiance

Join a clan gathering in the highlands of Scotland. Keep the lighting bright like you're out of doors, and the sound of bagpipes and Celtic music are a must. When the heather blooms in Scotland, it has an unmistakably, lovely smell. Use this scent in the room.

Colors

Use "Blackwatch" colors of deep blue, deep green, red and black.

Suggested Attire

The suggested attire is "watching a Scottish tatoo" casual.

Invitations

"Failte" (Gaelic for welcome). "Slàinte mhath" (Gaelic for cheers). Use a tartan pattern, a thistle, or Celtic artwork for your invitation. Or, send heather seeds that guests can plant in their gardens.

Decorations

Set the tables with navy blue tablecloths, Blackwatch tartan napkins, green place settings and tartan coffee cups. Scotland is famous for its distinctive square castles. For centerpieces, find replicas of the more recognizable castles, such as Edinburgh, Sterling, St. Andrew's or Eilean Donan. There are also famous Abbey ruins in Scotland, such as Jedburgh or Melrose — where the heart of Robert "the Bruce" is buried.

Keywords

Edinburgh, St Andrews, Stirling, Fife, Argyll, Skye, Arran, bagpipes, kilt, tartan, sporran, castles, Nessie, Loch Ness, clans, chief, clan plaids, crest, golf, rugby, heather, haggies, Scotch whisky, claymore, Caledonia, Alba, Hadrian's wall, Firth of Forth, Saxons, Picts, Celtic, Tweed river, Gaelic, Bannockburn, Flodden field, Highlands, Lowlands, lochs, glens, mountains, oceanside cliffs, cairns, stone walls, stone huts, bogs, Celtic cross, spiral-tailed dragon, Aran sweaters, St Aidan, Stone of Scone, Macbeth, William Wallace, Robert the Bruce, Mary

Scotch heather

Scottish

Scotland is also known for its highland scenery — dramatic island coastlines, snowy peaks, castle walls, Pictish ruins, clan strongholds, Roman encampments and breathless vistas over the long lochs. Create mural-sized posters of the highland scenery for your wall decorations.

Menu

Consider this Scottish "chippie stand" menu.

- appetizers: traditional Scottish royal mile stew
- main course: paper cones filled with hot, deep-fried fish and chips served with salt and vinegar
- dessert: deep fried Mars bars (they're awesome!) or Cranachan which is a traditional harvest dish. The table is laid with oatmeal, cream, heather honey, whisky and raspberries. Guests take a dish of oatmeal and add the toppings of their choice.
- Specialty drinks: Highland Coolers (scotch, sparkling water, sugar, ginger ale, lemon twist)

Entertainment

Celtic music is very popular today. Arrange for a Celtic group to perform or put together a collection of Celtic music to play. You can find a very large collection of Celtic, Scottish, Irish and Cape Breton music online at www.harpandthistle.com.

Ask a local Scottish dance troupe to perform step dancing and give your guests a lesson in this most "fleet of feet" dancing style.

Souvenirs/Party Favors

Give each guest a Blackwatch tartan scarf rolled up in a Blackwatch tartan coffee cup.

Fund Raisers

If you need to raise funds, auction a trip to Scotland or sell tickets to a local Highland Games festival. Check with the Association of Scottish Games and Festivals for a complete listing. You'll find them online at www.asgf.org.

Keywords

Queen of Scots, mountain plateaus broken up by broad valleys (straths) and narrower valleys (glens), fertile coastline, wild scenery, rounded hills, sandy coast, narrow sea lochs, salmon fishing, glacier-gouged valleys, Jacobite rising, open circular towers, massive stone fortresses, thatched roofs, heather honey, haggis, tea bread, cakes, scones, shortbread, jams, blue flag with white cross, horse-racing, walking trails, unspoiled peninsulas, coastal scenery, Loch Lommond, Eilean Donan, **www.celebration-solutions.com/scotland.html**

Governmental Themes

Introduction

The term "cavalry" comes from the Latin word for horse (caballus). Mounted troops have been in use since horses were domesticated and were often used for reconnaissance since they could travel more quickly than troops on foot. In early times, since horses were relatively scarce and valuable, only the wealthy nobility could afford them, helping to establish the cavalry as an elite military unit. After the U.S. Civil War, the cavalry was stationed in forts dotted across the wide, open west. Bring your guests along for a rough and tumble time with the cavalry.

Ambiance

Picture a frontier fort in the old west. Keep the lighting high like you're out of doors and think about the sounds you might have heard in a frontier fort — horses galloping, cooking fires roaring, men relaying orders, and blacksmiths pounding on anvils. A real cavalry camp would have the unmistakable smell of horse ... . We don't recommend this, although the scent of leather might be nice.

Colors

Use traditional "U.S. Cavalry" colors of Union blue and saddle brown.

Suggested Attire

The suggested attire is "riding across the high plains" casual.

Invitations

"Saddle up and ride over our way!" Use a photograph of an historic fort or a closeup photograph of cavalry artifacts for your invitation. Or, send a small, leather pouch that looks like a saddle bag with your message inside.

Decorations

Set the tables with Union blue tablecloths and napkins, and metal place settings. Use metal cups instead of glasses. Stamp or embroider "U.S." around the bottom edge of the cloth and on the napkins. For centerpieces, create fringed, leather Cavalry dress gloves to lay in the middle of the table. If you've ever seen a picture of General George Custer, you'll know what the gloves looked like. He often wore them.

Keywords

horsemen, mounted, George Armstrong Custer, Battle of Little Big Horn, reconnaissance, counterreconnaissance, delaying action, raid, pursuit, regiments, saber, long sword, equitation, hand-to-hand combat, dragoons, uniforms, saddle, reins, bits, bridle, breeches, boots, mounted infantry, Colonel, Captain, Lieutenant, Corporal, Quartermaster, Troopers, Bugler, galloping charge, melee, squadron, ammunition, sites for camping, watering and pasture, riding patrol, flags, standard, gloves, leggings, hat, clash, firepower and cold steel, rally the troops,

Cavalry

Ask the waitstaff to dress in frontier Cavalry dress — leather boots, riding pants, denim shirts and suspenders, big moustaches and broad-brimmed hats.

Work with a historical museum to create displays of Cavalry artifacts. You'll need glass cases and adequate security in order to get a museum to lend you the pieces and keep the pieces safe.

Menu

Consider this menu of "Civil War favorites."
- appetizers: green pea soup
- main course: chuck wagon BBQ (beef or pork ribs and chicken)
- dessert: green apple pie
- specialty drinks: ginger beer (ginger brandy and dark beer) or Mule's Hind Leg (apple brandy, gin, apricot brandy, Benedictine, maple syrup)

Entertainment

Hire a group to play traditional bluegrass music. Bluegrass has its roots in the "mountain music" of the pioneers as they moved west across the continent. Music was a large part of life in the Cavalry, both on the trail and in the forts. The fiddle, banjo, and guitar were the most popular instruments because they were so easily portable.

Souvenirs/Party Favors

Give your guests a pair of suede, fringed gloves, like those worn by Cavalry officers way back in the day.

Fund Raisers

If you need to raise funds, auction a trip to an historic, western fort. Some of the forts run by the National Park Service and available for tourist trips are: Fort Smith (AR), Fort Bowie (AZ), Camp Lockett (CA), Bent's Old Fort (CO), Forts Larned and Scott (KS), Fort Snelling (MN), Forts Selden, Sumner and Union (NM), Fort Gibson (OK), Fort Clatsop (OR), Forts Brown, Chadbourne, Clark, Concho, Davis, and Stockton (TX), and Fort Laramie (WY).

Keywords

gave the order, line of fire, musket fire, hussars, saddle-makers, smiths, fighting spirit, detachments, flags unfurled, cartridge box, fire a volley, aide-de-camp, reinforcements, at the front, pursuit, charge!, outflanked, wall of bayonettes, sabers flashing, repulse an attack, Colt six-shooter, lance, carbine, breech-loading rifle, saddlebag, clash at full gallop, advancing, battalion, regiment, brigade, heavy artillery, sharpshooters, troops, platoon, bandoleer, bridle, saddle, rifle, saber, trenching tools, **www.celebration-solutions.com/cavalry.html**

Governmental Themes

Introduction

From the defeat of the Spanish Armada in 1588 to the Napoleonic Wars, Great Britain was known for its superior Imperial Navy. Great literary works such as *Horatio Hornblower* tell the tale of the men and battles of the British Navy. Imagine the sound of the guns and the smell of gunpowder as a "mighty 40-pounder" gave a charge during one of the great naval sea battles. Can you see the officers, smartly dressed in woolen uniforms with high white collars, the feathers in their three-corner hats fluttering in the sea breeze? Imagine the magnificence of a party aboard a royal man-o-war.

Ambiance

Dance on the deck of the HMS Renown of *Horatio Hornblower* fame. Use fans to keep the air moving and the sails whipping. Play the sounds of waves crashing, the captain giving orders, the creak of the deck and the snap of the sails, and give the room the smell of the salt sea air.

Colors

Use "high-seas" colors of navy blue, white and red.

Suggested Attire

The suggested attire is "navy crisp" casual.

Invitations

"Come aboard for a special celebration." Use a picture of a man-o-war sailing ship or send along a DVD of a movie featuring the British Royal Navy such as *Horatio Hornblower* or *Master and Commander*.

Decorations

Set the tables with navy blue tablecloths and napkins, white china, gold utensils and gold-stemmed glassware. For centerpieces, use items that would be found on a 17th Century sailing ship — a sextant, jumble compass, weathervane, tide clock, barometer, anchor bell, ship strike clock, Galileo thermometer, hour glass, lantern, nautical map, scrimshaw carving, telescope or sundial. You can find rep-

Keywords

HMS (His/Her Majesty's Ship), sailing ships, rigging, masts, cannons, frigate, merchantman, lateen sails, mizzen mast, topmast, timbers, flags, gunwhale, porthole, halyard, mainmast, Barquentine, fully-rigged, gun deck, officers, sailors, gunners, soldiers, spritsail, flagship, windlass, fireboxes, hull, muzzle-loaders, bow, stern, warship, gold, oarsmen, Galleon, gangway, bulkhead, bowsprit, swivel guns, pavisades, armament, forecastle, cannon royal, planking, Galley, Francis Drake, armada, spar deck, mariner, circumnavigate, coat of arms,

Imperial Navy

licas of these items at shops that sell nautical items.

Use large diameter piping filler cord to create "rigging." Soak the piping in tea to give it a weathered look. Hang lines of nautical flags around and between the rigging.

Menu

Consider this "British Sunday lunch" menu.

- appetizers: ginger bread with sweet butter
- main course: roast beef and browned roast potatoes
- dessert: Yorkshire pudding or summer pudding (bread pudding with fruit and whipped cream)
- specialty drinks: Anchors Aweigh (bourbon, triple sec, peach brandy, cherry liqueur and half and half) or mead

Entertainment

At the Captain's mess, you might hear a string quartet playing for his pleasure. Hire actors to play the role of the Captain and his officers in full, dress Navy regalia.

Give your guests a chance to wage a naval battle. Let them play the popular game *Battleship*. Win the game by locating and sinking the enemy's fleet before your ships go down. You'll find game boards and instructions on the web page for this theme.

Souvenirs/Party Favors

Give your guests a sailor T-shirt and one of the many Patrick O'Brian novels that the movie *Master and Commander* was based upon or an episode of *Horatio Hornblower* on DVD.

Fund Raisers

If you need to raise funds, auction a trip to see the tall ships in harbor and sell a complete model of an historic naval warship as well as the kits for the model.

Keywords

between wind and water, port, poopdeck, whipstaff, helmsman, cargo hatch, bilge, ballast, armament, capstan, square sail, laden, armed escort, cargo, barge, broadside, sloop, battery, turrets, ornate, shot, stern chasers, bowel chasers, carrack, Sir Walter Raleigh, commanding officer, deck, caravel, patache, tri-corner hat, epaulettes, waistcoat, knee-length breeches, hose, brass buckles, sword, sidearm, Lord High Admiral, Admiralty, falconet cannon, aye aye, westerly gale, helmsman, watch, **www.celebration-solutions.com/hrnavy.html**

Governmental Themes

Introduction

The Pentagon, headquarters of the Department of Defense, is one of the world's largest office buildings at 3,705,793 square feet. It is twice the size of the Merchandise Mart in Chicago, has three times the floor space of the Empire State Building in New York, and the National Capitol could fit into any one of the five wedge-shaped sections. Built during the early years of World War II, it is still thought of as one of the most efficient office buildings in the world. Despite 17.5 miles of corridors it takes only seven minutes to walk between any two points in the building. Bring your guests along for a night honoring the nation's finest men and women.

Ambiance

Walk the Pentagon's Hall of Heroes. Keep the lighting low to put a highlight on the artwork. Marches of the military's bands would be appropriate for background music.

Colors

Use "military" colors of navy blue, khaki tan, army green and dress white.

Suggested Attire

The suggested attire is anything you might see at the Pentagon — from dress blues or dress whites to camouflage.

Invitations

"From the halls of Montezuma, to the shores of Tripoli … you won't find a celebration that rivals this one." Use a closeup of the stars and stripes or the seals of the different branches of the service for your invitation. Or, take a trip to the army surplus store and attach unit insignias to the invitation.

Decorations

Set each table with a color scheme for each of the four main branches of the military according to the colors of their dress uniforms. For the Navy, set the tables with white tablecloths, navy blue napkins and white china. For the Marine Corps, set the tables with navy blue tablecloths, red napkins and white China.

Keywords

five-sided, Arlington, Virginia, Potomac, Department of Defense, military, Joint Chiefs of Staff, combat command, defense forces, built in 1941, War Department, Honor Guard, soldiers, sailors, airmen, Marines, Coast Guard, seals, eagle, Secretary of Defence, Under-Secretary, war room, uniforms, organize, train, equip, operations, Commandant, officers, enlisted, dress uniforms, stars, bars, oak leaves, medals, flags, battle streamers, Executive Corridor - Dwight D Eisenhower Corridor, Army Executive Corridor - Gen. George C Marshall Corridor,

Pentagon

For the Air Force, set the tables with Air Force blue tablecloths, light blue napkins and white china. For the Army, set the tables with Army green tablecloths, lighter green napkins and black place settings.

To create the Hall of Heroes, use prints of paintings of America's early war heroes like General George Washington. Use an image editing program to give each "portrait" a gilded-looking frame.

Menu

Consider this menu from the "mess halls of any of the armed forces."

- appetizers: Sailor Seafood Salad from the Navy
- main course: Up, Up and Away (cider-sauteed chicken breasts on a bed of rice) from the Air Force
- dessert: Trench tarts (mincemeat tarts with whipped cream) from the Army
- specialty drinks: Grunts with Grenadine from the Marines (aka an American Beauty made with brandy, dry vermouth, orange juice, grenadine, and white crème de menthe)

Entertainment

Play music performed by a military band or choir. Play games for the Commander-in-Chief's cup. All of the tables decorated similarly will play as one team. Find some mind bender puzzles and let each table play as a group. Give points for the fastest table to solve the problem, or give a point to each table with the right answer. Then add up the points for each of the four branches — Navy, Army, Air Force and Marines.

Souvenirs/Party Favors

Give each guest a T-shirt from the branch of service that their table is decorated to commemorate.

Fund Raisers

If you need to raise funds, auction off a trip to Washington, D.C. including a tour of the Pentagon or copies of *Medal of Honor*, a coffee table book honoring the nation's medal of honor winners.

Keywords

Air Force Executive Corridor - Gen 'Hap' Arnold Corridor, Commandant of the Marine Corps Corridor, Navy Executive Corridor, pride, honor, courage, commitment, globe, anchor, discipline, wings, Supreme Commander, strategic, Hall of Heroes, Congressional Medal of Honor, valor, Buffalo Soldiers, Tuskegee Airmen, freedom, Navajo Code Talkers, honor, loyalty, commitment, For God and Country, Hall of Heroes, POW/MIA corridor, Faces of War Exhibit, award, badge, decorated, medal, valor, heroism, **www.celebration-solutions.com/pentagon.html**

Governmental Themes

Introduction

On May 23, 1873, the Mounties were formed calling for the enlistment of "able-bodied men of good character, between the ages of 18 and 40, who could ride a horse." They have been responsible for law and order in every corner of Canada since. The Royal Canadian Mounted Police were more than the law. They were also doctors, nurses, social workers, tax collectors, game wardens, judges, map-makers, parsons and explorers. In full regalia, Mounties cut a splendid figure with peaked Stetson hats, gold chevrons and glistening collar badges. Send your guests on a trek to a Mountie post.

Ambiance

Picture a rugged outpost in the great white north. Use lamps to give the space a cozy, log cabin feel and play sounds of the wind howling, the occasional wolf howling, or a bugle call in the background. Use the scent of pine or firewood burning to complete the effect.

Colors

Use "RCMP" colors of red, black and white.

Suggested Attire

The suggested attire is "Mountie" red. Let your guests figure out what that means. You may get anything from smartly-pressed dress reds, to red ties, to red sports coats, to red hearts on funny boxer shorts.

Invitations

"We always get our man ... or woman ... " Use a photograph of a Mountie or a closeup of something that would be found on a Mountie uniform like a medal or gold chevrons.

Decorations

Set the tables with red tablecloths, black napkins and white china. Create napkin rings out of black satin ribbon and use colorful military-looking medals to clasp the ends of the ribbon together to form a napkin ring.

Keywords —

Mounties, horseback, red and black, Ottawa, outposts, scarlet red jackets, blue breeches with gold stripes, black boots, riding pants, hats, homesteaders, cabins, bears, Yukon, northern lights, canoes, Polar mariners, wilderness police, Motto: "Maintiens le Droit - Uphold the Right," buffalo-hide greatcoat, hat of muskrat pelts, gold-striped breeches, lonely log outpost, headwaters of the Yukon River, dog sled, Inspector, Constable, "never send two men to do one man's job," pony soldiers, explorers, map-makers, snowshoe along trap lines, mail

Royal Canadian Mounted Police

Create light balsa wood "windows." Stain the wood, so that it looks like the frame of a log-cabin window and place snowy, winter scenes in the window panes. Hang a few Canadian flags around the walls as well.

Menu

Consider this "we always get our man (or our man's stomach ...)" menu.
- appetisers: mini pizzas with Canadian bacon (ham)
- main course: Beer-can chicken on the grill (beer batter BBQ sauce)
- dessert: the Great White North (coconut merengue pie)
- specialty drinks: Molson beer or Trois Rivieres (Canadian whiskey, Dubonnet rouge, Cointreau, orange twist)

Entertainment

The Maritime provinces of Canada have a rich tradition of celtic music. Hire a group that knows how to put on a good ceilidh (pronounced kay-lee -- meaning celebration). You can find information about Cape Breton music at the Ceilidh Trail School of Music site online at www.ceilidhtrail.com.

Give your guests a chance to "get their man" too. If you like the game *Clue*, you'll like our version of *Mountie's Mystery*. To win, you'll need to follow the clues as you make your way across the frozen tundra of the great white north to capture the crook. You'll find a game board and instructions on the web page for this theme.

Souvenirs/Party Favors

Give each guest a cozy, warm sweatshirt with a Canadian maple leaf on it.

Fund Raisers

If you need to raise funds, auction off a trip on the 4,000 mile coast-to-coast Trans-Canada railroad from Vancouver to Halifax. Travel the length of great rivers, across a thousand miles of rolling prairies, through the vast forest regions and atop the great ranges of mountains. Who wouldn't want to bid on such a great adventure!

Keywords

carrier, crack shots, sharpshooters, radio, ski troops, "the thin red line of heroes," out of teach of mail and telegraph, stout-hearted, in full crimson kit, treaty, proud, saddle, rugged mountains, glacial streams, clear mountain air, jagged summits of snow and ice, dangerous rapids, square-jawed, erect stature, broad-shouldered, pioneers in scarlet and gold, Klondike, valiant red coats, "We always get our man, "insignia, gendarme special constable, sharpshooter, commissioner, sergeant major, **www.celebration-solutions.com/rcmp.html**

Governmental Themes

Introduction

Built between 1792 and 1800, the White House is the official residence of the President of the United States. Originally, it was known as the President's Palace, although it has been known as the President's House, the Executive Mansion and finally, the White House, its official designation since 1901. It has been the home of every President in American history with the exception of George Washington, although he approved the act that led to its construction. Take your guests to a state dinner at the number one residence in the land.

Ambiance

Dine in the state dining room of the White House. Keep the lighting low to make the room feel formal. Play a recording of *Hail to the Chief* as your guests first come into the room and instrumental music in the background through dinner.

Colors

Use "presidential" colors of white and blue.

Suggested Attire

The suggested attire is "sitting down to a state dinner" formal.

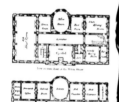

Invitations

"Hail to the Chief." Use a photograph of the inside or the outside of the White House or a graphic of the presidential seal for your invitations. Or, use an image editing program and superimpose photographs of your guests at the podium in the press briefing room.

Decorations

Set the tables with Oval Office blue tablecloths and napkins, white china, gold utensils and gold-stemmed glassware. Use white candles on a round mirror for your centerpieces. Take a 6" tall, large diameter candle for the center candle and use graduated candles around the outside of the center candle down to a stubby 1" candle at the bottom.

Keywords

1600 Pennsylvania Ave, President, First Lady, Chief Executive, world leader, semi-circular portico, Oval Office, Blue Room, Executive Wing, China Room, East Room, Red Room, Green Room, State Dining Room, Rose Garden, South Lawn, South Portico, intricate stonework, glassware, china, furniture, on the Potomac, Marine guards, protocol, Caroline Kennedy's pony Macaroni, apex of political power, network of expert advisers, trusted staff, top advisers, dignitaries, map room, war room, chandeliers, signing ceremony, fireside chats, political

WASHINGTON, D.C.

White House

Use prints of presidential portraits to adorn the walls. Label the prints with the president's name and the years he served. Hang them at regular intervals down the walls separated by shoulder-high white, plaster columns. Create fabric swags in Oval Office blue to hang along the walls at ceiling level.

Menu

Consider this "fit for a state dinner" menu.

- appetizers: seared pears and prosciutto
- main course: peppered scallops, coconut shrimp, marinated salmon on rice
- dessert: mango and grapefruit sorbet
- specialty drinks: Diplomats (dry vermouth, sweet vermouth, maraschino liqueur, bitters, lemon slice, maraschino cherry) or Stars and Stripes (cherry Heering, half and half, blue Curacao)

Entertainment

Hire a chamber music group to entertain your guests. If you need a recommendation for a local chamber music group, contact Chamber Music America online at www.chamber-music.org.

What better game to play in the White House, than *Risk* — the classic game of strategy and world power by Parker Brothers! Lead your armies across vast continents; launch daring attacks against your enemies, but keep any eye on your flanks! You never know when your power could be taken by a swift move.

Souvenirs/Party Favors

Give each guest a commemorative plate. Many of the Presidential china patterns are available as replicas. You can see examples of all of the Presidential china at the official White House site online at www.whitehouse.gov.

Fund Raisers

If you need to raise funds, auction a trip to Washington, D.C. with a tour of the White House or sell coffee table books about the White House.

Keywords

insiders, Situation Room, Marine One, Air Force One, Press Secretary, 'museum of a nation,' presidential portraits, Secret Service, Executive Office, portico, National Community Christmas Tree, Sherman Square, reflection pool, presidential portraits, ellipse, oath of office, military aides, Truman balcony, Presidential seal, show place, chauffeurs, telephone operators, house staff, social secretaries, telegraph operators, Macaroni (Caroline Kennedy's pony), Lafayette Square, diplomatic reception, state, **www.celebration-solutions.com/whhouse.html**

Holiday Themes

Introduction

April Fool's Day is one of the most light hearted days of the year, but it didn't start off that way. Since ancient times, people celebrated New Year's Day on April 1st, but on April 1, 1582, the Pope ordered a new calendar to be followed placing New Year's Day on January 1st. In France, many people either refused to accept the new date, or did not learn about it and continued to celebrate New Year's Day on April 1st. People made fun of these traditionalists, sending them on "fool's errands" or trying to trick them into believing something false. Today, on the first day of April it is customary to play jokes on friends and foe alike, causing them to believe a tall tale or go on a wild goose chase. April Fools — the perfect subject for a night of joy and laughter.

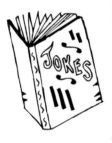

Ambiance

This theme is laugh-out-loud funny. Keep the lighting high and cheery and play "spoof" songs in the background. There are groups that perform only spoof songs — politics being the most popular target.

Colors

Use "fool's lot" colors of shades of purple.

Suggested Attire

The suggested attire is formal or foolish...or foolishly formal.

Invitations

Have fun with these invitations. Send different invitations to each guest and request a different type of attire for each, or send guests on a wild good chase with a list of silly items to bring, or make your invitation a riddle.

Decorations

Set the tables with different colors of purple tablecloths and napkins. Use many different colors for the place settings and cups. Have the wait staff bring around trays of marzipan cockroaches and offer them to guests along with the appetizers. Put out a tray of rubber band sandwiches or toothpaste Oreos. Use fake hands holding onto the serving trays. Set the table with fake brandy glasses (they look like they're full, but you can't drink from them) or dribble glasses, and deliver foaming sugar with the coffee.

Keywords

practical jokes, pranks, comic, jester, funny prizes, jokes, fool's errand, dupe, fall for the joke, playing the fool, wisecrack, witticism, quip, one-liner, jest, bon mot, pun, play on words, comedy, humor, facetiousness, drollery, whimsy, goofiness, ridiculousness, gag, prank, trick, irony, satire, parody, lampoon, farce, trick, cartoon, caricature, funnies, nonsense, rib-tickler, silly, schtick, kidder, banter, quipster, pun, pitfall, prankster, spoof, stand-up, life of the party, giggle, snicker, ha-ha, tee-hee, rolling on the floor, doubled over, guffaw, yuk it up, chortle,

April Fools Day

Hang a sign on the front door asking guests to use the back door. On the back door, hang a sign that says "April Fools" please use the front door. Put wet paint signs on the bathroom doors with an asterisk. Down at the very bottom of the sign in small type, print "April fools." Think about places where you could use some of these popular practical joke items: clocks with backwards numbers, fake blood, bullet hole decals, tablets that create colored tap water (in the bathrooms), double-sided "heads" quarters, exploding pens, Groucho glasses, hand buzzers, jumping spiders, Mexican jumping beans, million dollar bills, paint ball splats, snake in a can, squirt flowers, water balloons.

Menu

Consider this "full of fun" menu.
- appetizers: banana and mandarin orange salad served on a chilled banana peel
- main course: ham and asparagus fettucini
- dessert: strawberry shortcake with chocolate sauce and whipped cream
- specialty drinks: Stingers (brandy, white crème de menthe, lime juice) or Jolly Rogers (light rum, Drambuie, lime juice, scotch, sparkling water)

Entertainment

Create a puzzle prize tangle. Wrap a souvenir gift in a small box and attach a long string to it. Place all of the prizes in the middle and create a web by tangling up all of the strings. Ask each guest to grab the end of a string and they have to work their way to the prize by untangling the string while the other guests are doing the same. You can do this for the whole group, or table by table. The more people involved, the more room you'll need to spread the web out.

Souvenirs/Party Favors

The list of gag gifts is simply unending.

Fund Raisers

If you need to raise funds, hold a mystery auction. Wrap boxes in different sizes. The bigger the box the higher the cost. Give guests a list of what it's possible to win in each size category. For example you might wrap 20 small boxes. The cost to purchase the box is $5. Two of the boxes contain prizes worth $25 and the others have gifts worth $1.

Keywords

chuckle, cackle, roaring with laughter, funny, amusing, risible, comical, splitting one's sides, all a titter, joviality, joyous, hollity, glee, high spirits, hilarity, laughingstock, butt of the joke, schnook, schlemiel, boob, greenhorn, soft mark, sucker, patsy, pigeon, fall guy, pushover, puppet, stooge, trick, caper, stunt, mischief, antics, shenanigan, tomfoolery, horseplay, madcap adventure, lark, Dumb but True, Laughable Lawsuits, Oddly Enough News, News of the Weird, Whack-a-Fool, salt in sugar bowl, bamboozle, **www.celebration-solutions.com/aprfool.html**

BANG

Celebration Solutions

Introduction

Cinco de Mayo, Spanish for the 5th of May, is a national holiday in Mexico. It commemorates the badly outnumbered Mexican Army's defeat of French forces, on May 5, 1862, in the Battle of Puebla. The triumph became a symbol of Mexican unity and patriotism. Mexico has a rich heritage in art and architecture and is recognized for its murals. Mexico's blend of indigenous and European influences has contributed to the development of notable musical styles, folk art and cuisine, all of which are found throughout the world and celebrated on Cinco de Mayo. Engage your guests in this celebration of Mexico.

Ambiance

Picture an open-air market. Keep the lighting high like you're out of doors and play traditional Mexican folk music in the background. Give the room a scent of cinnamon — a spice commonly used in Mexican desserts.

Colors

Use Mexican "flag" colors of green, white and red.

Suggested Attire

The suggested attire is "colorful celebration" casual.

Invitations

"¡vámonos de juerga!" (Let's party! - in Spanish). Use photographs of colorful Mexican dancers or musicians, or send your invitations along with a pretty glazed tile or an embroidered cloth.

Decorations

Set the tables with alternating tablecloths of green, white and red. Use decorative Mexican pottery for the place settings and cups. For centerpieces, create oversized tissue paper flowers.

From the ceiling, hang streamers of white paper cut like lace. These decorative streamers are easy to create if you have paper punches in different shapes. Simply fold the paper over a few inches and cut a pattern. Repeat the pattern down

Keywords

Fifth of May, Mexico, sports events, parades, mariachi music, dancing, picnics, beauty contests, Pacific Ocean, Gulf of Mexico, Caribbean Sea, Sierra Madre mountains, volcanic peaks, snow-capped mountains, tropical rain forests, famous beaches, rugged terrain, Rio Bravo, Aztecs, Spaniards, Baja, Yucatan Peninsula, Acapulco, Mazatlan, Cancun, cactus, desert scrub, oak, pine, fir, silver, copper, gold, textiles, intricate designs, bright colors, pottery, murals, silver jewelry, folk-dance, Chapultepec Park, bright colors, serapes, sombreros, bright

Cinco de Mayo

the length of the streamer or make every few inches different.

Set up displays like you would find in an open-air market in Mexico. Use colorful woven fabric from Mexico to cover the tables and extend up the walls. Find colorful pottery, tiles, decorated masks or photographs of matadors to make up your displays.

Menu

Consider this "mostly" Mexican menu.

- appetizers: spicy guacamole with tortilla chips and black bean soup
- main course: fresh corn tamales and empanaditas de Picadillo (turnovers with beef, almonds and olives)
- dessert: flan (crème caramel) or crepes with fudge sauce
- specialty drinks: hot chocolate with a touch of cinnamon or Mexicana (silver tequila, pineapple juice, lime juice, grenadine)

Entertainment

Hire a Mariachi band to play traditional music. If you need help finding a Mariachi band contact Gig Masters at www.gigmasters.com. They list more than 15,000 musical acts.

Teach your guests to play the game of *Conquian* — a fast-moving, two-player Rummy-like card game popular in Mexico since the mid-19th Century. The game is played with a 40-card Spanish deck that has numbered cards from 1 to 7, and four face cards, roughly equivalent to Jack, Queen, King and Ace.

Souvenirs/Party Favors

Give your male guests a tooled leather wallet and the female guests an embroidered blouse from Mexico.

Fund Raisers

If you need to raise funds, sell pre-stuffed pinatas, decorative tiles or pottery and other folk crafts from Mexico.

Keywords

costumes, chiles, corn, picturesque villages steeped in tradition, monumental remains of the ancient cultures, colonial architecture, warm, hospitable people, handicrafts, brightly colored animal figures, embroidered blouses, ponchos, red glass goblets, earthenware crockery, colorful, wooden figures, black pottery, leather ware, shell designs, precious stone work, silverwork, colorful parades of floats, musical bands, people in costumes, masked dancers, fireworks, Maximillian, Carolota, French dragoons, **www.celebration-solutions.com/cinco.html**

Holiday Themes

Introduction

Holi is an Indian festival lasting up to a week that celebrates the beginning of spring and commemorates the burning of Holika, an evil sorceress who once tormented the people of India. On the first night of the festival, the night of the full moon, everyone gathers around a huge bonfire. They bring offerings of coconuts, wheat and other grains which are thrown into the fire. Once the fire is burning, the sound of drums, horns and singing fill the air. Parents walk with their children once around the fire praying for the children's good health and happiness, as a way of receiving a blessing from God for their children. During subsequent days, processions of carts and decorated floats wind their way through the streets. Sometimes the holiday is called the "festival of colors" because people spray one another with colored water. Tricks and mischief are common during the festival of Holi to remind the people of God's playful nature. Show your guests how to celebrate the joy of Holi.

Ambiance

Travel to a small village in India. The best way to hold this theme party is out of doors so that you can take part in the customs of the holiday. If you must hold it indoors, keep the lighting high like the part of the festival that takes place during the day and play up the bright colors. Play traditional Indian music in the background. Go to an Indian market and purchase packets of fresh spices to give the room an exotic smell.

Colors

Use a "rainbow" of colors for this theme.

Suggested Attire

The suggested attire is "every color in the rainbow" casual. Explain to your guests that this celebration is all about color and encourage them to wear their most colorful clothing.

Invitations

Just about anything with a lot of color will do for this invitation — a kaleido-

Keywords

Indian, Hindu full moon festival, carnival of colors, bonfires, end of winter, beginning of spring, sanskrit, street processions, music, festival of colors, a time to thank the gods for the harvest to come, fire and light, fire is used to purify and cleanse, coconuts, colored cloth, stands selling snacks, sweet treats, merry-go-rounds, puppet shows, music, drums, wind instruments, dancing, curry, rice, lentils, fried bread, lanterns, colored powder, colored water, full moon, heralds the spring, carnival, colorful, joyous, sweets, Thandai - a drink made with

Holi

scope pattern or abstract art. Send nice, Indian silk scarves along with your invitation for the female guests to wear during the party.

Decorations

Set the tables with multicolored tablecloths, napkins and place settings. Part of the tradition of Holi are bowls piled high with colored powder. Use these for your centerpieces. Use a powder that doesn't permanently stain, though. Just in case! If you can, use colorful fabrics from India. If not, cover the walls in different colored gauze material. Let it overlap for a rainbow effect.

Menu

Consider this "tasty treats from India" menu.
- appetizers: fry bread with dosai chutney (yogurt chutney)
- main course: Khat Mithi Machchi (sweet and sour fish), Alu Keema Tikki (potato and meat puff), and Panir Channa Biriani (a three-colored rice dish)
- dessert: Balu Shahi (sugared-covered doughnuts)
- specialty drinks: Madras (vodka, cranberry juice, orange juice) or Melon Balls (vodka, melon liqueur, pineapple juice, slice of honeydew)

Entertainment

Play Indian folk music and ask Indian dancers to perform traditional dances. At an actual Holi celebration, guests would spray squirt guns full of colored water at each other. If you're holding your celebration indoors, the facility might not appreciate such activities. But you can give guests a chance to play with color. Set up stations where guests can tie dye a T-shirt.

Souvenirs/Party Favors

In addition to the tie dyed T-shirts, send your guests home with a gift box of coconut candy popular in India. Wrap the box in brightly-colored paper.

Fund Raisers

If you need to raise funds, sell dinners at an Indian restaurant or tickets to a local Indian festival.

Keywords

almonds and milk, music, dancing, parades, festival, dusk, coconuts, wheat, offerings, decorated floats, tricks, mischief, blessings and good fortune for the year to come, feast, banquet, revel, fete, wassail, festivities, ceremony, rite, ritual, rejoicing, amusement, regalement, celebration, observance, carnival, fair, get-together, gathering, soiree, bash, fair, merrymaking, mirth, glee, kaleidscopic, bright-hued, rich, brilliant, lustrous, many-colored, shades of color, ecstatic burst of color, exuberant festival, **www.celebration-solutions.com/holi.html**

Introduction

Oktoberfest is the world's largest and most celebrated popular festival. It's held every year at the end of September and beginning of October on the Theresienwiese in Munich, Germany. Oktoberfest was celebrated for the first time in 1810 at the marriage of King Ludwig I and Princess Therese of Saxony-Hildburghausen. The only attraction at the time was a horse race. Side shows have been added continuously ever since. Today, more than six million visitors are expected at each Oktoberfest celebration to take in the great beer tents, swings and giant ferris wheels. Give your guests a real "taste" of Oktoberfest.

Ambiance

Imagine a big beer tent at the famous festival. Lower the lights slightly. Since beer doesn't have the most pleasant smell, perhaps the smell of fresh pretzels would be better.

Colors

Use "lederhosen" colors of loden green and grey.

Suggested Attire

The suggested attire is "sitting down for a liter or two" casual.

Invitations

"Wilkomen" (Welcome in German). Use the traditional blue and white diamond pattern found in the flag of Bavaria where the Oktoberfest is held or use a closeup photograph of beer in a mug. Or, send a liter-sized beer mug that guests can bring with them to the party.

Decorations

In the real Oktoberfest tents, guests sit at long, picnic-style tables. If you can manage this in your facility, great. If not, set the tables with loden green tablecloths, wood place settings and deep grey napkins. Every place should, of course, have a beer stein. The most popular beer steins in Germany are ceramic, although glass steins may be easier to find and less expensive. In the center of the table create a big pile of large, soft pretzels. Talk to a travel agent about acquir-

Keywords

German, Munich, Hofbräuhaus, beer tents, beer, foam, beer stein, pretzels, chicken song, lederhosen, sausage, autumn, beer tasting, horse radish, beer garden, beer cellar, bonfire, vendors, tents, dirndl, loden, antler, hats with bone buttons, feather, edelweiss, oompah, tuba band, slap dancing, grilled chicken (brathendl), veal sausage (Münchner weisse), white sausage (Weisswurst), pork sausage, grilled trout, five million liters of beer, games, carousels, roller coasters, bands, traditional costumes - lederhosen and dirndls, cloaks, hats with

Oktoberfest

ing posters advertising Oktoberfest or Bavaria, Germany for your wall decorations. Some of the larger brewers also send posters to beer distributors, another source for "official" Oktoberfest posters. At Oktoberfest, you'll see tall decorated poles that mark the entrance of the tents. Take some light PVC pipe and cover it with 4" wide, alternating, blue and white ribbon. Create crossbars through the pipe using 1" dowels. On the dowels secure graphic pictures of people in traditional German costumes or of German castles. Secure the "poles" at both the ceiling and the floor.

Menu

Consider this "beer hall" menu.
- appetizers: beer bread with beer cheese soup
- main course: roast sauerbraten (marinated roast beef), spaetzle (dumplings) and green beans with sweet and sour dressing
- dessert: black forest torte (chocolate cake with cherry filling)
- specialty drinks: Weisbeer or Liebfraumilch (white crème de cacao, half and half, fresh lime juice)

Entertainment

Hire a German band familiar with the traditional "chicken dance" always played at Oktoberfest to come and perform for your guests. Chances are pretty good, that your guests will need a quick lesson in the dance before they can perform it themselves but it's quick and easy to learn. Of course, if it's Oktoberfest, you must sing German beer drinking songs while you enjoy the music and the food. Ask the band to lead you in a few.

Souvenirs/Party Favors

Send your guests home with the beer stein from their place setting.

Fund Raisers

If you need to raise funds, auction off a trip to Munich during the annual Oktoberfest, pictures of Germany castles or cases of German beer.

Keywords

tassels or bone ornaments, Bavarian Alps, ramparts and moats, stone gates, baroque buildings, grand canals, pavilions scattered throughout the grounds, (beer types) - Altbier, Biergarten, Bock, Dunkel, Kolsch, Dortmunder, Marzen, Pilsner, Rauschbier, Sezuen, Steinbier, Hefeweizen, Dunkelweizen, malt, hops, yeast, cuckoo clocks, ancient castles, Neuschwanstein, medieval towns, frothy beer, heady wine, hearty food, cobblestoned streets, old towns, frothy beer, heady wine, hearty food, Romantic Road, **www.celebration-solutions.com/oktoberf.html**

Professional Themes

Introduction

Money, money, money. People dream about it, write songs about it, fight over it. Money is almost as old as recorded history. From Continentals issued to finance the American Revolution, to Confederate currency backed by cotton, to today's Federal Reserve notes backed by faith in the U.S. government, the story of American history is told in its currency. Bankers deal with the trade of money — the upside, money lent to buy things, and the downside, counterfeiters and thieves. Some of the wildest stories ever told have to do with money. Give your guests a night of opulence.

Ambiance

Imagine the richest "bank" ever — the vault at Fort Knox. Keep the lighting high to show off the gold and play background sounds like the "cha ching" of a cash register, or bills going through a money-counting machine.

Colors

Use "show me the money" colors of green and gold.

Suggested Attire

The suggested attire is "pinstripe and power tie" cocktail.

Invitations

"The color of money is green … but we'll be blue if you can't attend." Use funny money for your invitations. Put your own face on some bills or coins, or make up some currency in absurd amounts. Send along money bags with chocolate coins or a new wallet with your invitation inside.

Decorations

Set the tables with green tablecloths, gold metallic fabric napkins, gold utensils, gold-rimmed place settings and gold-stemmed glasses. For centerpieces, create the "pot of gold" you might find at the end of the rainbow. Fill the pot heaping full with gold (chocolate) coins.

Keywords

FDIC, charter, deposit, debit, credit, loans, tellers, teller cage, safety deposit box, old money, cash, mortgage, currency, exchange, foreign, interest, rates, robbers, financial services, accounts, investment, pension, securities, dealers, trusts, free market, cash, credit cards, checking, savings, borrow, savings and loan, credit union, assets, liabilities, bonds, underwriting, mutuals, depositors, capital, vault, goldsmith, dollars, cents, schillings, shekels, pounds, francs, lire, kronor, deutchmark, yuan, yen, pesos, rupees, legal tender, guilders, silver, gold,

Banking

For your wall decorations, use a photograph of an "old-money" bank — marble floors and columns, fancy wooden desks, or tellers behind cages. Blow these up to mural size. You can use different pictures if you want to create a gallery or use a single picture and repeat it for a pattern effect.

Menu

Consider this "wealth on a plate" menu.

- appetizers: polenta pie with gorganzola
- main course: steak Diane with marinated and grilled assorted vegetable stacks with mint chutney
- dessert: white chocolate and pistachio cheesecake
- specialty drinks: Golden Dreams (Galliano, Cointreau, orange juice, half and half) or Grand Occasions (light rum, Grand Marnier, white crème de cacao, lemon juice)

Entertainment

Show movie clips of bank heists and chase scenes on screens around the room. Teach your guests to play *Acquire* by Avalon Hill — a classic business game. The game is fast-moving and easy to learn. The object of the game is to grow your company or acquire others. As your company grows, you build until you can top your building with a skyscraper roof creating a mini skyline on the game board.

Souvenirs/Party Favors

Send each guest home with a decorative money clip full of funny money or an old-fashioned piggy bank.

Fund Raisers

If you need to raise funds, sell proof sets of coins and collections of paper currency from different places around the world. Contact a numismatic dealer to help you find sets to sell.

Keywords

wampum, barter, coinage, exchange rate, revenue, gold coins, gold bricks, Fort Knox, bullion, bills, greenbacks, counterfeiters, money lending, coins, currency, legal tender, barter, goldsmith, inflation, Mint, bank notes, bullion, Federal Reserve, faces on bills, In God We Trust, silver certificates, checkbook, engraving, commodity, stocks, bonds, T-bills, Treasury, affinity cards, daily balance, credit, collateral, discounts, rates, overdraft, surcharge, amortization, appreciation, ATM, balance, bank run, broker, **www.celebration-solutions.com/bank.html**

Professional Themes

Introduction

Chemistry is the study of composition, structure, properties, and interactions of matter. Chemistry arose from alchemy, an attempt to transform metals into gold. As the field of chemistry developed, chemists learned how to create new substances that have many important applications in our lives. Experimenting with chemicals can also stir the imagination. Give your guests a "lab-level" look at the world of chemistry.

Ambiance

Imagine a mad scientist's lab. Keep the lighting "clinical" bright white and play background sounds of clinking glass beakers, chemicals bubbling, bunson burner's burning and chalk being used on a chalkboard. If you're going to give the room a chemical smell, make it a pleasant one.

Colors

Use one color — "lab coat" white.

Suggested Attire

The suggested attire is "experimental" casual. If you want to emphasize the "sterile" white environment, ask your guests to dress only in white. If you do, any color you use in the room will jump out.

Invitations

"The formula for a terrific celebration is …" Use a scientific photograph of an atom or an electron, or give your directions using the diagram of a compound. Or, send a beaker full of candy along with your invitation.

Decorations

Set the tables with white tablecloths, white napkins, white plastic utensils and white china. For centerpieces give your guests snacks that are white, such as yogurt covered peanuts, pretzels dipped in white chocolate and white chocolate fudge. Ask the wait staff to dress in lab coats, white shirts and white pants.

From the ceiling hang a network of colorful styrofoam balls connected by white

Keywords

laboratory, periodic table, test tube, beakers, chemicals, compounds, elements, atomic mass, atomic weight, metals, salts, nuclear, bunson burner, microscope, experiment, lab coat, goggles, safety glasses, matter, alchemy, experiment, gas, liquid, solid, alchemy, gas, liquid, solid, alloys, polymers, magnets, elements, compounds, atoms, molecules, radioactive particles, microscope, nucleus, proton (positive), electron (negative), isotopes, orbitals, ions, metals, bonds, polarity, electronegativity, formulas, isomers, equations, reactions,

Chemists

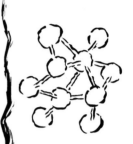

dowels like a fantastical chemical formula.

Create a beaker pyramid. Champagne glasses are often stacked this way during the holidays to create a champagne fountain. Use beakers of all the same size, fill them full of white substances — sugar, salt, shaving cream, soap shavings or fake snow. Use something different for each row.

Menu

Consider this menu a "formula for success!"
- appetizers: hot whole wheat bread with sweet honey butter
- main course: pork loin stuffed with apples
- dessert: hot hazelnut brownies with vanilla ice cream
- specialty drinks: Grapeshots (gold tequila, white Curacao, white grape juice) or 10-Gallon Cocktails (gin, coffee liqueur, sweet vermouth, egg yolk)

Entertainment

Cranium is a good game for this theme. *Cranium* features 14 riot-filled, fun activities. Your guests will be splitting their sides as they hum, whistle, sketch, sculpt, act, puzzle, and even spell backwards to win. Play rounds with the different card decks: Creative Cat, Star Performer, Word Worm and Data Head. Award prizes for each round.

Souvenirs/Party Favors

Send your guests home with a "formula for success" puzzle. Figure out what you think is the formula for a successful life (marriage, company, etc.), and have it printed on a puzzle blank.

Fund Raisers

If you need to raise funds, sell copies of the game *Cranium* by Cranium Cranium, or other popular games like *Mindtrap* by Pressman Toys, *Coda* or *Pente* by Winning Moves, *Outburst, Trivial Pursuit* or *Jenga* by Parker Brothers, *Pictionary, Scattergories,* or *Taboo* by Milton Bradley.

Keywords

solutions, acid, base, salt, oxide, laws, crystal, conductivity, melting point, freezing point, solutions, sugars, starches, kinetic energy, electrolytes, concentration, mole, degrees, organic, inorganic, equilibrium, electron sharing, biochemistry, photochemistry, electrochemistry, molecular chemistry, minerals, electron pairs, atomic number, acid, base, catalyst, equation, combustion, isotope, double bond, empirical formula, constant, free energy, half life, geiger counter, acid, base, bonding, elements, **www.celebration-solutions.com/chemist.html**

Professional Themes

Introduction

How we live depends very much on what we can create. In early civilization, inventors were anonymous. We will never know who invented the wheel or sparked the first fire, but these basic innovations lead to other discoveries. Throughout human history, creative, imaginative people have been the mainspring of new inventions. As our livestyles change, so do our inventions. Necessity, they say, is the mother of invention. Invite your guests for a night of "inventive" celebration.

Ambiance

Picture an inventor's workshop. Keep the lighting low like you're in an old garage. Use background sounds of metal against metal, hammer against wood, nails being pounded, screws being screwed, gears turning and engines backfiring. Give the room a dusty, slightly oily smell to complete the effect.

Colors

Use "tinkering around" colors of grey green, tan and brown.

Suggested Attire

The suggested attire is "inventive" casual.

Invitations

"The best way to predict a great party is to invent it!" Choose a picture of a famous invention or a closeup of gear-driven machinery.

Decorations

Set the tables with grey green tablecloths, stoneware place settings and tan napkins. For centerpieces, build a tabletop sculpture using lots of gears and knobs. The childrens toys, Lego™, Tinkertoys® or K'Nex, are good for this.

Use the walls to create a hall of famous inventions. Either use pictures of the real thing, along with a notation about the inventor, or give your guests their own inventions. Turn on the TV or rent a few sci-fi movies to get ideas about inventions of the future. Then give your guests credit for having invented the

Keywords

idea, product, patent, device, process, object, procedures, accidental discovery, Alexander Graham Bell, Sir Isaac Newton, Eli Whitney, chance discovery, inspiration, solution of a problem, experiment, insight, gifted, new use for an old product, 1759 first accurate time piece, 1769 first steam powered vehicle, 1793 cotton gin, 1800 batteries, 1800 gas lighting, 1805 railroad locomotive, 1807 steamboat, 1818 bicycle, 1831 regular train service, 1835 revolver, 1837 telegraph, 1839 photograph, 1851 Singer sewing machine, 1874 Levi's, 1876 telephone, 1877

Inventors

"dilithium engine" or "warp drive." Or look at some of the funny household inventions from the television show the Jetsons — Rosie the robot, the space car, the moving sidewalk clothes closet.

Menu

Consider this " … interesting … very interesting" menu.
- appetizers: poached salmon with egg and caper sauce
- main course: shrimp and crab etouffee
- dessert: chocolate walnut pie
- specialty drinks: Ramos gin fizz (gin, orange flower water, egg whites, confectioner sugar, lemon juice, half and half, vanilla extract and soda water) or Whiskey Sangaree (blended whiskey, Ruby port, sugar, sparkling water)

Entertainment

Pile each table high with Lego™, Tinkertoys®, Erector sets or K'Nex. Give each table a picture of what you want them to construct and see which table can finish first. You can either have the group put together small objects and construct three or four of them, or you can give the table a larger project that will require them to work separately in order to put together a larger sculpture quickly. Give a prize to the table that finishes first. Or, let the guests come up with their own inventions. Give a prize for the most imaginative one.

Souvenirs/Party Favors

Give each guest one of the greatest inventions of all time — a clock. Find a replica piece that has all of the gears showing like the early clocks did.

Fund Raisers

If you need to raise funds, auction off a consultation with a invention/patent specialist. You might be surprised how many of your guests want to find out of their idea for an invention is a good one. You'll find the U.S. Patent and Trademark Office online at www.uspto.gov.

Keywords

phonograph, 1883 electric lighting, 1893 Sears and Roebuck catalog, 1895 first motion picture, 1901 color printing, 1903 Model T Ford, 1903 first airplane flight, 1906 vacuum cleaner, 1907 color photograph, 1907 helicopter, 1913 zipper, 1928 penicillin, 1929 first television program, 1938 xerography, 1944 IBM computer, 1946 Polaroid, 1948 transistor, 1948 contact lens, 1957 velcro, 1958 video game, 1960 laser, 1961, robot, 1968 calculator, 1970 computer chip, intellectual property, copyright, **www.celebration-solutions.com/invent.html**

Professional Themes

Introduction

To the earliest photographers, cameras challenged the painter's brush as a way to create a realistic image rather than an impression. The first picture was taken in 1826, so photographs have only been around about a century and three quarters. In the 1880s a great number of small, hand cameras were produced. The Eastman Kodak Company's motto, "You press the button, we do the rest," started the revolution of modern photography. Today, we record our everyday activities and the most important events in our lives with a camera. Give your guests a "snapshot" in time at a picturesque celebration.

Ambiance

Create a photo gallery. Keep the lighting low except for spotlights on the pictures. Play background sounds of flashes popping and shutters clicking.

Colors

Use "old-fashioned picture" colors of shades of sepia.

Suggested Attire

The suggested attire is "a snapshot in time" casual.

Invitations

"You ought to be in pictures! … and you will be, if you join us!" Use old-fashioned pictures, or pictures you have of your guests for your invitation. Or, send a picture frame with the details of the party and tell guests that they'll receive a picture to put in the frame.

Decorations

Set the tables with tablecloths of unbleached cotton or muslin. You can use photo transfer paper or transfer solution to put photographs onto the table cloths in different sizes and at different angles. Put a photograph of each guest on a napkin and use placecards to direct individuals to sit at the setting with their picture. For centerpieces, create photo bouquets.

Create a gallery of pictures on the walls. It's easy to add a sepia tone to pic-

Keywords

light, optics, chemistry, developing, snapshots, portrait, news photographs, landscapes, travel photographs, astral photographs, scientific photos, architectural photographs, camera obscura, daguerreotype, visible images, action of light, souvenirs of occasions of personal significance, film, lens, camera, prints, slides, artistic, exposure meter, filters, electronic flash, viewfinder, focus, shutter speeds, shutter release, self-portrait, 35mm, single-lens reflex, double exposure, focal length, f-stop, telephoto, depth of field, negative, macro lens, ASA,

Photography

tures using an image-editing program. If you're gathering friends or colleagues, make the gallery about them. Gather pictures of guests in different scenes at different ages. If it's your family you're gathering, feature your ancestors. Label the pictures so everyone will understand where the person pictured fits into the family tree. If your guests don't have a close connection to one another, use historic photographs of the area.

Menu

Consider this "enlightening …" menu.

- appetizers: spinach salad with raspberry vinagrette
- main course: lime shrimp, chicken and roasted pepper fajitas with a choice of salsas, from fruity mile to hell-blazing hot
- dessert: coffee and vanilla ice
- specialty drinks: Anatole Coffee (cognac, coffee liqueur, Frangelico, iced coffee, whipped cream, chocolate shavings) or Café Romano (white Sambuca, coffee liqueur and half and half)

Entertainment

Almost everyone wishes that they could take better pictures. Give your guests a quick lesson in photography. Give them a disposable camera to practice with. Set up props that guests can practice on such as a still life for a closeup, a model for a portrait, a dancer for an action shot or objects at a distance for a landscape. Encourage guests to use the rest of the roll to take pictures of themselves or other guests at the party.

Souvenirs/Party Favors

Send guests home with a decorative photo frame.

Fund Raisers

If you need to raise funds, auction off sittings with a photographer. Offer different packages such as couples portraits, glamour shots, family portraits, or senior pictures.

Keywords

color balance, lighting, exposure, shutter speed, composition, darkroom, processing, enlarger, printer, contrast, mask, tone, zoom, subject, lighting conditions, color, harmony, contrast, sunset, backlighting, silhouettes, patterns, depth, perspective, camera angle, cropped, details, close-up, fish-eye, framing the shot, positioning the subject, pose, isolating detail, showing movement, fill flash, local color, candids, waterscapes, skyscapes, changing light, weather, air brush, ambient light, camera angle, **www.celebration-solutions.com/photo.html**

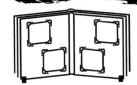

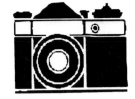

Professional Themes

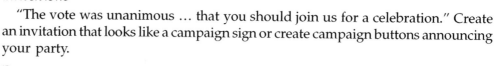

Introduction

"Tippecanoe and Tyler Too!" That was the slogan for the presidential election in 1840. Never before had an election been so nationally celebrated. Lincoln waged an election campaign from his front porch in Illinois and the 1860 election started a tradition of candidate debates. Lincoln's opponent, Stephen A. Douglas, also started a tradition that lasted into the 1940s — the whistle-stop tour. Douglas traveled by train to different areas around the country rousing support for his candidacy. In 1920, Warren G. Harding used the power of radio to get elected, and in 1960, the power of television handed the White House to John Fitzgerald Kennedy. Today, the internet is a way for candidates to get their message to the people. Take your guests back a few decades to a time when you could only hear a campaign speech if you lived "on the mainline."

Ambiance

Join the "stump" of an old-fashioned whistle-stop campaign. Keep the lighting high like you're out of doors. Play background sounds of a locomotive coming up the tracks, steam coming off the engine, the train's whistle sounding, and of course, a firebrand political speech or two. Make the speeches fun. Record your support for funny, obscure causes. Be careful about taking a stand on political hot-button issues, though, your guests might not feel the way you do.

Colors

Use "flag-waving" colors of red, white and blue.

Suggested Attire

The suggested attire is "fat-cat" formal.

Invitations

"The vote was unanimous … that you should join us for a celebration." Create an invitation that looks like a campaign sign or create campaign buttons announcing your party.

Decorations

Set the tables with blue tablecloths, red napkins and white china. For center-

Keywords

campaign, stump, speech, buttons, hats, microphone, platform, slogan, lies, legislation, Electoral College, candidates, government, Congress, Senate, House of Representatives, scandal, spending limits, election, judges, checks and balances, Federal, State, influence, power, policy, voter support, Watergate, raise money, plan strategy, electors, votes, pigsty politics, fat cats, handbills, pamphlets, posters, torchlight parades, rallies, dirty tricks, image, triumph of the masses, Republican, Democrat, Independent, Whig, nominating convention,

Politicians

pieces, create red, white and blue balloon bouquets. Anchor them in the center of the tables inside an upside down campaign hat.

Find historic pictures of Presidential candidates making whistle-stop tours. Blow these up to mural size and hang them on the walls. Use red, white and blue material to create swags across the tops of the walls all the way around the room.

Menu

Consider this "good 'ole boys" menu.

- appetizers: iceberg wedges with blue cheese dressing, and herb-crusted cherry tomatoes
- main course: pan-fried flank steak with roasted garlic mashed potatoes
- dessert: cheesecake with blueberry and strawberry toppings
- specialty drinks: Strawberry margaritas, White Way (gin, white crème de menthe), or Blue Devils (gin, fresh lime juice, maraschino liqueur, blue Curacao)

Entertainment

Ask each table to come up to nominate a "candidate" from their table. Give them the means to create a campaign sign and ask them to come up with a slogan for their candidate. Ask each candidate to come to the microphone and give their slogan and show their sign. Ask the crowd to vote for the best candidate. Give the winning table a special souvenir. Hire actors to give campaign speeches on funny topics. Steer clear of any "hot button" political topics.

Souvenirs/Party Favors

Send each guest home with a nice coffee table book about a piece of the nation's history — George Washington's Mount Vernon or Thomas Jefferson's Monticello.

Fund Raisers

If you need to raise funds, ask for "campaign" donations. Or, sell tickets for a trip on a scenic railroad.

Keywords

parades, whistle-stop tour, parade floats, "Slippery Jim," "Tricky Dick," "Slick Willie," press corps, campaign hats, buttons, balloons, ribbons, flags, banners, primaries, caucus, Iowa, New Hampshire, image, parties, "I Like Ike," "Dewey Wins," exit polls, voter registration, ballot, boss, bandwagon, convention, elector, electorate, flier, impeachment, inauguration, incumbent, landslide, majority, nominate, party, plurality, poll, pollster, precinct, sound bite, suffrage, ticket splitting, anarchy, sine die, unicameral, **www.celebration-solutions.com/photo.html**

Progressive Themes

Introduction

Thank goodness for holidays! They give us a reason for celebrating. We celebrate the seasons, the feast days, planting and harvest — even the cycle of life. Holidays also provide traditions and a link across history. How much would you know about the Pilgrims without the celebration of Thanksgiving? Would Count Dracula have faded into obscurity without Halloween? Pick a group of holidays and celebrate them all at once. Or celebrate one holiday right after another for a progressive theme.

Ambiance

Create a happy holiday atmosphere. If you're going to progress from one holiday to another, change the lighting scheme as you do by putting the decorative lights on a timer. Just about every holiday has music that is representative of either the holiday itself, or the time of year of the holiday. Put together a collection of holiday favorites to play in the background.

Colors

Use "cheery holiday" colors.

Suggested Attire

The suggested attire is "holiday party" cocktail.

Invitations

"Yes, Virginia … there is a Santa Claus." Create a photo composite for each of the holidays you will celebrate or send your invitation in something that represents a holiday — a snow globe, an Easter basket, a pumpkin or a cornucopia.

Decorations

Set the tables in rows from holiday to holiday. In other words, if you have chosen to celebrate a holiday a month from January to December, set the first row of tables for New Year's, the second row for Valentine's Day, and so on throughout the year. For the centerpieces, choose something that represents the holiday, like valentines chocolates for Valentine's Day, or use the same centerpiece for all tables. Either way, if the centerpieces are edible, make sure the ap-

Keywords

New Year's Day, Twelfth Night, Chinese New Year, Groundhog Day, Lantern Festival (Taiwan), IckChan Lee (Korean New Year), President's Day, Valentine's Day, Lupercalia (Greece), Mardi Gras, Purim (Jewish), Saint Patrick's Day, Anzac Day (New Zealand), April Fool's Day, Arbor Day, Good Friday (Christian), Easter, Hakata Dontaku (Japanese Golden Week), Passover (Jewish), Beltaine (Celtic), Cinco de Mayo (Mexico), May Day, Memorial Day, Mother's Day, Vesak (Buddhist), Dragon Boat Festival (China), Father's Day, Flag Day, Queensland

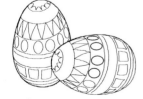

Holiday

peal of the food items are the same for all tables so that no table will feel slighted.

Menu

Consider this "holiday treat" menu.
- appetizers: smoked salmon on sliced potatoes with dill sauce
- main course: pork loin and onions on brown rice pilaf with pecans
- dessert: warm lemon-rice custard and decorated holiday cookies
- specialty drinks: Wassail bowl (ale, cream sherry, sugar, allspice, cinnamon, nutmeg, ginger, lemon slide)

Entertainment

Put together a collection of music representative of each of the holidays you've chosen for this theme. If you're holding a progressive theme, use the music to indicate to your guests that you're moving on to the next holiday.

Give each guest a nice notecard and a decorative envelope. Ask them to write a New Year's resolution and address the envelope to themselves. Send it to them after the next New Year.

Play an around-the-year guessing game. Give guests a headline and see if they can guess what month the headline appeared in. In addition to headlines, think about using movie releases, events, and international or unusual holidays. Or, give guests a date and see if they can correctly place events that took place on that day in history.

Souvenirs/Party Favors

Wrap a small gift for each guest that is appropriate for the holiday represented at their table. For example, watches for New Year's, candy for Valentine's, or green beer mugs for St. Patrick's Day.

Fund Raisers

If you need to raise funds, conduct a silent auction for romantic dinners for two — one for each month of the year, or one in every month.

Keywords

Day (Australia), Bastile Day (France), Canada Day, 4th of July, Nag Panchami (Hindu), Labor Day, Mid-Autumn Festival (China), Yom Kippur (Jewish), Chusuk (Korean Harvest Festival), Columbus Day, Dasara (Hindu), Ghandi Jayanti (India), Halloween, Samhain (Celtic), Sukkot (Jewish), All Saint's Day (Christian), Shichi-go-san (Japan), Day of the Dead (Mexico), Guy Fawkes Day (England), Ramadan (Muslim), Sadie Hawkins Day, Thanksgiving, Hanukkah (Jewish), Christmas, Boxing Day (England), celebrate, **www.celebration-solutions.com/holiday.html**

Kufi

Progressive Themes

Introduction

We called this progressive theme a mirror party because it's intended to go in reverse. Start with dessert, end with breakfast. Say good-bye when your guests enter and tell them you're glad they had a good time. Play games where winners lose and losers win. If it's summer wear snowshoes and galoshes, and if it's winter wear shorts and sandals. It's all about the weird, wacky and unexpected.

Ambiance

This theme is topsy turvy — mixed up, reversed, upside down and backwards. Keep the lighting high to show off the decorations. Use the kind of background sounds that you hear in animated cartoons like a slide whistle followed by a cymbal crash.

Colors

Use "reflective mirror" colors of metallic silver, metallic gold and red to spice things up.

Suggested Attire

The suggested attire is backwards … or upside down.

Invitations

"Mirror, mirror on the wall … where's the greatest party of them all?" Send your invitation on shiny silver mylar paper or print the words backward so that it has to be read in a mirror.

Decorations

Set the tables with red tablecloths, silver utensils and silver metal place settings. For centerpieces, create bouquets of hand mirrors. Surround the bottom of the mirrors with metallic silver and gold mini-balls in a red glass bowl.

From the ceiling, hang mirror balls to reflect the light. Don't skimp. Use plenty of them. Take pictures of the back of people's heads and hang these backwards portraits on the walls. Sprinkle glitter on the floor. The mirror balls will make the glitter on the floor sparkle.

Keywords

mirror image (exactly backward), distorted images, looking backward into the future, backward glances, reading right to left, count backwards from 100, the Great Leap Backwards, looking at the world in the rearview mirror, mirror mirror on the wall …, the mirror has two faces, the mirror cracked, looking glass, Through the Looking Glass, The World Turned Upside Down, pineapple upside down cake, Turn the thing on its head, hanging upside down, upside down and backwards, upside down - inside out, From the inside out, indoor-outdoor, back to front,

Mirror Party

Naturally, you'll need mirrors. If you can find them, use the distorted mirrors found at carnivals. It's fun to see your reflection in these mirrors.

Menu

Consider this "all backwards" menu.
- appetizers: apple brown Betty (dessert)
- main course: fried chicken and corn (lunch)
- dessert: poached eggs in tarragon sauce, sauteed mushrooms (breakfast)
- specialty drinks: Tutti-Fruitti (gin, amaretto, cherry liqueur, apples, pears, peaches)

Entertainment

Play a game of *Mirror Hunt*. Split the room into two parts. Have each group choose representatives in multiples of two. If you want to play one round, then they would choose two representatives, if you want to play three rounds then you'll need six representatives from each group, and so on.

Ask the players to step outside of the room. Prior to the party, hide as many objects as rounds of the game you would like to play. Ask the first two players from each team to enter the room. Remind them that they're playing "mirror" hunt, but don't give them any further explanation. Give them clues to find the objects, but they should be *opposite* clues. In other words, when you say look up, they should look down. When you say go right, they should go left. If they should look on page 753, it's really 357. The fastest group to find the object, wins.

Souvenirs/Party Favors

Create address books that are bound on the opposite side from normal and that go from Z to A. Put a "back of the head portrait" on the cover of the address book.

Fund Raisers

If you need to raise funds, sell products from somewhere on the opposite side of the globe from where you are.

Keywords

reflecting surface, cheval glass, replica, echo, repeat, in reverse, rearward, vice versa, upside down, topsy-turvy, assbackwards, reversed, opposite, inverse, retro, counter, broken mirror, lost in the mirror, man in the mirror, magical mirror, smoke and mirrors, mirror me, mirror image, shattered mirror, mirror in time, looking backward, backwards and forwards, a face turned backwards, mirror image, back to the future, reflection, round about, in reverse, a smooth or polished surface of metal or glass, reflector, **www.celebration-solutions.com/mirror.html**

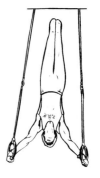

Celebration Solutions

Progressive Themes

Introduction

Mystery stories are loved like no other genre. The chief aim mystery stories is to create suspense. Throughout the story, some kind of evil lurks, creating uncertainty and portending ominous things to come. Floors creak; lightning, thunder, and rain are the standard weather; and mysterious winds ruffle papers and extinguish the candlelight. Meanwhile, the detective must follow a trail of clues to solve a puzzle involving crime, usually murder. Make this theme a progressive party by creating a mystery where a new clue is revealed at each new location or time. "Clue" your guests in to a good time.

Ambiance

Imagine a creaky, old mansion with hidden doors and passageways and dark, forbidding recesses. Keep the lighting low to enhance the mysteriousness of the room and play sounds like those mentioned above in the background. Remember, old mansions often have a dusty, musty smell.

Colors

Use "plot-twister" colors for this theme of black, brown and grey.

Suggested Attire

The suggested attire is "detective story" casual.

Invitations

"It's a mystery … why anyone would miss this party!" Use a picture of a spooky, old house or the chalk outline of a body. Or, buy copies of your favorite mystery books in paperback and send them with your invitation as a bookmark.

Decorations

Set the tables with black tablecloths, grey napkins and black place settings. Take inspiration from the game *Clue*™ and created tabletop sculptures using potential murder weapons. Use toy guns arranged handle grip up and tied together to create the base for a floral arrangement. Make a bouquet of jewel-handled daggers. Use candlesticks on pedestals of different heights. Use your imagination for other "murder weapon" bouquets.

Keywords

clues, who dunnit, detective, murderer, Inspector, cops, Bobbies, Sherlock Holmes, the faithful Watson, Professor Moriarty, Hercule Poirot, Charlie Chan, Nick Carter, Mickey Spillane, Dick Tracy, ancient documents, tracking skills, legends, Agatha Christie, Edgar Allan Poe, Arthur Conan Doyle, Charles Dickens, Dorothy Sayers, a battle between good and evil, the solution, pit your own wits against those of the criminal, weaving a spell, private eye, pulp magazines, homicide, criminal gang, suspect, confession, victim, high drama, rogue, street urchin,

Mystery

To pull off an "old mansion" look, you'll need props. Create a bookcase that is slightly ajar so that it looks like the entrance to a secret passageway and windows that are shuttered tight. Put up a couple of doors that open into brick or solid black walls.

Menu

Consider this "anybody's guess ..." menu.
- appetizers: green corn dumplings and fried green tomatoes
- main course: bubble and squeak (beef, potatoes, carrots, onions, leeks and cabbage)
- dessert: shoofly pie
- specialty drinks: White Spiders (a favorite of the crowd in the Algonquin Hotel in New York during the 1930s — vodka and white crème de menthe) or Moonlight (apple brandy, lemon juice, sugar)

Entertainment

Play old time radio mysteries like the *Green Hornet*, *Suspense*, *A Man Called X*, or the *Shadow* ("only the shadow knows ... "). Or, hire actors to play out a mystery for you. Choose a dime-store mystery that can be turned into a simple four-act play. Control the lights and you control the drama. Out go the lights, a shot rings out, up come the lights, there's the murder victim ... and everyone is a suspect. Let your main detective character step out of the play to get ideas from the audience for solving the crime.

Souvenirs/Party Favors

Send each guest home with a paperback mystery novel. Wrap them in plain brown wrapping paper and mark them "For Your Eyes Only."

Fund Raisers

If you need to raise funds, sell tickets to a mystery weekend at a local Bed & Breakfast, resort or hotel.

Keywords

underworld, villains, discovery of the body, masked robber, highwayman, vivid and sensational tale, unscrupulous, twists and turns of the plot, hero, courageous exploits, gang of thieves, forensics, engrossing storyline, poisoner, resolve the case, blackmail, counterplot, masterpiece, dime novels, master of disguise, super sleuth, dead man, secret, seemingly unsolvable, ingenious, gas-lit streets, evil deeds, jewel thief, modus operandi, rogues, highwaymen, swindlers, villains, hidden passageways, **www.celebration-solutions.com/mystery.html**

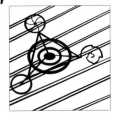

Progressive Themes

Introduction

A thousand years ago, man had no need to know the exact time. Sure there were sundials, but it wasn't until 1714 when the British government sponsored a contest to find a clock that would solve the problem of longitude, that a precise time keeping machine was created; and that clock took nearly 50 years to build! Today, we have clocks in everything from our computers, to our automatic coffee makers, to every conceivable souvenir. In this progressive theme, you'll make the minutes pass like time lapse photography — in record time.

Ambiance

Picture a clock in motion from dawn to dusk. Change the lighting as to correspond to the time of day. Think about sounds you hear at different times of the day. Early in the day you might hear sounds like roosters crowing and later in the day you might the sound of the whistle at quitting time.

Colors

Use "sunrise and sunset" colors for this theme.

Suggested Attire

The suggested attire is "up with the sun" casual.

Invitations

"Time flies ..." "Rock around the clock." Create a composite of pictures of timepieces or send a logo watch with the time and date of the party on the face along with the rest of the invitation details.

Decorations

Set the tables with bright yellow tablecloths, orange red napkins and red place settings. For centerpieces, of course, you will need some time pieces. Scour the flea markets for as many different kinds of clocks as you can find. Clocks in ... lamps, toys, souvenirs ... wall clocks, mantle clocks, wrist watches, pocket watches ... whatever.

Hang clocks of different styles and colors on the walls around the room and

Keywords ———————————

Around the Clock, clock, alarm clock, watch, time piece, sundial, hour glass, dusk, dawn, morning, noon, night, midnight, a measure of change, before and after, temporal notions, moment to moment, stitch in time, daylight savings time, time zone, standard time, Greenwich Mean Time, mid-day, timekeeper, sun in the sky, shadows, canonical hours- matins with lauds, prime, tierce, sext, nones, vespers and compline, candle clocks, chroniclers, the clock struck midnight, ante meridien - before noon, post meridien - after noon, the face of the clock, the

Time of Day

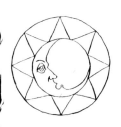

set each to a different time. Since bringing in real grandfather clocks would be difficult, create mural-sized posters of grandfather clocks to hang on the walls.

Menu

Consider this "day-long" feast.

- appetizers: an assortment of muffins with sweet butter (breakfast)
- main courses: avocado and tomato mini-omelettes and scones (brunch) and spicy shrimp and mushroom papardelle on fettucini noodles (dinner)
- dessert: almond cookies and coffee
- specialty drinks: Midnight Sun (aquavit, grapefruit juice, grenadine, orange slice) or Tequila Sunrise (silver tequila, orange juice, grenadine)

Entertainment

Play a game of *Beat the Clock*. This was a popular television show in the 1970s. Put together your own version where participants have to perform a stunt before the clock runs out.

Or play a game of *Clockwise Dice*. You'll need two dice for each person. All players roll their dice and the player with the highest number rolls first. After the first roll, players go in order clockwise around the table. On the first throw, players try to get a total of two on their dice (snake eyes). After that they must roll the numbers 3 through 12 in order. If they don't get the number they need during their roll they must keep trying in subsequent turns until they get the next number. The first player to roll to 12 wins.

Souvenirs/Party Favors

Choose a logo that will remind guests of the party and have it printed on the face of a logo watch.

Fund Raisers

If you need to raise funds, sell tickets to a sunset cruise, a sunrise horseback ride or a movie showing of *High Noon*.

Keywords

hands moved slowly, sounding the hours, phase of the moon, pendulum, grandfather clock, cuckoo clock, chronometer, the beat of time, prime meridian, London's Big Ben, punctual, late, gears, works, watchmakers, pocket watch, wrist watch, timetable, time zones, "I'm late, I'm late, for a very important date," time warp, atomic clock, quartz crystal, carriage clocks, chimes, clock's hands, pendulum, snooze alarm, alarm clock, Grandfather clock, chimes, on the hour, quarter hour, pendulum, military time, **www.celebration-solutions.com/time.html**

Regional Themes

Introduction

It is said that the Amazon river pulls life itself along with it to the sea. A seemingly endless, impenetrable and forbidding wall of jungle lies on either side of the Amazon, teeming with life. The Amazon basin is a tropical wilderness filled with countless species of plants and animals. Beyond the river settlements, the rainforest is so thick and difficult to travel through, that many areas have never been explored or mapped. Take your guests along to the Amazon river basin — a land of beauty and mystery.

Ambiance

Travel to the misty, steamy heart of the jungle. Play sounds of birds and other wildlife as well as rain falling against leaves in the background. Keep the temperature high and use a misting machine to raise the humidity in the room. Lower the lights a bit as if you're under the canopy of a thick jungle. Use potting soil or peat to give the room an earthy smell.

Colors

Use "deep, dark jungle" colors of leaf greens and bright accent colors.

Suggested Attire

The suggested attire is "hacking your way through the jungle" casual.

Invitations

"It's a jungle out there … and in here too." Use a closeup of colorful parrot feathers or tropical vegetation on the cover of the invitation. Or, send along a colorful bandana that guests could wear to the party.

Decorations

Set the tables with bright green tablecloths and bright, multi-colored napkins and place settings. The jungle around the Amazon is known for its exotic plant life. Use sweet-smelling orchids for your centerpieces. Ask the wait staff to dress in khaki shorts and shirts and wear "bush" hats.

Rent or borrow large-leafed plants, like banana plants, to place throughout the

Keywords

Amazon River, rio Amazones, tributaries, delta, tropical rain forest, tree canopies, dark green carpet of forest, hundreds of tributaries, tribes of hunter-gatherers, jaguars, vampire bats, headhunters, clouds rolling with sound and fury, lush vegetation, hot, humid, equator, palm trees, banana trees, pitcher plants, corpse flowers, moss, orchids, bromeliads, rattan palms, beetles, leafcutter ants, monkeys, macaw birds, water lilies, piranha fish, anaconda snakes, crocodiles, vultures, electric eels, butterflies, manatee, toucan, tree frogs, egret, firefly,

Amazon

room. Fill in the gaps with smaller variegated plants to give the "jungle" additional color and texture. Place colorful, stuffed parrots in the leaves of the larger plants. Let stuffed animals like pumas and large snakes peek out from between the plants.

Menu

Consider this menu that you might find in Brazil.

- appetizers: puree of pumpkin and cassava root fries (you'll find these on every Brazilian pub menu) with tomato relish
- main course: black bean and meat stew
- dessert: tropical fruit salad with coconut pudding
- specialty drinks: Brazilian chocolate (unsweetened chocolate, boiling water, hot half and half, strong coffee, vanilla extract, grated cinnamon)

Entertainment

Play Brazilian folk music. You'll find a large collection of Brazilian traditional and contemporary music online at www.cdnow.com.

Give your guests a chance to play a round of Jungle Jump. If you've ever played the game of *Snakes and Ladders* (or *Chutes and Ladders*™ by Milton Bradley), you'll enjoy this game. Players must climb the ladders to move forward or recover from a slide backwards down the chute to be the first to the heart of the jungle.

Souvenirs/Party Favors

Send guests home with a "jungle survival kit." Fill a bush hat with a water bottle, a bandana, a compass, an all-purpose knife, mosquito netting, bandaids, sunscreen and bug spray.

Fund Raisers

If you need to raise funds, sell an adventure trip to the Ariau treetop resort in the Amazon. This resort consists of about 210 rooms in wood towers connected by walkways suspended about 130 feet above the jungle floor.

Keywords

heron, dolphin, owl monkey, tarantula, rhinoceros beetles, leeches, cities of gold, conquistadors, malarial swamps, jungle humidity, insects, spiders, scorpions, snakes, macaw, toucan, blow pipe, poison arrows, cloves, cinnamon, brazilwood, turtles, rubber trees, beans, sweet potatoes, peppers, pineapples, hollowed-out canoes, flood plain, sand banks, islands, canopy, forest floor, face painting, photographic, jungle trekking, Teriano Indians, alligator hunting, one of the world's mightiest rivers, **www.celebration-solutions.com/amazon.html**

Regional Themes

Introduction

Unearthly and immense, Death Valley has seized the imagination of travelers ever since men first looked over the valley and viewed the spectacular mountains and deserts that surround it. Death Valley was given its name by one of 18 survivors of a party of 30 attempting to find a shortcut to the California gold fields in 1849. After intense suffering, the explorers made their way out of the valley by climbing the steep slopes of the Panamints mountains to the west in January 1850. Death Valley is filled with spectacular scenery, unusual wildlife, and at its lowest point, 282 feet below sea level, it is the lowest point in the Western Hemisphere. Give your guests a date with Death Valley — a fascinating and beautiful place.

Ambiance

Imagine a dry, dusty ghost town in the desert. Play sounds of the wind blowing, boards creaking, saloon doors banging, ghostly gunfights and coyote's howling in the background. Keep the lighting "sun in the sky" high and give the room a slight scent of desert sage.

Colors

Use "parched to the bone" colors of shades of sandy brown.

Suggested Attire

The suggested attire is "hotter 'n Hades" casual.

Invitations

"What makes the desert beautiful is that somewhere it hides a well" — Antoine de Saint-Exupery (1900-1944). Use a photograph of the desert in bloom, sand dunes, cactus, or a deserted landscape.

Decorations

Set the tables with light tan tablecloths, tan napkins and light-colored stoneware place settings. For centerpieces, use things you might find in a ghost town — a coiled up rattlesnake, old cowboy boots, cactus, an old water bucket, or antique liquor bottles.

Keywords

Hole in the Wall Gang, cactus, desert, western pants, jackelopes, tumbleweeds, hot and dry, the sound of wind, parched, watering hole, stagecoach stop, highest temperature ever recorded, sandstorm, dust, dunes, horned toads, lizards, desert bighorn sheep, rattle snakes, gold, silver, copper, lead, borax, Badwater, Dante's view, pale mudhills worn by water gullies, towering peaks, salt flats, mesquite clumps, prickly pear, devil's pincushion, crickets, grasshoppers, rabbits, pinyon nuts, bighorn sheep, dunes, high buttes, barren country, grand desola-

Death Valley

For the walls, create windows looking into the dusty remains of ghost town buildings. You'll find a gallery of photographs and information at the following websites: www.ghosttowns.com and www.GhostTownGallery.com.

Bring in hay bales, old pairs of cowboy boots, cactus and wagon wheels for empty spaces in the room.

Menu

Consider this "southwest" menu.
- appetizers: blue corn pancakes with green chili chutney
- main course: black bean soup with chile-marinated pork
- dessert: apricot empanadas
- specialty drinks: Creamsicle (vanilla liqueur, fresh orange juice, half and half, orange slice) or Curacao Coolers (dark rum, white Curacao, fresh lime juice sparkling water, orange slice)

Entertainment

Play music from a "ghost" band. Use the sound system to pipe in music from the 19th Century that fades in and out.

Hire a storyteller to regale your guests with spooky, ghost stories. Try Roald Dahl's *Book of Ghost Stories* or *Best Ghost and Horror Stories* by Bram Stoker (more famous for his story of Dracula).

Souvenirs/Party Favors

Send guests home with a small cactus in a decorative terra cotta pot or a copy of *The Explorer's Guide to Death Valley National Park* by T. Scott and Betty Tucker Bryan, or *Lost in Death Valley: the True Story of Four Families in California's Gold Rush* by Connie Goldsmith.

Fund Raisers

If you need to raise funds, auction a trip to visit Scotty's Castle and Death Valley National Park.

Keywords

tion, panning for gold, rumors of silver, abandoned wagons, ox yokes, bleached skeletons, sunburn, carrion crows, poison springs, mining camps, buzzard circling, gun fighters, stake a claim, mule team, wagon wheels, grub, burros, narrow gauge railroad, hooch, saloon, boom towns, rust-red earth, rain pool, mesquite flat, water pump, bobcat, coyote, forbidding and gloomy, badlands, rugged canyons, shimmering valley floors, severe environment, heat, deep, arid basin, salt flats, rock formations, **www.celebration-solutions.com/dvalley.html**

Regional Themes

Introduction

New England is the collective name given to Maine, New Hampshire, Vermont, Massachusetts, Rhode Island, and Connecticut. The region is best known for fishing, shipbuilding and many of the major events of America's colonial period, including the start of the American Revolution. New England in the fall is the stuff of stunningly beautiful calendars, travel books, and postcards. Whisk your guests away for an afternoon in crisp, cool New England.

Ambiance

Visit a scenic, rural New England town in the fall. Take the temperature in the room down a few degrees and keep the lighting bright. Give the room the scent of fallen leaves and play background sounds of rustling leaves and the wind blowing gentle breezes.

Colors

Use "brilliant fall" colors of orange, red, brown and green.

Suggested Attire

The suggested attire is "cool, crisp autumn" casual.

Invitations

"Meet us for a night in New England." Use a photograph of the fall foliage or postcards from the area for the invitation. Or, find a good symbol of fall like small pumpkins or big, ripe apples and send one wrapped in colorful tissue paper along with your invitation details.

Decorations

Set the tables with dark green tablecloths. Set each table with different colored napkins and place settings, either red, brown or orange. For centerpieces, fill small "bushel" baskets with things that you would commonly see in the fall — apples, Indian corn, small pumpkins or gourds. Place silk leaves in fall colors on the tables so they stick out from under the baskets.

Keywords

Maine, New Hampshire, Vermont, Massachusetts, Rhode Island, Connecticut, covered bridges, mill wheels, country inns, white churches, shipbuilding, American Revolution, colonial, patriots, Samuel Adams, Lexington and Concord, Shaker furniture, real maple syrup, weathered wooden barns, fields of wildflowers, tree-lined avenues, old-fashioned lampposts, long ancestries, shuttered windows, boats, church steeples, coastal communities, white picket fences, colorful shop signs, white clapboard, stained glass windows, dory, ferries, bell

New England

For wall decorations, use photographs of rural scenes in New England in the full blaze of fall colors. Blow the photographs up to poster size. Give the pictures a silk-leaf frame by covering the edges of the photograph with silk leaves of different colors. Paste them on at random, but be sure to completely cover the edges of the picture.

Menu

Consider this New England "Shaker" menu.

- appetizers: green salad
- main course: roast wild turkey on a bed of wild rice with mini cheese souffles
- dessert: Shaker cranberry pie
- specialty drinks: Damn the Weather (gin, sweet vermouth, triple sec, fresh orange juice) or Fair and Warmer (light rum, sweet vermouth, white Curacao, lemon twist)

Entertainment

See how well your guests would have fared a century or two ago during the harvest. Show pictures of 19th Century farm implements and see if your guests can guess how the tools would be used. Give your guests a matching list of canning instructions and see if they would have been able to put their garden goods up for the winter. Or, see if they would know how to dry and store food for the winter. Look at the book *Everyday Life in the 1800s* by Marc McCutcheon for ideas.

Souvenirs/Party Favors

Send each guest home with a basket of fall goodies — wine, ripe apples, pumpkin tarts, ripe grapes, and cheese.

Fund Raisers

If you need to raise funds, sell tickets to a scenic "fall colors" tour in New England.

Keywords

tower, high tide, low tide, fishing gear, lobster, Puritans, Pilgrims, clerestory windows, little red schoolhouse, small towns, town commons, 'on the common,' lighthouses, piers, fish market, white columns, old cannons, war monuments, old gravestones, island communities, cobble-stoned lanes, brilliant fall colors, scarecrows, pumpkins, fall leaves, winter festivals, sleigh rides, pine-bough garlands, Atlantic, mountains of fall colors, beautiful beaches, skiing in winter, fertile valleys, colonials, Salem, **www.celebration-solutions.com/newengl.html**

Regional Themes

Introduction

Since ancient times, people have dreamed of leaving their home planet and exploring other worlds. In 1961, that dream became reality when man first stepped on the moon. Studies in space have yielded a bounty of scientific discoveries about the solar system, the Milky Way Galaxy, and the universe, but nowhere has space been more explored than in the imagination. Fantastic creatures and remarkable spacecraft fill the pages of sci-fi novels and the screens of movies and television. Give your guests an opportunity to take their place "in space."

Ambiance

Create a futuristic space station. Keep the lighting low and bring on the blinking lights, buzzing buttons and flashing dials. Sci-fi movies are the birthplace and breeding ground of weird sound effects. Use these for background sounds.

Colors

Use "out-of-this-world" colors of midnight blue and white.

Suggested Attire

The suggested attire is alien. Encourage your guests to come up with the wildest and wackiest space alien costumes they can imagine.

Invitations

"Blast Off!" Have fun with this invitation. Send the details on a circuit board, toy space ship, or a laser gun.

Decorations

Set the tables with midnight blue tablecloths and napkins, and white china. Create a logo for your fictional space station and create placemats with the logo and "Launch Pad" on them.

From the ceiling, hang wire forms that look like instrument panels. Use all different shapes and sizes. Poke colored, blinking Christmas tree lights through black paper or material on wire forms. At the entrance, hang a "take off" timetable with all of the evening's events listed. On the walls, hang star charts.

Keywords

asteroids, planets, Moon, Mars, Pluto, Jupiter, solar systems, galaxies, constellations, astronaut, NASA, telescope, aliens, space walk, space station, rocket, zero gravity, spacecraft, Columbia, Challenger, Discovery, Atlantis (shuttles), Gemini (1961-1963), Apollo (1965-1966), Mercury (1968-1975), NASA, astronaut, rocket, solar system, stargazers, astronomers, lightyear (6.2 trillion miles), telescope, radio waves, Hubble Space Telescope, Saturn, rings, comets, moons, orbit, corona, arches of fire, sunspots, eclipse, dark side of the Moon, phases of

Outer Space

Arrange for large screens to play moving stars video files on so that the screen looks like a window looking out of the ship. These files are fairly easy to create on a computer or use a computer screensaver that looks like moving stars.

Menu

Consider this "outa' sight!" menu.
- appetizers: hush puppy planets
- main course: baked tuna stuffed avocado space ships with solar system stew (clam chowder)
- dessert: Pluto's own pecan pie
- specialty drinks: Jupiters (gin, dry vermouth, crème de violette, fresh orange juice) or Moonlight (apple brandy, fresh lemon juice, sugar)

Entertainment

Hold an "Alien Ball." Make the first dance something traditional, like the waltz. It will be plenty amusing to watch a bunch of aliens dancing in 3/4 time. Then liven the music up with more modern tunes. Give prizes for the best costumes. Vote on the guest "Least Likely to be Recognized as Human" or "Most Likely to be Mistaken for a Vulcan." Be creative with your awards and prizes.

Souvenirs/Party Favors

Send every guest home with a good photograph of themselves in costume. Set up a space background for them to stand in front of, or set up a situation that would be ridiculous like a corporate office. Seeing an alien sitting behind a desk conducting business would be amusing. Look for ideas at www.sciencefiction.com.

Fund Raisers

If you need to raise funds, sell science fiction memorabilia as well as complete seasons of the popular *Star Trek* series or science fiction movies. Or, auction a trip to Las Vegas to attend the *Star Trek Experience* at the Las Vegas Hilton Hotel. This hotel has one of the largest collection of *Star Trek* memorabilia in existence.

Keywords

the Moon, Man in the Moon, gold-coated visor, Martian, great red spot, meteorites, asteroids, nebula, white dwarf, super giant, super nova, Andromeda, Milky Way, galaxy, cosmic, splashdown, Soyuz, space walk, space station, Mir, escape pod, Skylab, satellite, meteor shower, Roswell, NM, Klingon, Borg, extraterrestrial, Star Trek xenology, putting a man on the Moon, nebula, gravitational pull, black hole, galaxy, orbit, satellite, solar flare, ultraviolet rays, nebula, neutron star, parallax, orbit, perigee, pulsar, **www.celebration-solutions.com/space.html**

Regional Themes

Introduction

The South Pacific is made up of more than 25,000 islands and islets of 25 nations and territories spread over the western and central Pacific Ocean. The tradewinds bring the monsoons for the rainy season and take them away for the dry season. The tradewinds also brought a diverse population of hunters, fishermen and farmers to the islands. Take your guests to a place of spectacular beaches and unspoiled beauty.

Ambiance

Picture a warm, summer evening on a deserted island. Use fans to create a slight breeze and keep the lighting high like a cloudless island day. Play the sound of waves hitting the beach and the call of sea birds in the background. Give the room the scent of the salt sea air.

Colors

Use "gentle, sea breeze" colors of pink, yellow and blue.

Suggested Attire

The suggested attire is "relaxing at a beach resort" casual.

Invitations

"Set sail for a remote and inaccessible island in the South Pacific." Use a photograph of a picturesque, white sand beach or palm trees against a cloudless, blue sky or send a decorative jar filled with sand and shells along with your invitation details.

Decorations

Set the tables with sea blue tablecloths, pink napkins and yellow place settings. For centerpieces, use a tall square vase filled with multi-colored sand and a large exotic blossom at the top. Place the vase in a low bowl with floating votive candles. If you want something a little more playful, put a pile of sand in the center of the table and place a bottle with a message in it among shells, starfish and sand dollars.

Keywords

Tahiti, islands, palm trees, coconuts, bananas, beaches, tropics, birds, Oceana, New Zealand, Fiji, Bali, Papua, New Guinea, Polynesia, Balboa, Magellan, Captain James Cook, cannibalism, head-hunting, Micronesia, New Caledonia, Solomon Islands, Fiji, south of the equator, atolls, archipelago, exotic, romantic, tropical, reefs, uninhabited islands, desert isles, volcano caldera, lagoons, high humidity, trade winds, leeward, windward, jungle interiors, rainfall, monsoon, typhoons, hurricanes, breadfruit, pandini, papayas, taro, yams, arrowroot,

South Pacific

If you want your guests to feel like they're on a deserted island, you'll need some murals. Find a panoramic view out from a beach over the water. Break the picture up into sections. Blow these pictures up into mural-sized posters and lay them side-by-side all the way down the walls. Use potted palms throughout the room and aim the fans at the leaves to keep them in motion.

Menu

Consider this "sweet, soft breezes of a beach somewhere" menu.
- appetizers: shrimp with papaya and pineapple chutney, and scallops with chili ginger oil
- main course: Asian mahi mahi salad on a bed of rice
- dessert: Bananas Foster
- specialty drinks: Aloha (rum cream liqueur, dark rum, fresh lime juice, pineapple juice, orange juice, coconut syrup and vanilla ice cream) or Island Coolers (lemon juice, orange juice, papaya juice, pineapple juice, grenadine, sparkling water, maraschino cherry, pineapple spear)

Entertainment

Play traditional island music or the soundtrack from the musical *South Pacific*. See how much your guests know about the this island region. Put together a guessing game and see how many of the following countries your guests can get right: Tuvalu, Tonga, Guam, Vanuatu, Tahiti, Fiji, New Caledonia, Cook Islands and Kiribati.

Souvenirs/Party Favors

Send each guest home with a beach bag stuffed with a sun hat, sunglasses, tanning lotion, sunscreen, a pair of flip flops and a tank top.

Fund Raisers

If you need to raise funds, raffle a trip to Bali. Give each person who buys a ticket a sealed airline ticket wallet. At an appointed time, have everyone open their wallets to determine a winner.

Keywords

fish, lobsters, shrimp, eels, octopus, sea creatures, snakes, lizards, sea birds, cacao, coffee, vanilla, sugar, pineapple, citrus fruits, hospitality, mosquito nets, carved boar's tusks, porpoise teeth, pierced stone disks, fed feather belts, shells, red shell necklaces, white shell armbands, rituals, fishing, drums, canoes, body paint, headdresses, costumes, masks, Bali, Bora Bora, Tuvalu, Cook Islands, Solomon Islands, Kiribati, Guam, Vanuatu, Tahiti, Fiji, New Caledonia, wood carving, wood inlay, animal figures, **www.celebration-solutions.com/spacific.html**

Regional Themes

Introduction

The process of winemaking is as old as the most ancient civilization. Wine was considered a gift from the Gods because it was often safer to drink than the water. One of the most important wine growing regions in the United States are the Napa and Sonoma Valleys in northern California, although many other wine growing areas exist around the country. Give your guests a wine tasting tour of a valley vineyard.

Ambiance

Imagine a vineyard just before the grape harvest. Keep the lighting high like a cloudless late summer day and bring in rich potting soil to give the room an earthy smell. Uncorking the wine bottles will also give the room a fruity vineyard bouquet.

Colors

Use "hillside harvest" colors of deep purple and shades of green.

Suggested Attire

The suggested attire is "barrel tapping" casual.

Invitations

"Wet your whistle …" Paste labels off different bottles of wine to your invitations, or use a closeup photograph of grapes or wine casks. Or, send wine glasses along with your invitation details.

Decorations

Set the tables with deep purple tablecloths and white china. Use fabric with grape leaves and grapes on it for napkins. Create a centerpiece of grape bunches. Use all different types of grapes from green to red to purple. On the serving tables, "pot" silk grape leaves in decorative pots using real potting soil for an earthy fragrance.

Use wooden barrels to create displays of different wines. Use fabric-covered boxes to display the wine bottles at different heights. Station a host at each dis-

Keywords

grapes, cultivated vineyards, fermentation, Bacchus, viticulture, corks, vintage, trellis, wine tasting, barrels, casks, Chardonnay, Merlot, Zinfandel, Cabernet, Riesling, Pinot Noir, foggy in winter, warm in summer, Inglenook, Mondavi, Beringer, Louis Martini, Charles Krug, Calistoga, aroma, robust, full-bodied, body, bouquet, snappy, tart, brisk, dry, sweet, fruity, neat long rows of vines, surrounded by rolling hills, dining among the vineyards, scenic, country view, wine jellies, chutney, tapanades, pack an empty stomach and a week's worth

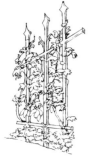

Wine Country

play to pour wine for your guests, rather than allow guests to serve themselves. Print a guide to each of the wines served to tell guests a little bit about what to expect when they taste it. The book *Good Wine Made Simple: Straight Talk from a Master Sommelier* by Andrea Immer will help get you started.

Menu

Consider this "day trip through the wine country" menu.

- appetizers: summer salad with Gewurtztraminer wine dressing
- main course: risotto with oven-roasted tomatoes and basil served with Pinot Noir
- dessert: Zinfandel-poached pears with spiced zabaglione (creamy wine-flavored topping)
- specialty drinks: Wine — of course!

Entertainment

Give your guests a lesson in wine tasting. Show them how to recognize a good wine. Define what gives a wine balance, length, concentration, finish and aftertaste. See if your guests know which champagne to drink with seafood, or which wines should go with which course of the meal. Does red wine go better with chocolate or Asian food? Does white wine go better with pasta or beef? Many people are intimidated by choosing a wine for themselves or their guests at a good restaurant. A lesson in wine tasting will answer many of their questions.

Souvenirs/Party Favors

Send each guest home with a bottle of wine in a wine basket. Attach two glasses to the basket with a purple satin ribbon.

Fund Raisers

If you need to raise funds, sell weekend getaways to northern California along with tickets for a trip aboard the Napa Valley Wine Train. You can find information about the many different excursions of the Napa Valley Wine Train at www.winetrain.com.

Keywords

of aspirin, winery hopping, the state's hottest culinary destination, balloon rides, farmer's market, cooking school, cappuccino stops, grape-crushing, cheese, perfect picnic fare, gorgeous gardens, rustic, cooking classes, food festivals, concerts, art exhibits, French bistro fare, charming tables, cozy fireplaces, wild mustard, lupines, poppies, Chinese pistachio trees, barrel, tasting, grape growers, cask, fermentation, sediment, tannin, Beaujolais, Chablis, clinking glass, toast, Champagne, Claret, **www.celebration-solutions.com/wine.html**

Transportation Themes

Introduction

The first hot-air balloon flight took place in France in 1783, when the sons of a wealthy papermaker sent up a paper-lined linen balloon that rose 6,000 feet into the air. When the local peasants saw the balloon floating in the sky, they believed that the moon had fallen from the heavens as a sign of the Last Judgement. When it landed, they attacked and destroyed it. Ever at the mercy of the winds, hot air balloons enabled explorers to survey the countryside in a way they never had before — from above. Today, hot air ballooning is a popular recreation activity. Give your guests an evening of "up, up and away" fun.

Ambiance

Visit a balloon festival. It's hard to decide which is more spectacular, the sight of balloons filling a cloudless blue sky or the balloons all lit up at night. You choose which lighting scheme you prefer. In the background play the sounds you would hear around hot air balloons — the burner creating hot air, the nylon flapping as the balloon is inflated and the tug on the tether lines as the balloon lifts into the air.

Colors

Use "soaring to new heights" colors of blue, green, red and yellow.

Suggested Attire

The suggested attire is "wild, blue yonder" casual.

Invitations

"Up, up and away ..." Some of the most stunning pictures of hot air balloons are those taken at night. Use a nighttime photograph or pictures of a balloon festival for your invitation. Or, send your invitation in a balloon. Use clear balloons that you can slip your invitation details into before blowing the balloons up with helium.

Decorations

Set the tables with tablecloths of blue, green, red or yellow. Match the napkins and place settings to the tablecloths. Make cloth bags out of white muslin with a

Keywords

Born on the wings of the winds, airship, aeronauts, dirigibles, blimps, ballast, basket, helium, lighter-than-air, silk, rubber, pilot, rarified air, flying machine, gust of wind, sheroid of linen and calico, aeronauts, clouds, baskets made of willow, bamboo, rattan or reed, rope restraints, ballast, aviation, meteorology, ascent, descent, onlookers, wind speed and direction, windsock, light breeze, hydrogen, hot air, the four corners of the earth, rise majestically above the clouds, chase vehicle, fierce northly wind, a view of the countryside, flight, altimeter, Jules

Hot Air Balloons

drawstring at the top. Fill them with non-helium balloons and hang them from the edges of the tablecloths like ballast bags.

From the center of the tables, use piping filler cord to create tie lines. Bunch the tie lines together in the center of the table and attach the other ends to a ring suspended from the ceiling. In the center of the ring, use a photograph so that when guests look up from the table, it will seem like they're looking up into a hot air balloon.

Menu

Consider this "up, up and away" picnic fare.
- appetizers: roasted potatoes and tomatoes with garlic mayonnaise
- main course: sausage and pepper turnovers
- dessert: riesling-soaked, warm, roasted nectarines with cherries and almonds
- specialty drinks: Strawberry Sangria or Heavenly Days (hazelnut syrup, fresh lemon juice, grenadine, sparkling water, orange slice)

Entertainment

Put together a collection of songs about flying or balloons. "Up, up and away in my beautiful balloon …." "I can fly, I can fly, I can fly" — Peter Pan, *Flying High* or *Flying without Wings*. Arrange to show the film *Around the World in 80 Days* taken from the Jules Verne classic tale. Your guests no doubt will enjoy the exploits of Phileas Fogg and his lovable sidekick Passepartout.

Souvenirs/Party Favors

Give each guest a beautiful photograph of a balloon in flight. Use clear photo corners to attach the photograph to a colored matte on a stand-up backing.

Fund Raisers

If you need to raise funds, sell tickets for rides on a hot air balloon or tickets to a local balloon festival. You can find a lot of information about hot air balloon companies and festivals at Hot Air Ballooning's home on the web at www.launch.net.

Keywords

Verne, stratosphere, great heights, rip cord, stowaway, marvellous adventure, aerial map, picturesque villages below, inflated, storm clouds, balloon festival, departure, visibility, barometer, altitude, duration, distance, navigation, atmospheric conditions, sportsmen, air currents, resistance, lifting force, guide rope, adventure, patterns - chevron, sawtooth, vertical, gondola, burners, basket, envelope, skirt, balloonatics, enthusiasts, hobbyists, ballast, fly way up high in the sky, hydrogen, hot air, **www.celebration-solutions.com/balloons.html**

Transportation Themes

Introduction

Imagine back to a time when the first automobiles took to the dusty roads that would someday become our public highways. In those days, driving was sport. You had to teach yourself to drive because not many people knew how, and before you took to the road you had to charge the tanks with water and gasoline, and make sure that the crankcase was filled with lubricating oil. To start the car, you had to insert the plug that would start the ignition and vigorously turn the handle until the engine cranked. If all went well, you took off for parts unknown. If not, you might wish you hadn't turned the horse out to pasture. At his Michigan plant in 1908, Henry Ford made the first "Tin Lizzie" — the Model T — the car you could have in any color you wanted, as long as it was black. Take your guests for a nostalgic look at the beginning of the auto era.

Ambiance

Imagine a turn of the century auto race. Keep the lighting high like a perfect summer day. Play audio clips of cars backfiring, tires groaning, an old engine running, crowd noise, and, of course, the official calling, "Gentleman, start your engines." A real race would smell of dust and exhaust. Definitely steer clear of the exhaust, but there's nothing like that new car smell.

Colors

Use "Tin Lizzie" colors of black, chrome, brass and mahogany brown.

Suggested Attire

The suggested attire is "turn of the Century" cocktail.

Invitations

"Go for a joy ride." Use the Model T logo or a picture of a mint-condition vehicle. Or, send a DVD of the movie *The Great Race*. That ought to get your guests in the mood for an evening of Model Ts on the move.

Decorations

Set the tables with black tablecloths and napkins. Use wooden place settings and chrome utensils. The earliest cars used brass lanterns for headlights. Use

Keywords

Henry Ford, Tin Lizzie, antique automobile, assembly line method, fire chariots, self-propelled road vehicle, chassis, rubber tire, battery, liquid fuel, horseless carriage, combustion engine, closed coach, lantern lighting, tiller for steering, crankshaft, flywheel, steering stick, bone-shaking vibration, Daimler, Benz, Olds, Renault, transmission, hand-squeezed horn, carriage springs, tiller steering, at the edge of town the pavement disappears, buggy, patent leather dashboard, mudguards, nickel-plated wire wheels, straight-line body work, sau

Model T

replica lanterns for your centerpieces. Beside the lamps, place old-fashioned driving gloves and driving goggles.

For wall decorations, use historic pictures of people out for a drive in their new Model Ts. Go to a car museum and take pictures of the license plates used before 1920 to create a poster-sized collage.

Menu

Consider this menu of "motorway treats."
- appetizers: Chrysler Chowder — corn chowder with red pepper cream
- main course: Ford Fill Up — marinated chicken breast on toasted sourdough bread
- dessert: Dodge Dessert — nectarine blackberry cobbler
- specialty drinks: Chevrolet Champagne (champagne with crème de peche) or American Flyers (light rum, fresh lime juice, sugar and champagne)

Entertainment

If you didn't send the DVD as an invitation, arrange for a showing of clips from the *Great Race (1965)* starring Jack Lemmon, Tony Curtis and Natalie Wood.

Play *Mille Bornes* by Winning Moves. *Mille Bornes* is a card game for two to six players. Players are in a cross-country auto rally through France filled with real-life traffic hazards. If you run out of gas, you'll need a Gasoline card. If you get a flat tire, you'll need a spare. Keep moving by playing mileage cards, or place an obstacle in an opponent's path. It's a fast-paced, fun game. If your tables will hold more than six, use more than one deck per table.

Souvenirs/Party Favors

Send each guest home with a pair of driving gloves and a scarf.

Fund Raisers

If you need to raise funds, sell tickets for a country tour in a Model T complete with a gourmet picnic.

Keywords

sage-thin pneumatic tires, one cylinder engine, handles and knobs, wheel steering, convertible, buggy roof, heated from the muffler, white knuckles, goggles, scarf, cap, leather gloves, great clouds of dust, running boards, cylinders, start button, brass speedometer, mahogany dashboard, hand and foot brakes, sleek, sporty, Rolls Royce Silver Ghost, "they can have any color they want, as long as it's black," rumble seats, fenders, aprons, frame, mirror, honk of the horn, speed, running boards, **www.celebration-solutions.com/modelt.html**

Transportation Themes

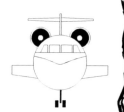

Introduction

The passport is a document issued by a country permitting its citizens to leave and reenter the state, and requesting protection for him or her abroad. Passports have been used for centuries as a means of identification. Today, the passport represents the ability to travel the wide world, to reach the edges of civilization … and beyond … far beyond. Give your guests first class service and a "passport" to the world.

Ambiance

Picture an imaginary journey around the world. Keep the lighting high to show off the decorations and think about the sounds you would hear if you were traveling — train whistles, a ship's captain calling, "All aboard," the sound of a paddlewheel engine ferrying you across a wide river, or the sound of an old diesel truck engine running. Exotic incense will help make guests believe that they're in a far away place.

Colors

Use "show the blue and go right through" colors of blue and white.

Suggested Attire

The suggested attire is "whirlwind tour" casual.

Invitations

"A journey of a thousand miles … begins with a good send-off!" Create a souvenir passport or cover your invitation with stickers or stamps from one region, or all around the world.

Decorations

Set the tables with blue tablecloths and napkins, and white china. For centerpieces, choose hand-crafted items from all over the world. Make each centerpiece different.

Hang giant passports on the walls. Give them a hinge or binding so that they can be opened. In the interior of the passports, use photographs and "passport

Keywords

Travel documents, visa, permit, stamp, customs, immigration, passport-size (2"x2") photographs, consular officials, citizenship, apply for a visa, embassy, consulate, departure fees, issued on arrival, currency exchange, tickets, travel itinerary, application forms, entry-tickets, transit visa, residence permit, tourist cards, immunizations, traders, markets, vibrant, colorful, fascinating, crafts, bargaining, local music, mystique, adventure, rugged conditions, sights, trekking, meandering along, humble villages, spectacular cities, tranquil lagoons,

Passport

stamps" of exotic locations. Create a couple of these giant passports big enough to stand alone in bare spots in the room.

Throughout the room, place sign posts that shows names of famous or exotic cities and the distance from where you are to that location.

Menu

Consider these "taste treats" from around the planet.

- appetizers: gazpacho from Spain
- main course: beef bourguignonne from France with Portuguese bread rounds
- dessert: trifle (wine soaked sponge cake with layers of custard crème) from England
- specialty drinks: Shanghai Cocktails (dark rum, Pernod, lemon juice, grenadine) or Savoy Hotels (dark crème de cacao, Benedictine, cognac)

Entertainment

Play traditional music from all around the globe. Give your guests a chance to play the legendary board game *Diplomacy* by Avalon Hill. Wits must be as sharp as swords, as each of the seven pre-WWI superpowers, England, France, Germany, Italy, Russia, Turkey, and Austria-Hungary negotiate their way to the top. To win, players must beg, threaten, plead and argue their way past nations where friends become pawns and enemies become allies. You can find *Diplomacy* online or at stores where games are sold.

Souvenirs/Party Favors

Arrange for a photographer to take passport photographs of your guests. Give them their pictures, a passport application and leather luggage tags as a souvenir of the event.

Fund Raisers

If you need to raise funds, auction a trip around the world, sell travel guides or pictures from exotic locales.

Keywords

great rivers, dense rainforests, snow-crowned mountains, windswept dines, savannah plains, lush vegetation, mosquito net, luggage, maps, festivals, bush taxi, travel light, travellers checks, black market, pickpockets, hiring a car, translator, tour guide, locals, foreigners, curio stalls, souvenirs, telegram, field guide, jet lag, travel book, culture, art, museums, hotels, inns, food stalls, restaurants, festivals, local color, fares, accommodations, hostels, reservations, travel guide, hiking, hitch, touring, trekking, **www.celebration-solutions.com/passport.html**

Transportation Themes

Introduction

Although people have been skiing for about 5,000 years, the sport didn't become a popular form of recreation until the 20th Century. Today, millions of people worldwide enjoy skiing for its exhilaration, sense of freedom and physical challenge. People ski Alpine-style (downhill), Nordic-style (cross-country) and for those skiers who are not gravitationally challenged, there is extreme skiing (flying down difficult slopes under extremely dangerous conditions). Once the skiing is done, the apres-ski partying begins.

Ambiance

Picture the club car of a ski train in the 1950s. Play sounds of trains moving along the tracks, the train's whistle blowing and the snow coming down the mountain in the background. Use tabletop lamps for the ambient lighting. Use pine scent to make the room smell like the mountains.

Colors

Use "winter wonderland" colors of white, white and more white.

Suggested Attire

The suggested attire is "relaxing in front of an fire" casual.

Invitations

"Après Ski …" Use pictures of people in '50s-era ski wear like stretch pants, fur-lined hoods, or wooden skis. Or, send ski area pins attached to your invitation.

Decorations

Set the tables with white tablecloths, napkins and china. If possible, use square tables for four people, like you might find on a dining car in a real train. Use crystal candle lamps with white candles for the centerpieces. Ask the wait staff to wear "dress whites" as well — white short coats, white shirts and ties, and white pants. If you want to add a little color, give the waitstaff blue cumberbunds with white snowflakes on them.

Keywords

like a Swiss chalet on a train, chrome-frame windows, '50s skiwear, wooden skis, fur hats, big sunglasses, winter scenes, poles with rings held by webbing, leather boots, strap bindings, fur-lined hoods, lift tickets, waxed boards, schussing, telemark, snowplow, stem turns, slalom, ski jumping, moguls, ski jumps, snow tunnel, knee-deep in snow, downhill, herringbone climbing, apres-ski, snowshoes, tough trails, groomed slopes, challenging winters, snow depth, avalanches, blizzards, skis made from barrel staves, daring feats, ski racing, starting

Ski Train

The train will need windows with snowy, mountain, winter scenes. Frame the windows in chrome like you would have found in a '50s-era ski train. Check out the photography section of the website www.mountainzone.com for ideas.

Use a projector on a screen at the front of the room to show scenes of a train moving slowly through the snowy mountains.

Menu

This menu is designed to warm the heart (or the hands!).

- appetizers: tortilla corn soup
- main course: warm roast beef sandwich with red onion, red pepper and basil mayonnaise, potato salad
- dessert: warm ginger cake with peaches and cream
- specialty drinks: Hot Spiked Chocolate (hot chocolate, brandy, dark crème de cacao, nutmeg) or Hot Mulled Wine (cloves, nutmeg, allspice, cinnamon stick, sugar syrup, dry red wine, lemon twists)

Entertainment

Show clips from ski races, past Winter Olympics or extreme skiing. Warren Miller, one of the most prolific ski-genre filmmakers, has been filming for more than 50 years. Many of his ski titles are available on DVD.

Let your guests try their hand at *Lifts and Avalanches*. If you're familiar with the game *Chutes and Ladders*™, you'll understand how challenging it can be to make it past the avalanches and up the lifts to get to the top of the mountain. You'll find a game board and instructions on the web page for this theme.

Souvenirs/Party Favors

Send your guests home with a ski hat with a ski area pin attached to it.

Fund Raisers

If you need to raise funds, sell tickets for a ski weekend including tickets for the Ski Train from Denver, Colorado to Winter Park.

Keywords

gates, finish line, spectacular peaks, winter carnival, lodge, fireplace, hot toddies, sweaters, mittens, gloves, warm socks, hats with pompons, winter sport center, tramway car, gondola, T-bar, pomma lift, chair lift, rope tow, mountains, snow fields, hot mulled wine, slopes, Giant Slalom, snow cat, sitzmark, winter's isolation, summit, bowls, making a run, condominiums, glacier, backcountry, bunny slopes, moguls, double diamond, freestyle, slalom, schussing down the slopes, lift, freestyle, jump, sitzmark, **www.celebration-solutions.com/skitrain.html**

Transportation Themes

Introduction

Romanticized in the works of American writer author Mark Twain and others, early steamboats were rough and uncomfortable. Later steamships were luxurious with elaborate woodwork and decorations. As the transcontinental railroads pushed west across America, seagoing ships pushed east across the Atlantic to Europe. Within a decade of the Civil War, ships created a system of transatlantic trade, immigration and luxury travel. Take your guests aboard a "Titanic-class" luxury liner for an evening of elegance.

Ambiance

Imagine the dining room of an early 20th Century luxury liner. Use oil lamps to light the room and play audio clips of a ship's horn and waves crashing in the background. The scent of the salt-sea air will make your guests feel like they're making a transatlantic crossing.

Colors

Use luxury "White Line" colors of white, grey and red.

Suggested Attire

The suggested attire is "Titanic-legend" formal.

Invitations

"We will commence sailing on … " Use pictures of the golden era of luxury liner travel — pictures of passengers on deck or postcards showing the great ships. Or, send white cotton gloves holding a formal invitation.

Decorations

Set the tables with white tablecloths, napkins and china. Use a red napkin ring or a fancy napkinfold. Use oil lamps with fancy globes for your centerpieces. Ring the bottom of the lamps with miniature red rose buds. Ask the waitstaff to dress in formal attire, like that the staff would have worn on a luxury liner early in the 20th Century — black pants, white shirts, white ties, white waistcoats and white gloves. Create beaded chandeliers, the fancier the better. Use a wire frame

Keywords

ocean-going steamships, river boats, water wheels, steam whistles, paddle-wheels, iron-hulled, passengers, freight, trunks, flag-ships, transportation magnates, trans-Atlantic, Anchor Line, cargo, terminus, dock, landing, steamers, port, port of call, ship yards, propeller, first-class, steerage-class, keel, coal-fired, danger of icebergs, launch, ocean mail service, maiden voyage, the Bridge, Ladies' Saloon, Smoking Room, Dining Saloon, in the hold, captain, quartermaster, seamen, stewards, pursers, pantrymen, barbers, porters, waiters, musicians,

Steamships

to hang strings of crystal beads that will reflect the light. You'll need portholes for the walls. Place pictures of the open sea or other grand sailing ships in round, brass frames.

Menu

This menu comes right off the dining cards of the glamorous, transatlantic steamers.

- appetizers: crostini with salmon and lemon zest and tomato bisque
- main course: braised leg of lamb with garlic roasted potatoes, asparagus, snap peas
- dessert: chocolate macadamia souffle cake with whipped cream
- specialty drinks: Sink or Swim (brandy, sweet vermouth, bitters) or Ruby Fizz (sloe gin, lemon juice, grenadine, sugar syrup, egg white, and sparkling water)

Entertainment

Hire a live orchestra to play music for ballroom dancing. Ask a dance troupe to come and perform some of the less well known ballroom dances that would have been popular at the turn of the century such as the Landler (the dance seen in the *Sound of Music*), the Volta (similar to the Waltz but in 5/4 time) and the Tango (based on the Flamenco dancing of Spain). Then give your guests a chance to learn the steps from the pros.

Souvenirs/Party Favors

Give each guest a copy of a hardback copy of the book *Ghosts of the Abyss*, a DVD of the movie *Titanic* and a paperback copy of the book *A Night to Remember*. Wrap them together with an elegant combination of white, grey and red ribbons and a White Line sticker.

Fund Raisers

If you need to raise funds, sell tickets for a transatlantic crossing on the Queen Mary2 or sell tickets to a showing of the IMAX movie *Ghosts of the Abyss*.

Keywords

cooks, engineers, firemen, coal passers, steamer (deck) chairs, lifeboats, White Star Line, ballast, dressed out with flags, sailing schedule, summer holiday abroad, fine china, grand staircase, ballroom, musicians, gangplank, bells clanging, whistles booming, cabin, berth, gray-green waves, steaming full speed forward, floating palaces, polished mahogany woodwork, silk brocade upholstery, leather library chairs, crisp-white uniforms, Titanic, Noordland, Anchoria, Furnessia, Oceana, wine-dark sea, **www.celebration-solutions.com/steamsh.html**

Transportation Themes

Introduction

Submarines were objects of fantastic fiction in the 1570s, although a number of scientists at the time thought they were feasible. By 1620, a Dutch inventor created a submersible of watertight leather. An American submarine attempted to sink a British vessel during the Revolution and subs were used more extensively during the Civil War. During WWII, submarines were crowded, uncomfortable vessels, but today the modern nuclear subs have pools, running tracks and movie theaters. Submarines have also been the subject of fiction like the much-loved adventure tale of Captain Nemo and his submarine, the Nautilus. Give your guests a trip down to the "depths" of your imagination.

Ambiance

Visit the command center of a fictional submarine. Use twinkle lights and strip lighting to set the scene and play audio files of underwater sounds, sonar pinging and propellers turning in the background.

Colors

Use "in-the-drink" colors of black, grey and deep green.

Suggested Attire

The suggested attire "fantastic voyage" casual.

Invitations

"Run silent, run deep … and join us on …" Send the invitation in clear, blue plastic balls that look like bubbles or use a picture that looks like what you would see through the eyepiece of a periscope.

Decorations

Set the tables with grey tablecloths, black china and deep green napkins. For centerpieces, ask a baker to make cakes covered with dark chocolate frosting that look like the top of a submarine sticking out of the water.

From the ceiling, hang periscopes. Hang them on a loose spring so that they can be pulled down to eye level. Put a different picture in each periscope — ships in the distance, girls on the deck … whatever will give your guests a giggle.

Keywords

periscope, underwater, radar, propeller, Navy, running silent, submerge, dive, surface, torpedoes, mines, crew, captain, depth charge, U-boat, snorkel, rudder, stern, ballast, sonar, dead reckoning, gyroscope, global positioning, cramped spaces, whale-shaped warship, raised dorsal structure, antennas, snorkel tubes, effective deterrent to general war, mine laying, reconnaissance, rescue of downed aircraft crews, supply of isolated garrisons, landing and debarking agents on enemy territory, warship, oceanography, operations well below 400

Västergötland
Sweden

Submarine

To make the room look like a submarine, use grey butcher paper tacked to the carpet and then run the paper up the wall in a gentle curve. Do the same for the walls to the ceiling. Use this technique on the longest length of the room to emphasize how long and round a sub is.

Around the room, create a few panels of blinking lights. Place small tables near the walls and let your "command" panels cover the tables and extend up the walls.

Menu

This menu is "from the deep," not from a sub's mess hall.

- appetizers: honeydew and shrimp salad, mussels on the half shell with avocado salsa
- main course: trout with tomato-yogurt-curry sauce on a bed of pilaf
- dessert: white chocolate mousse in white chocolate sea shells
- specialty drinks: Salty Dogs (vodka, grapefruit juice, sugar, lime wedge) or Quarter Deck cocktails (dark rum, cream sherry, lime juice)

Entertainment

Show scenes from movies about submarines such as *U-571* or *Operation Petticoat* or a submersible visiting ancient shipwrecks. The classic naval warfare game *Battleship* can be easily adapted for the underwater world. You'll find game boards and instructions on the web page for this theme.

Souvenirs/Party Favors

Send guests home with a hat from one of the U.S. Navy's subs. You will find the Submarine Warfare Division online at the U.S. Navy's website, www.navy.mil.

Fund Raisers

If you need to raise funds, sell tickets for trips to the Submarine Force Museum in Groton, CT and a tour of the USS Nautilus (SSN 571), or to areas like Hawaii or Aruba where guests could take a submarine tour.

S.O.
Submarine Flotilla

Keywords

feet (120 meters), speeds of well over 20 knots, nuclear, attack, armament, missiles, torpedoes, hull, ballast, buoyancy, seawater, conning tower, power plant, watertight, below the surface, propellers, batteries, reactor, rudder, dive, climb, berth, warheads, depth charge, mines, run silent, run deep, fore, aft, pressure, silent hunter, ship's log, U-boat, "Dive! Dive! Dive!" radar, depth charge, gyro, surface, buoyancy, bridge, brig, commander, control room, deckhouse, U-boat, USS Nautilus, nuclear, enigma, **www.celebration-solutions.com/sub.html**

Yesteryear Themes

Introduction

WWI was over … and along came a prosperous, free-wheeling time known as the Roaring Twenties, the Jazz Age, or the Age of Wonderful Nonsense. It was a time of assembly-line production, mass consumption, easy credit, and mass advertising. Millions of people read *The Saturday Evening Post* and listened to the same music, comedy shows, and commercials on the radio. Young and uninhibited, the flapper represented much of what typified the age — youthful rebellion, female independence, bobbed hairdos, short skirts, makeup, and cigarettes. Dance clubs of the '20s were an explosion of color, the wailing sounds and fast rhythms of jazz and energetic dancing. Take your guests back to the free-wheeling days of "wonderful nonsense."

Ambiance

Picture a Prohibition-era honkey tonk at the height of the flapper craze. Keep the lighting low so the room feels close and intimate and let the energetic music of the time fill the air. The clubs of that era were smoke-filled. We don't suggest that you ask your guests to light up just for the effect, but you could recreate that kind of atmosphere with a fog machine that sprays up high.

Colors

Use "Gatsby sophisticated" colors of teal, peach and yellow.

Suggested Attire

The suggested attire is "flapper" formal. If you want your guests to come in '20s attire, send along a picture so they will have something after which to model their attire.

Invitations

"Belly up to the bar for some giggle water." Use a picture of people doing the Charleston — a popular dance in the '20s or send a small flask with "bathtub" gin along with your invitation details.

Decorations

Set the tables with teal tablecloths, peach napkins and yellow place settings.

Keywords

F. Scott Fitzgerald, flappers, Great Gatsby, Zelda, devil-may-care pursuit of pleasure, carefree attitudes, female independence, Charleston dance, bobbed hair, heavy makeup, drop-waisted very short dresses, elegant, silhouette, gangster, gentlemen's bar, grand piano, speakeasy, paper moon, bathtub still, vintage Rolls Royce, Cole Porter, Gershwin, Rodgers and Hurt, swing band, crisp white linen, silver beaded candle lamps, white china, prohibition, beaded tops for women, Paul Whiteman, Guy Lombardo, Al Jolson, Sophie Tucker, Eddie

1920s

Use artsy and decorative glassware at each place for cocktails and wine. For centerpieces, use small Art Deco-style, standing stained glass pieces.

From the ceiling, hang oversized lampshades with beaded fringe. The artwork of the 1920s had a very distinctive style. On the walls, hang old (or replica) posters of shows that were popular in the '20s, such as Zigfield follies or photographs of the stars who were popular back then.

Menu

Consider this "Great Gatsby" menu.
- appetizers: vidalia onions stuffed with corn bread and parmesan cheese and lobster bisque
- main course: peppered beef fillet with stilton cheese and red onion salad
- dessert: rhubarb and apple Charlotte (stuffed cake)
- specialty drinks: Raquet Club Cocktails (gin, dry vermouth, orange bitters), Polo Club Dreams (bourbon, orange juice and almond syrup) or Rolls Royce (gin, dry vermouth, sweet vermouth, Benedictine)

Entertainment

Ask a dance troupe to come and give a demonstration of the Charleston — one of the most popular dances in the 1920s. Give your guests a lesson and then let the dancing begin!

In the '20s, before the age of the boombox, dance clubs always featured live bands. If you can find a band to play music the era, hire them. If not, ask a DJ to put together a collection of era-appropriate music.

Souvenirs/Party Favors

As guests enter, give male guests a pocket flask and female guests a garter flask. Flasks were very popular during Prohibition days.

Fund Raisers

If you need to raise funds, sell replica Tiffany lamps, Art Deco stained glass or rides in a '20s roadster.

Keywords

Cantor, Rudy Vallee, Maurice Chevalier, bobbed hair, short mini skirts, makeup, long cigarette holders, fringe, Saturday Evening Post, Reader's Digest, Ladies' Home Journal, radio shows, Jazz Age, youthful rebellion, movie stars, Scopes Trial, Prohibition, "a chicken for every pot and a car in every garage," Black Monday, stock market crash, women's suffrage, art, music, literature, Art Deco, first transatlantic flight, dough boys, the lost generation, slicked back hair, wingtips, white gloves, top hats, tycoons, **www.celebration-solutions.com/1920s.html**

Yesteryear Themes

Introduction

A 1970s theme is a nostalgic and funny way to flash back to the past. Even though you've got to be over 30 to really appreciate the '70s, the retro phenomenon has caught on and hip huggers, wild colors and long, straight hair are back. Mood rings were all the rage and the 8-Track tape player was supposed to revolutionize the music industry. *M*A*S*H*, *The Godfather* and *Star Wars* were playing in the movie theaters. The Vietnam War ended, Nixon resigned, OPEC held oil hostage and there was a near nuclear disaster at Three Mile Island. On the TV we were watching *Charlie's Angels*, *Mary Tyler Moore*, and *The Waltons*. The '70s began with the Beetles and ended with Disco — a decade that was just plain "far out."

Ambiance

Imagine a hippie hangout. Use blacklights to show off the '70s-era artwork and keep the rest of the lighting low. Let the music of the time fill the air. We don't suggest you recreate the actual smell of a hippie "joint," but a touch of incense might help.

Colors

Use "psychedelic" colors of orange, pink and yellow.

Suggested Attire

The suggested attire is "hippie" casual — love beads, peace signs, bell bottom jeans and tie dye shirts.

Invitations

"Turn on, Tune in, Drop Out — Timothy Leary … or drop in on our celebration." Use psychedelic artwork, yellow smiley faces or album cover art for your invitations.

Decorations

Set the tables with psychedelic paisley tablecloths. The wilder the better. Tear fabric remnants into ragged-edged napkins. Use plastic place settings of whatever bright, day-glo colors you can find. Tie dye shirts were mandatory hippy wear during the era, so place a tie-die shirt at each place setting. For centerpieces, use lava lamps. Believe it or not, they're making a come back! Mirror balls hanging from the ceiling are a must, especially if you'll be playing disco music. Cover the walls with posters — black light, Saturday

Keywords

retro, hip huggers, wild colors, long straight hair, hippie, tie dye, bell bottom jeans, peace sign necklaces, round, yellow smiley faces, lava lamps, macrame decorations, mood rings, 8 Track tape player, Rowan & Martin's Laugh In, pet rocks, Jonathan Livingston Seagul, Love Story, M*A*S*H, The Godfather, The Poseidon Adventure, The Sting, Jaws, One Flew Over the Cuckoo's Nest, Grease, Rocky, Star Wars, the Vietnam War ended, Nixon resigned, OPEC held its oil hostage, hostage crisis, near nuclear disaster at Three Mile Island, Marcus Welby,

1970s

Night Fever, Farrah Fawcett, yellow smiley faces, psychedelic — there's no limit. Find or create at least one macrame wall hanging.

Build a shrine to '70s fashion. Pile on jazzed up jeans (i.e. jeans with studs, emblems, patches, smiley faces or paint), short shorts, bell bottom jeans, hip huggers, platform shoes, angel flight suits, mood rings, platform shoes, toe socks. If you can find them (try eBay), put out a pair of egg chairs. If you lived during the '70s, you'll know what these are.

Menu

Consider this "picnic in the back of a VW bus" menu.

- appetizers: black-walnut bisque
- main course: tomato, sweet onion and cheese quiche with snap beans
- dessert: gooseberry tarts
- specialty drinks: Strawberry or Melon margueritas and Purple People Eaters (vodka, purple grape juice, lime juice, sparkling water)

Entertainment

Hire a DJ to put together Top 40 hits from the '70s. Play a game of *What Year was That?* Make a list of well-known events, songs or movies and give the guests a choice of three different consecutive years. Create a slide show where you can show the headlines, play the songs or show the movie clips. Play the slide show on a large screen. Have the audience vote, then reveal the correct answer.

Souvenirs/Party Favors

Give each guest their own Pet Rock. Wrap the pets in a box with smiley faces on them. Pet rocks in the '70s came with a Training Manual that instructed new owners on the care and maintenance of their pets.

Fund Raisers

If you need to raise funds, hire artists for face painting or temporary tattoos and someone for hair braiding. Or, hold a disco dance off. Ask each couple to pay an entrance fee and award a prize to the winner.

Keywords

MD, Charlie's Angels, Mary Tyler Moore, All in the Family, Sonny and Cher, Barnaby Jones, Hawaii 5-0, The Waltons, The Six Million Dollar Man, the Bionic Woman, Kojak, Mork and Mindy, Happy Days, Beetles, disco, the Partridge Family, Three Dog Night, Carole King, Chicago, Stevie Wonder, the Jacksons, Donnie Osmond, Simon & Garfunkel, The Carpenters, The Bee Gees, Elton John, Paul McCartney and Wings, short shorts, bell bottom jeans, angel flight suits, ankle boots, go go boots, big hair, wide belt, **www.celebration-solutions.com/1970s.html**

Yesteryear Themes

Introduction

For centuries, the Barbary Coast was a haven for pirates. The most renowned of the Barbary corsairs were the Barbarossa brothers. Fierce fighters and adroit sailors, the Barbary Coast pirates extorted payment from many governments, including England, France and the United States. In July 1785, the pirates captured two American vessels and held their crews for ransom. Negotiations were finally concluded 10 years later after most of the prisoners had died. The pasha of Tripoli decided that the treaty of 1796 was not paying well enough, and when the U.S. refused to pay more, he declared war. The U.S. dispatched a fleet to the Mediterranean to settle the "treaty" question once and for all. The age of the Barbary Coast pirates was over. Give your guests a chance to indulge themselves in the romantic era of "masked devils and sea dogs."

Ambiance

Visit the rolling deck of a Barbary Coast pirate ship. Keep the lighting high like a cloudless summer day and play seafaring background sounds such as crashing waves, drunken pirates and sword fighting. We don't imagine that pirates smelled very good, so give the room the scent of the open ocean.

Colors

Use "shiver-me-timbers" colors of black, red, blue and white.

Suggested Attire

The suggested attire is "yo-ho and a bottle of rum" pirate wear.

Invitations

"Ahoy maties!" Send your invitation as treasure map leading to the location of the party or send it as a note in a bottle.

Decorations

Set the tables with black tablecloths, napkins and place settings. Use gold utensils and gold-stemmed glassware. For centerpieces, fill a treasure chest to overflowing with bright, shiny baubles and pieces of eight (coins).

Keywords

Barbary Coast (North Africa), note in old bottle, nautical flags, treasure chest, gold doubloons, beads, gems, ship's rigging, ship's wheel, plank, pirate flags, ragged clothes, stripped shirts, black patch over one eye, wooden leg, hook arm, Buccaneer, Corsair, Privateer, Sea Dogs, plunder, riches, capture, Tunis, Tripoli, Barbarossa (red beard), skull and crossbones, cove, harbor, inlet, capture, Sultan Selim of the Ottoman Empire, gold, silver, jewels, pearls, Pasha, ravage the coasts, galley ship, galley slaves, four men to an oar, cannons, guns, spears,

Barbary Coast

Hang pirate flags and treasure maps on the walls. Use brown ink on parchment paper and burn the edges, so they look old.

Against one wall, secure a giant ship's wheel. Use large diameter piping filler cord to create a ship's rigging. String the rigging from the ceiling a few feet away from the walls to the floor against the walls.

Menu

Consider this feast fit for a "party of pirates."
- appetizers: molohia (a thick green pea soup)
- main course: tangine of chicken with onions, ginger, prunes on saffron rice
- dessert: sweet couscous (like rice pudding)
- specialty drinks: Pirate's Julep (gold rum, white curacao, almond syrup, mint sprigs) or Barbary Coast (light rum, gin, scotch, white crème de cacao, half and half)

Entertainment

Introduce your guests to the game of *Mutiny* by Fantasy Flight. It's a high-stakes game of rum and riches on the high seas. You will try to become captain by an act of mutiny and must win the trust of the five most senior members of the crew in the only way you can — bribery! You'll need plenty of doubloons and rum to gain the loyalty of this treacherous crew, and a pirate's word is only good until the money is spent. You can find *Mutiny* at stores where games are sold.

Souvenirs/Party Favors

Give each guest a copy of the popular movie *Pirates of the Caribbean* and a paperback copy of *Treasure Island* by Robert Louis Stevenson. Tie the book and the movie together using black fishnet material and a black ribbon.

Fund Raisers

If you need to raise funds, auction a cruise in the waters of the Mediterranean. Or sell tickets to a pirate tour. Cities like Charleston, South Carolina have a history of pirates and buccaneers and host their own pirate tours.

Keywords

enemy ships, boarding the ship, fleet of pirate ships, turbans, Pasha, tribute, menace to shipping, marauders, privateers, plundering and slave raiding, Barbarossa brothers, fierce fighters, adroit naval strategists, sea rovers, outlaws, easy profits, shanghaiing, smuggling, duels, swords, pistols, walk the plank, boarding ships, give no quarter, buried treasure, booty, profit, pickings, boodle, goods, swag, sea rover, sea dog, corsair, freebooter, rustler, highwayman, robbery, looting, to the victor go the spoils, **www.celebration-solutions.com/pirates.html**

Yesteryear Themes

Introduction

The legend of King Arthur represents chivalry and ideal manhood embodied in romantic knights, ladies, giants, and dragons. Camelot was the place where King Arthur held his court and where the Round Table was located. It was where Arthur drew the sword from the stone, where Perceval left to search for the Holy Grail, where Galahad and Gawain fought legendary dragons, and where Lancelot loved the beautiful Gwenevere. Camelot holds a place in the hearts of everyone who believes in legend and fantasy.

Ambiance

Imagine the grand hall of the castle of Camelot. Use an abundance of candles and keep the lighting low. The burning candles will also fill the room with a scent. Play audio files of clinking armor, horses, hoof beats, hammers hitting iron anvils, footsteps on stone, and sword fighting in the background.

Colors

Use "King Arthur" colors of metallic gold, sage green and purple.

Suggested Attire

The suggested attire is "fair damsel and brave knight" medieval.

Invitations

"A proclamation from the King." Use Old English script for the lettering on a sheet that looks like an illuminated manuscript, or stick toy daggers through an invitation on parchment paper.

Decorations

Set the tables with sage green tablecloths, purple napkins and gold place settings. For centerpieces, ask a baker to create cakes that look like the "round table" of legend and lore. The table is sometimes pictured with alternating stripes and other times with swords inlaid into the table with points at the center.

On the walls, create a mural that looks like stone blocks with castle battlements. Hang tapestries or brass rubbings over the stonework. Real tapestries

Keywords

swords, chain mail, armor, weapons, castle, knights, King Arthur, Gwenevere, Lancelot, Holy Grail, Uther Pendragon, Merlin, sword in the stone, Excalibur, Lady of the Lake, Mordred, Avalon, Charlemagne, Morgan LaFey, lords, ladies, coronation, banners, coat of arms, herald trumpets, horse-drawn carriage, cone hats with veils, shield, sword, colors: red, purple, royal blue, gold, candelabra, sconces, chandelier, throne, metal goblets, plates, banquet table, chivalry, parchment scroll, calligraphy, wax seal, jousting, heraldry, banner, flags, throne,

Camelot

may be too heavy to hang, but a good mural-sized print will work. If it's truly Camelot, you'll need a sword in the stone. Buy a few "movie" rocks and sink a plastic sword into one of them. Place the "Excalibur" somewhere prominent in the room.

Menu

Consider this feast fit for King Arthur's table … or King Henry VIII's for that matter.

- appetizers: Cullen Skink (Gaelic for soup) — haddock, onion, potato and leak soup
- main course: turkey legs, roast beef, roasted corn, baked potatoes
- dessert: fresh fruit tarts, warm gingerbread muffins with sweet butter
- specialty drinks: King's Peg (cognac and champagne), Prince of Wales (brandy, Madeira, white curacao, bitters and champagne), or ale in tankards

Entertainment

Entertain your guests the way they would have been at King Arthur's court. Have heralds trumpet the arrival of your guests. Hire musicians to sing madrigal music and play mandolin, dulcimer or harp music or ask a DJ to put together music from the Dark Ages or Renaissance. Hire street performers such as jugglers and fortune tellers to entertain the crowd.

Souvenirs/Party Favors

Give each guest a copy of the Mark Twain classic, *A Connecticut Yankee in King Arthur's Court* and a copy of *A Knight's Tale* on DVD.

Fund Raisers

If you need to raise funds, set up stations where guests can create brass rubbings or illuminated manuscripts. Work with local artists that sell products at Renaissance festivals to set up booths to sell Camelot-era replica products to your guests. You'll find a directory of Renaissance Faires with links to product vendors online at www.faires.com.

Keywords

stoneware, crockery, earthenware goblet, beer tankard, whole chicken roasted on pit, turkey leg, wooden serving platters, monks, cathedrals, Bishops, Romanesque, Gothic, bans, proclamations, illuminated books, bubonic plague, kings, queens, coronation, abbey, crusades, craftsmen, trade guilds, cosmology, devil, empires, estates, fealty, peasants, fiefdoms, alchemy, hermits, homage, liege, lords, ladies, icons, insignia, chain mail, minstrels, masons, prince, princess, page, stone carvers, **www.celebration-solutions.com/camelot.html**

Yesteryear Themes

Introduction

The Civil War began on April 12, 1861 when soldiers of the Confederate States of America fired on Fort Sumter in Charleston Harbor, South Carolina. Known as the War Between the States, the War of the Rebellion, the War of Northern Aggression and the War for Southern Independence, it lasted until 1865. It was the most destructive war in American history pitting brother against brother, neighbor against neighbor, citizen against citizen. In the end, the Union was preserved, slavery was abolished and America emerged from the valley of the shadow of war. Bring your guests to a brush with the battlefield.

Ambiance

Visit a Civil War battle camp. Keep the lighting high like a midsummer day and play the sounds of far off cannons, gunfire, horses and the clash of battle in the background. Use potting soil to give the room an earthy scent and use glove oil on pieces of leather to create the scent of saddles.

Colors

Use "Yank and Johnny Reb" colors of blue and grey.

Suggested Attire

The suggested attire is Union blue or Confederate grey.

Invitations

"Four score and seven years ago …" Use a picture of Abraham Lincoln or create a composite, grey on one side, blue on the other using military insignia from the Union and Confederacy for you invitation graphics.

Decorations

Set one side of the room in Union blue and the other side in Confederate grey. Set all tables with white china. For centerpieces use old-fashioned oil lamps with plain, non-decorative globes.

Hang tin-type photographs from the Civil-War era and battle maps on the walls. Use canvas material to create open tent flap(s) on one or more walls. Use

Keywords

Abraham Lincoln, Jefferson Davis, confederate, union, abolitionist, slavery, seceded, Confederate States of America, Fort Sumter, Bull Run, Gettysburg, Robert E Lee, blue and grey, Ulysses S Grant, Sherman's March to the Sea, Army of the Potomac, Johnny Reb, Yankee, War between the States, War of the Northern Aggression, War of the Rebellion, Emancipation Proclamation, reconstruction, blue and grey, Johnny Reb, Antietam, Vicksburg, Gettysburg, infantry, casement, Grant, Lee, caissons, Bull Run, cotton, "a house divided cannot stand," rebellion,

Civil War

a poster-sized photograph in the opening of the tent flap that looks out onto a Civil War battlefield.

Menu

This menu is what might have been fixed for the troops on the battlefield.

- appetizers: Dutch potato pancakes with apple-cranberry chutney
- main course: Hopping John (black-eyed peas with sausage and rice) and New York-style baked beans
- dessert: Artillery pie (bread, shortening, apples and sugar and baked)
- specialty drinks: Applejack (applejack, grapefruit juice, grenadine) or Navy Grog (dark rum, light rum, Demerara rum, guava juice, lime juice, pineapple juice, almond syrup, tamarind syrup and lime slice)

Entertainment

Entertain your guests with Appalachian folk music. Ask a dance troupe to demonstrate Appalachian clog dancing. The music for this style of dancing features the fiddle, banjo, and guitar and is somewhat of a misnomer because it isn't performed in clogs. It's distantly related to the step dancing of the Scottish Highlands. Cloggers dance in teams and wear elaborate costumes similar to those of western square dancers and shoes with jingle taps. All dancers "clog" the same step at the same time.

Souvenirs/Party Favors

Send guests home with crafts that were popular during the Civil War. Fill a woven vine basket with notecards of old-fashioned quilt patterns, handmade soap, cornbread muffin mix, and recipes for country favorites — potato biscuits, red eye gravy, southern fried chicken and fried green tomatoes. You'll find these recipes on the web page for this theme.

Fund Raisers

If you need to raise funds, auction trips to some of the more famous Civil War battlefields, like Gettysburg or Vicksburg.

Keywords

slaves, plantations, abolitionists, cannons, secession, Confederate States, CSA, USA, Fort Sumpter, volunteers, fire a volley, Stonewall Jackson, marching, battle formation, blockade, camp, Matthew Brady, cavalry, iron-clad vessels, ordinance, guns, cartridge boxes, hard tack, muskets, artillery shells, reinforcements, hero's welcome, tents, drummer boys, Emancipation Proclamation, charge, rebels, yanks, cemetery hill, sniper's nest, Camp Misery, prisoners of war, carpet baggers, powder magazine, **www.celebration-solutions.com/civilwar.html**

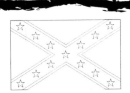

Yesteryear Themes

Introduction

Virginia was founded in 1607 as a trading outpost and became the first permanent English colony in the western hemisphere. In 1620, a group of Puritans arriving on the *Mayflower* established Plymouth colony in present-day Massachusetts and set up a system of political and religious self-rule, allowing each town and congregation to govern itself. Maryland's first town, St. Mary's, was established in 1634 when settlers, arriving on the ships the *Ark* and the *Dove*, chose a location high on a bluff near the point where the Potomac River flows into Chesapeake Bay. Take your guests back four centuries to an early colonial towne.

Ambiance

Picture the 17th Century settlement of St. Mary's in Maryland. Keep the lighting low as if you are inside an early Colonial home and play background sounds of things you might hear going on outside, such as chopping wood, cattle or horses moving, blacksmiths working and people talking as they go about their business. Use half-burned fireplace logs to give the room the smell of cooking fires.

Colors

Use "17th Century" colors of purple, deep magenta and mauve.

Suggested Attire

The suggested attire is "visiting historic monuments" casual.

Invitations

"In the year of our Lord …" Use a graphic of the Maryland flag or a portrait of Cecilius Calvert, Lord Baltimore for your invitations. Or, send the invitation engraved on a pewter plate.

Decorations

Set the tables with deep magenta tablecloths, purple napkins and pewter place settings, including tankards for ale. For centerpieces, use candle lanterns in punched tin holders. On the walls, hang pictures of people who would have been well-known back then, such as Calvert, Lord Baltimore or the crest that's used

Keywords

British colonies, British North America, New England, mid-Atlantic, South East, Puritans, Calvinists, Society of Friends, Quakers, Huguenots, plantations, tobacco, planters, town meeting, town square, quadrangle, commons, yeoman, Salem witch trials, timber houses, stone fireplaces, parlor, loft, detached kitchen, livestock, settler, artisans, shopkeepers, merchants, blacksmiths, wheelwrights, furniture makers, traders, Ordinary, barrels bills of exchange, shipbuilding, sail makers, Georgian style architecture, symmetrical façade, William Penn,

Colonial

on the state flag of Maryland. Also, create windows with frames that look like rough-hewn wood. In the windows, use pictures of likely scenes from that period, such as sailing ships at port or people in appropriate dress.

Menu

This menu uses recipes from early Colonial America.

- appetizers: Alsatian soup (this French vegetable soup was popular in early Maine), and green salad
- main course: Massachusetts mulligan stew with dumplings plus red cabbage with apples
- dessert: Vermont maple mousse
- specialty drinks: Grog (hot tea, dark rum, sugar syrup, nutmeg and lemon zest) or Colonials (gin, maraschino liqueur, grapefruit juice)

Entertainment

Hire a group to play Baroque music of the 17th Century — either a group of Madrigal singers or instrumentalists who can play the instruments of the day such as the harpsichord, lute or mandolin. You will find a good database of early music at www.classicalarchives.com. You should be able to find exactly the music you want there.

Arrange for a demonstration of a Colonial-era craft such as spinning, weaving, wood or metal working.

Souvenirs/Party Favors

Let the guests take home their pewter ale mugs and as they leave, give them a gift bag filled with spices for a meat and vegetable stew, dry lentil soup mix, and cranberry bread mix.

Fund Raisers

If you need to raise funds, auction a trip to St Mary's and other colonial sites in the area such as Jamestowne or the plantation homes.

Keywords

New Netherland, Poor Richard's Almanac, John Locke, Mennonites, James River Plantations, representative government, religious toleration, economic growth, cultural diversity, New Amsterdam, George Calvert - Lord Baltimore, John Winthrop, Massachusetts Bay Company, Boston Tea Party, William Penn, sugar trade to the West Indies, settlers, yeoman, freeholders, rum trade, tobacco trade, dyeing, weaving, soap making, furniture making, candle making, cotton, tobacco, handmade, quill pens, **www.celebration-solutions.com/colonial.html**

Yesteryear Themes

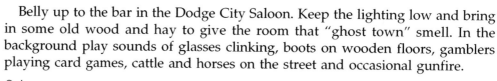

Introduction

Fort Dodge was an army post built in 1864. It provided protection for travelers and wagon trains on the Santa Fe Trail. Dodge City, the town that grew up around the fort, was infamous for its lawlessness and gun-slinging. Buffalo hunters, railroad workers, drifters and soldiers scrapped and fought. The most populated place in the city was Boot Hill Cemetery, where all of those who "died with their boots on" were laid to rest. Law enforcement came riding in with the likes of William Barclay 'Bat' Masterson, Bill Tilghman and Wyatt Earp. Fort Dodge was closed in 1882 and by 1886, the cattle drives had ended, but the legend of Dodge City lives on in its romantic and infamous past. At one time or another, every one of your guests has probably wanted to be a cowboy.

Ambiance

Belly up to the bar in the Dodge City Saloon. Keep the lighting low and bring in some old wood and hay to give the room that "ghost town" smell. In the background play sounds of glasses clinking, boots on wooden floors, gamblers playing card games, cattle and horses on the street and occasional gunfire.

Colors

Use "Wild West" colors of green, blue grey, deep green and deep red.

Suggested Attire

The suggested attire is "boot scootin" western.

Invitations

"Wanted …" Put the guest's face on an old west, wanted poster, or pin a toy Marshal's badge to your invitations.

Decorations

Set the tables with blue grey tablecloths, deep green place settings and deep red napkins. For centerpieces, create a tabletop display of the kinds of things you might have seen in the Dodge City Saloon — hands of poker laid out on the table, six-shooters in holsters, leather gloves, bottles or shot glasses.

Keywords

Wanted posters, metal cookware, Long Branch Saloon, cattle drive, horse thieves, cattle rustlers, outlaws, hobby horse, wagon wheel, sheriff's star, boots, bandanas, ghost town, saloon doors, chaps, cowboy hats, cattle, rodeo, horse thieves, bank robbers, trains, stagecoach, highwaymen, Wyatt Earp, Bat Masterson, buffalo hunters, peace officer, marshal, gamblers, mercantile, range wars, barbed wire, chuckwagon supper, western show, gunfighters, stage coach, hayrack rides, poker game, square dance, dancing girls, saloon, gunfight in the

Dodge City

Create a set of saloon doors for the entrance to the room. Make sure that the saloon door is braced and secured well so that it cannot fall.

On the walls, hang "Most Wanted" posters and pictures from the 1870s of cowboys and gunslingers. Create windows that look out onto Dodge City. Show classic old west scenes in the panes — horses at the rail, gunfighters at the ready, buckboards full of supplies, or the Mercantile across a dusty, dirt street.

Menu

Consider this "wild west saloon" menu

- appetizers: buffalo chili
- main course: smoky mesquite flank steaks with new potatoes
- dessert: cowboy biscuits with preserves and sweet honey butter
- specialty drinks: Cowboy Cocktails (rye and half and half) or Cowgirl's Prayer (gold tequila, fresh lemonade, fresh lime juice, lemon slice)

Entertainment

Hire a group to play country and western music or hire a DJ whose specialty is country and western for dancing.

Hire a dance instructor to give your guests a few lessons in the popular two-step, the Cowboy Hustle, Country Jazz, Honky Tonk Attitude, Walkin' Wazie and the Tumbleweed. After the dance lessons, strike up the band and let the dancing begin!

Souvenirs/Party Favors

Send your guests home with CDs of popular country and western music wrapped in a colorful bandana.

Fund Raisers

If you need to raise funds, create a cutout of a gun slinger and a dance hall girl. Let guests have their pictures made in the cutout and sell the pictures.

Keywords

street, holsters, hanging hill, cattle rustlers, dusty, wooden sidewalks, settlers, log cabins, stake holders, Boot Hill, six shooters, spurs, bandanas, wagon train, dust bowl, trade center, mercantile, Indian Territory, trigger, well water, tents, cannons, militia, bitter winters, hot, dry summers, posse, Dead or Alive, fort, cavalry, Jawhawkers, railroad, bandanas, chaps, 10-gallon hats, wagon trains, settlers, miners, riding the range, get along little doggie, boots, boomtowns, miners, life on the trail, train whistles, **www.celebration-solutions.com/dodge.html**

Yesteryear Themes

Introduction

According to ancient Egyptian legend, every night Ra, the Sun God, sails across the sky in his boat and every night he returns to the underworld. Osiris, the ruler of the underworld, has Ra's boat pulled along the other river Nile until it crosses the horizon and the sun rises again. The enduring images of Egypt — the great pyramids, golden sarcophagi, bearded pharaohs, hieroglyphics, underground burial chambers, sprawling temple complexes, and statues combining human and animal forms — captivate the imagination even today, twenty centuries after the collapse of the ancient empire. Let your guests "discover" the land of the pharaohs.

Ambiance

Travel to an archaeological dig in ancient Egypt. Sunshine is nearly a constant in Egypt, so keep the lighting high. Use audio files of hammers hitting stone, brushes against a dirt surface, people moving earth in wheelbarrows and the wind escaping ancient tombs for background sounds. Sand or dirt will give the room a dusty, earthy smell.

Colors

Use "stone-columned temple" colors of marble white, deep marble yellow and blue grey.

Suggested Attire

The suggested attire is "archeological dig" casual.

Invitations

Use hieroglyphic symbols along with a symbol guide to express your invitation message. Or, find a good photograph of the golden mask of King Tut or a sunset near the pyramids for your invitation graphics.

Decorations

Set the tables with blue grey tablecloths, stoneware place settings and marble yellow napkins. For centerpieces, let your guests take part in an archaeological

Keywords

hieroglyphs, sphinx, pyramid, treasure maps, lotus blossoms, Nile valley, tombs, temples, pyramids, mummy, desert sand, chariots, Tut, oil lamps, pottery jars, darkened eyelids, obelisk, animals with human bodies, scarab, papyrus rolls, Nile River, Prince of Egypt, agriculture, Pharaoh, architecture, large stone buildings, tombs, sculpture, paintings, hieroglyphics, Rosetta stone, archaeology, temples of Karnak, Valley of the Golden Mummies, monumental elegance, slender papyrus columns, mortuary complex, stone columns, thickets of dark

Egyptians

"dig." Place party favors in a box full or sand or create decorative sarcophagus boxes to hold the party favors.

For the walls, create mural-sized hieroglyphs and temple statues. Between the murals, use plaster columns to provide a platform for "artifacts" such as pharoah's masks, scarabs or model pyramids. You'll find incredible photographs of Egypt taken in 1856 in the Dover Photography Collections book *Egypt and the Holy Land Historic Photographs: Seventy-Seven Views.*

Menu

Consider this "Nile delta" menu.
- appetizers: falafel balls with cucumber yogurt sauce with raisins
- main course: stuffed peppers and stuffed grape leaves
- dessert: rice pudding with toasted almonds
- specialty drinks: Deltas (blended whiskey, Southern comfort, lime juice, sugar, orange slice) or Dinahs (blended whiskey, lemon juice, sugar, mint sprig)

Entertainment

Play traditional Egyptian music and arrange to show scenes of the movie *Cleopatra (1963)* starring Elizabeth Taylor.

Teach you guests how to play the game *Senet* — the most popular of the many board games of ancient Egypt. The wall paintings of many Egyptian tombs show the spirits of the underworld playing games of *Senet*. You'll find a game board and instructions on the web page for this theme.

Souvenirs/Party Favors

Give each guest a hieroglyphic of their name in a decorative metal frame. You can find a Egyptian name translators on the internet.

Fund Raisers

If you need to raise funds, sell tickets to an Egyptian art exhibit or auction a Nile River Cruise.

Keywords

green papyrus, ageless, Pharaoh, relics, grandeur, golden mask, braided beard masks, Tut, Ramses, Nefertari, Cleopatra, Ra, Amun, Horus, Osirus, Aton, sphinx, obelisk, awed by the size, golden chariots, white stone, tomb robbers, falcons, lion-headed goddess, cartouche, colossus, Memphis, Alexandria, eucalyptus trees, palm trees, ancient sites, amulet, ankh, Book of the Dead, caliph, colossus, false doors, tomb seals, tomb robbers, explorers, curse of the mummy, archaeologist, golden mummies. **www.celebration-solutions.com/egypt.html**

Yesteryear Themes

Introduction

J. Edgar Hoover was born in Washington D.C. in 1895. He studied law at George Washington University and became the Director of the Federal Bureau of Investigation where he worked for 48 years, serving every President from Coolidge to Nixon. The early FBI is probably most famous for the cases of Elliot Ness and the "Untouchables" who pursued gangsters in the 1930s. One of the most notorious captures during Hoover's time was the gangster John Dillinger, then considered Public Enemy Number One. Relive the dangerous days of Dillinger and the gallant G-men who chased him down.

Ambiance

Picture the office of the "Untouchables" — crime fighting central. Keep the lighting low like an old government office building and play audio files of typewriters and telex machines, phones ringing and gangsters being interrogated in the background.

Colors

Use "double-breasted pinstripe" colors of deep brown and light tan.

Suggested Attire

The suggested attire is "gangster vs. G-man" cocktail.

Invitations

"Most Wanted" Make up FBI Most Wanted posters or make your invitation look like a ransom note. Or, send your invitation in a file folder marked "Most Wanted" on the outside with a picture of your guest and the details of the party on the inside.

Decorations

Set the tables with deep brown tablecloths, white china and light tan napkins. For centerpieces, use items that might have been found in a 1930s FBI office, such as rotary telephones or typewriters. At each place setting, put a "case file" for the guest that has their name on the label, a photograph inside and a humorous

Keywords

crime fighters, gangsters, Untouchables, G-men, crime lab, fingerprints, sleuth, profiles, criminologist, crime detection, bad buys, investigation, violation, special agent in charge, detective, life, liberty, justice, nicknamed "Speed," guns blazing, collecting evidence, analyzing documents, trigger, pistol, shotgun, machine gun, firearms, notorious, surrender, witnesses, law enforcement, elite organization, fingerprints, proper procedures, identification, handwriting analysis, lipstick stain, top investigators, bomb blast, Quantico, Virginia, modus

J Edgar Hoover and the FBI

"charge sheet." Make up silly crimes, like "Buick molester" with a picture of a wrecked car, "fashion homicide" for bad '70s leisure suits, or "smuggling" for women who carry a lot of stuff in their purses.

On the walls, hang "FBI's 10 Most Wanted" posters from the era, featuring criminals like Dillinger, Pretty Boy Floyd, Machine Gun Kelly or Bonnie and Clyde. You can read about the FBI's most famous cases on their website at www.fbi.gov.

Menu

Consider this menu "right out of Al Capone's Chicago territory."
- appetizers: mini-Chicago-style hot dogs with cheese and a choice of salsas
- main course: Chicago-style pizza
- dessert: French silk cheesecake (made famous by Eli's of Chicago)
- specialty drinks: Chicago Fizz (gold rum, port, fresh lemon juice, sugar, egg white and sparkling water) or Whiskey shots and beer

Entertainment

Play famous outlaws trivia. Play audio files of famous lines from gangster movies ("You dirty rat!") and see if guests can correctly guess the actor and the movie from which it came. Add trivia questions about groups like the James Gang or see if your guests recognize the famous exploits of John Dillinger, Baby Face Nelson, Slick Willie Sutton or Al Capone.

Souvenirs/Party Favors

Create a cutout of Bonnie and Clyde and let guests have their pictures taken as the famous bandit pair.

Fund Raisers

If you need to raise funds, put guests pictures on the walls as mug shots. Offer to let guests "Get Your Face Off this Wall" if they ante up a donation.

Keywords

operandi, Ten Most Wanted List, captured, John Dillinger, Public Enemy Number One, bootlegger, prohibition, bank robbers, "Pretty Boy" Floyd, "Ma" Barker, "Baby Face" Nelson, "Creepy" Karpis, fugitive, tip, "Dead or Alive," surveillance, law and order, Lindburgh kidnapping, ransom note, "You Can't Get Away With It," "Don't shoot, G-men, don't shoot," " You dirty rat," incorruptible, conviction, moonshine, blue-ruin, hooch, sauce, juice, barley-bree, mash, home brew, giggle water, bump off, struggle buggy, **www.celebration-solutions.com/hoover.html**

Yesteryear Themes

Introduction

The Kremlin was founded in the 12th Century as a fortress within the city of Moscow, Russia. Red Square is a vast open space dominated by the onion-domed Cathedral of the Assumption, the place where the Czars were coronated and the burial place of the leaders of the Russian Orthodox Church. What the Kremlin came to symbolize was the seat and power of Communism and its security service, the KGB. Today, the Kremlin comprises government buildings, palaces, cathedrals and massive, fortified walls. Let your guests play a roll in this spoof on the Soviet "spooks" (spies).

Ambiance

Imagine KGB headquarters during the heyday of Communism. Play audio files of people speaking in Russian or people speaking in English with Russian accents, the sound of typewriters, telex machines spitting out secret communiques and telephones ringing in the background.

Colors

Use "Komisar" colors of Soviet Army green and Communist red.

Suggested Attire

The suggested attire is "communist drab" casual unless you want your guests to come dressed in costume as old Soviet officials.

Invitations

"By order of the KGB ..." Use the old symbols of Soviet Russia — the hammer and sickle, or pictures of Lenin with cyrillic lettering plus an English translation.

Decorations

Set the tables with Soviet Army green tablecloths, metal place settings and Communist red napkins. For centerpieces, find postage stamps from the Soviet era hailing the people, the people's heroes or the collective. Blow them up to 8x10 size and place them in standing frames on the tables.

Keywords

Red Square, Komisar, Komrade, Lenin, Stalin, USSR, CCCP, KGB, GRU, Kossak, Supreme Soviet, Counsel of Ministers, Cathedral of the Assumption, Russian Orthodox Church, Cathedral of Saint Basil the Blessed, May Day military parade, Russian Revolution of 1917, Cold War, espionage, listening devices, spies, saboteurs, KGB, communist, subversion, underground spy ring, red stars with hammer and sickles in them, grey-green uniforms, war medals, Komisar, Kossak, state security apparatus, foreign intelligence, covert action, counterintelligence,

Kremlin

No Soviet office would have been complete without a large portrait of Lenin and posters hailing the people's party or the workers. You'll find a large selection of posters and propaganda pieces in the International Poster Gallery online at www.internationalposter.com.

From the ceiling, hang plain, metal lampshades with single, bare light bulbs hanging from them. The sparser looking, the better.

Menu

Consider this menu for the "Komrades at the Kremlin Komissary."

- appetizers: spicy stuffed cabbage
- main course: roast turkey stuffed with walnuts and cherry puree
- dessert: baked, stuffed apples
- specialty drinks: Vodka, of course! KGB (kirschwasser, gin, apricot brandy, lemon twist), Russian Bears (vodka, dark crème de cacao, half and half) or Russian Quaaludes (vodka, Frangelico, Irish crème liqueur)

Entertainment

Play Russian folk music while your guests try their hand at one of the many spy-based games such as: *Inkognito* (by Fantasy Flight) where every player is a spy, and your first job is to figure out which of the other players is your partner; or *Top Secret Spies* (by Rio Grande Games) where players search for top secret information locked in a safe that is constantly moving.

Souvenirs/Party Favors

Send each guest home with a spy game.

Fund Raisers

If you need to raise funds, arrange for a sale of Russian folk crafts. You will find a large selection of Russian folk crafts — nesting dolls, lacquer boxes, woolen shawls, enamel jewelry, Russian fairy tales and hand-carved Santas — online at www.russian-crafts.com.

Keywords

counter-subversion, recruiting agents, intercepting foreign communications, data analysis, penetrate and disrupt the activities of the enemy, defections to the West, terrorist activities, assassinations, clandestine methods, dull green uniforms, black boots, dowdy women's clothes, fierce loyalty, fur hats, long coats, boyars, dragoons, Rus, human intelligence, signal intelligence, imagery intelligence, signature intelligence, targetted assassination, gulags, Checka agency, NKVD, SMERSH (death to spies), **www.celebration-solutions.com/kremlin.html**

Yesteryear Themes

Introduction

Dinosaur is the common name for extinct reptiles belonging to the group Dinosauria meaning "terrible lizards." For more than 140 million years, dinosaurs dominated the earth. They lived in a world very different from earth day. Surface temperatures were much warmer and there were no polar ice caps. The earth's crust was covered by one supercontinent where deserts were common across the equator and tropical areas extended much farther north than they do today. Today, only fossils remain to tell us about the dinosaurs' life on earth. Give your guests a chance to walk the trails of the dinosaurs.

Ambiance

Imagine the proverbial "primordial soup" in the land before time. The key to this theme is making your guests feel small against the scale of the decorations. In the background, play sounds of jungle life — birds, insects and small animals, and the sound of large, heavy feet crashing through plants. Raise the temperature in the room like a steamy jungle and dim the lights just a bit as if there is a dense jungle canopy above. Use scented candles to give the room the smell of a flowering jungle.

Colors

Use "Jurassic Park" colors of deep brown, deep green, and shades of leaf green.

Suggested Attire

The suggested attire is "caveman" casual.

Invitations

"Dinosaur Doings." Send an invitations that looks like a newspaper as if it had been written by a dinosaur. Or, send your invitation along with a toy or blowup dinosaur.

Decorations

Set the tables with leaf green tablecloths, deep green napkins and stoneware place settings. Use your centerpieces to help create the illusion that guests are in

Keywords

dinosaurs, swamp land, caves, cave painting, petroglyphs, stone tools, carbon dating, ice age, Neanderthal, cave dwelling, fire, spears, Mastodon, Stone Age, stone tools, Paleolithic, Mesolithic, Neolithic Age, hunter-gatherers, early man, Homo Erectus, fossils, bone fragments, armor plates, skeleton, bipedal, paleontology, Tyrannosaurus rex, Triassic Period, Cretaceous Period, carnivorous, more closely related to birds than to modern reptiles, warm-blooded, Theropoda, sauropod, feather-bearing dinosaurs, pterosaurs, crocodilians, Velociraptor,

Prehistoric

a great, vast jungle. Let large-leafed plants — real, silk or paper — flow out of the center of the tables. Make sure they reach at least 7" high, so that your guests won't be bumping their heads into the leaves all evening. You'll also need a heavy, steady base or pot for the leaves, so that they won't tip over.

Create giant dinosaur legs using nylon material. Create a cylinder shape at least 5" in diameter and sew round rings into the fabric to give the material a round shape. Hang the "legs" from ceiling to floor and give the legs giant claws.

Menu

Consider this "caveman's delight" menu.
- appetizers: swamp bowls (spinach and cheese dip in a bread bowl)
- main course: roast pig with baked apples and roasted corn on a stick
- dessert: fried bananas in crepes with honey
- specialty drinks: Yellow Parrots (brandy, Pernod, yellow Chartreuse) or Swamp Water (dark rum, blue Curacao, orange juice, lemon juice)

Entertainment

Set up computers at stations around the room and let your guests explore the very best dinosaur website we've found — the Jurassic Park Institute at www.jpinstitute.com or arrange for a showing of one of the classic *Jurassic Park* films directed by Stephen Spielberg.

Souvenirs/Party Favors

Send your guests home with fossil soap. Make nearly-clear, glycerine soap with small plastic dinosaurs in them. Wrap two or three bars of the soap in a large, silk banana leaf and tie it together with a colorful ribbon.

Fund Raisers

If you need to raise funds, sell annual passes to a local Natural History Museum or trips to the Jurassic Park exhibit at Universal Studios in Orlando, FL.

Keywords

plant-eaters, Jurassic Period, stegosaurs, dominate the land, horned, high-spined, catastrophic disaster, hatchlings, herbivore, herds, spikes and knobs, massive club at the end of their tail, fossilized footprints, tracks, fossils, tooth, bone, shell fragment, leaf, Pleistocene elephants, tracks and trails, ice age, amber fossils, badlands, bones, cold-blooded, crater, dinosaur eggs, extinct, ferns, carnivores, herbivores, Jurassic, lava flow, petrified forest, fossil, mastodon, Tyranosaurus Rex, skeleton, **www.celebration-solutions.com/dinosaur.html**

Yesteryear Themes

Introduction

Theodore Roosevelt was a soldier, statesman, adventurer, outdoorsman and a President of the United States. His dynamic presence left an indelible stamp on America. He was larger than life. He drank his coffee with seven lumps of sugar from a cup that his son Teddy, Jr. described as "more in the nature of a bathtub." He was a jolly man who roared with laughter, enjoyed spending time with his children, and walked with such a determined stride that even other military men had a job to keep up with him. Roosevelt was a rough-and-tumble, swashbuckling character who should do well entertaining your guests.

Ambiance

Picture the study in Teddy Roosevelt's Sagamore Hill home. Use lamps to light up the room and play early 20th Century instrumental music in the background. Use leather cleaner on small strips of leather to give the room that "rough rider" smell.

Colors

Use "turn-of-the-century" colors of grey blue, sage green and forest green.

Suggested Attire

The suggested attire is "hunting lodge" casual.

Invitations

"Bully for you … if you join us for a pint or two!" Use a good photograph of Teddy Roosevelt or a gentleman's study trophy room for your invitations. Or, create Teddy Roosevelt campaign stick pins to stick through your invitation sheets.

Decorations

Set the tables with sage green tablecloths, forest green napkins and grey blue stoneware place settings. For centerpieces, use table lamps with leather shades. Surround the bases of the lamps with coffee table books full of pictures of nature or the national parks.

For the walls, create mural-sized posters of bookshelves full of leather-bound

Keywords

"Bully for you," "Speak softly and carry a big stick," Rough Riders, San Juan Ridge, Spanish-American War, bespectacled, walrus mustache, force of presence, ebullient personality, he walked with a fierce, determined stride, daredevil, Sagamore Hill (family home), great victories and accomplishments, soldier, statesman, author, adventurer, big game hunter, outdoorsman, Oyster Bay, trophy room, doting father, wife Edith, children: Alice, Theodore, Jr, Kermit, Ethel, Archie, and Quentin, tireless, grit, The Turn of the Century, horseless carriages, driving

Teddy Roosevelt

books. Hang enough murals to make the room look like a library.

Menu

This menu is typical of the wild game Teddy Roosevelt would have bagged as a hunter.

- appetizers: green chile and roasted corn soup
- main course: stuffed, roasted quail with bourbon sauce and sweet potato puree
- dessert: Dutch apple-cherry pie
- specialty drinks: Huntsman (vodka, dark rum, fresh lime juice, sugar) or Hudson Bay (gin, cherry brandy, rum, orange juice, lime juice)

Entertainment

Hire a ragtime jazz band to entertain your guests. Ragtime jazz was popular from just after the turn of the century to the 1920s because of its syncopated rhythms and crazy lyrics. The most easily recognizable ragtime jazz piece is probably Scott Joplin's song the *Maple Leaf Rag*. It was popular when it was written in 1916 and made a comeback in the 1973 film *The Sting*. If you can't find a ragtime jazz band in your area, you will find CD recordings of minstrel and ragtime jazz at www.vintage-recordings.com.

Souvenirs/Party Favors

Give your guests a leather-bound edition of an adventure book like *Treasure Island* by Robert Lewis Stevenson, *Wild Bill Hickok Gunfighter* by Joseph G Rosa, *Last of the Mohicans* by James Fenimore Cooper, *White Fang* by Jack London, *Red Badge of Courage* by Stephen Crane or *Hondo* by Louis L'Amour, and an oversized coffee cup.

Fund Raisers

If you need to raise funds, sell tickets for a trip to Roosevelt's Sagamore Hill home in Oyster Bay, New York.

Keywords

hats and goggles, bowler hats, ice deliveries, women in long dresses, a splendid time, new inventions - telephone, typewriter, sewing machine, Kodak's brownie camera, Kewpie dolls, hometowns, bowler hats, stiff white collars, pocket watches, spectacles, women didn't work outside of the home, straight razors, men always wore hats, Sagamore Hill, Oyster Bay New York, adventurer, women wore long dresses with puffed sleeves and corsets for narrow waists, the last frontiers were explored, **www.celebration-solutions.com/TeddyR.html**

Yesteryear Themes

Introduction

The name "Viking" was used to describe men who fared by the sea to adventures of raiding, commerce and war. It was also used as a verb in the expression "to go I Viking" which described their favorite enterprise — trading and plundering. Being a Viking in that sense was considered highly honorable. The stories of the Vikings are told in numerous runic inscriptions scattered across the Scandinavian countryside. The Vikings were more than just legend, though, they were daring and adroit sailors, merchants, explorers, settlers, farmers, craftsmen, storytellers and poets. Let your guests enjoy an evening celebrating the rich culture of the norse Vikings.

Ambiance

Picture a Viking raiding camp. Keep the lighting low as Viking longhouses were quite dark inside. Play the sounds of someone hewing wood, lashing boats, stoking fires, striking iron and cooking food on a spit in the background. Use peat to give the room an earthy, outdoor smell.

Colors

Use "marauder" colors of green, white and red.

Suggested Attire

The suggested attire is "trading and plundering" casual.

Invitations

"We go a Viking …" Use a clip art graphic of a Viking or Viking weapons to use for your invitation. Or, use photographs from the L'Anse aux Meadows National Historic Site in Canada — the only known Viking settlement in the Americas. You can find information about this historic archaeological site online at whc.unesco.org.

Decorations

Set the tables with green tablecloths, red napkins and white china. For centerpieces, have runic symbols etched into flat slate tiles. You can find information about stone etching online at Ideas in Stone, www.ideasinstone.com.

Keywords

Norsement, clans, landowning jarls, freemen, fjords, freedom of the open sea, plunderer, raiders and traders, daring adventures, war gods, Odin and Thor, scourge of Europe, thieves and destroyers of life and property, colonizing, bawdy raids, rich stores of gold and silver and sacred objects, bloodthirsty warriors, plundering forays, conquer, burn, pillage, Leif Ericson, Eric the Red, explorers, tall blonde barbarians, horned helmets, dragon-headed ships, Erik Bloodaxe, Iceland, Faeroe Islands, Greenland, bronze pins, furs, hides, down, walrus

Vikings

Create displays of things that might be seen in a Viking raiding camp — clothing, weapons, fire pit or an iron forge. On the walls, place poster-sized pictures of famous Vikings, such as Leif Erikson or photographs of Viking ruins.

Menu

Consider this "land of the Vikings (Norwegian)" menu.

- appetizers: sour cream porridge
- main course: Nakkerrul (pork roulade with mustard sauce) and potato dumplings
- dessert: Fyrstekake (cake with hazelnut or jam filling)
- specialty drinks: Negus punch (ruby port, lemon zest, sugar, cinnamon, nutmeg, cloves, all spice, lemon juice) or Lallah Rookh (light rum, cognac, vanilla extract, sugar, whipped cream)

Entertainment

Play Norwegian folk music. Northside Records features music from Sweden, Finland, Norway, Denmark and Sámiland. You can find them online at www.noside.com.

Introduce your guests to the game of *Kvatrutafl*. *Kvatrutafl* is similar to modern backgammon and was played during the Viking Age. Viking warriors were not only judged by their skills on the battlefield but by their poetry and riddles. You'll find a gameboard and instructions for *Kvatrutafl* and Viking riddles to solve on the web page for this site.

Souvenirs/Party Favors

Give each guest a colorfully decorated runic stone symbol.

Fund Raisers

If you need to raise funds, fill "treasure chests" and hold a blind auction. Let guests know what it's possible to win, but don't open the boxes until after bidding closes.

Keywords

ivory, amber, nuts, honey, beeswax, gold, riding into battle, gilded bronze weather vanes, rows of painted shields on the sides of the ship, ice skates made of bone, cauldrons hanging over lit campfires, seas dotted with icebergs, long hall with turf roof, men in trousers with a belted tunic, women in long robes with shawls held closed by a brooch, carved picture stones, runes, storytelling tradition, skinning animals, long house, peat roof, carved stone, dwarfs, elves, giants, Gods, Valhalla, Valkyrie, **www.celebration-solutions.com/viking.html**

Celebration Solutions

Checklists

Task Tracker	Month 9	Month 8	Month 7	Month 6	Month 5	Month 4	Month 3	Month 2	Month 1

E-mail Meeting Reminder

E-mail tips
- Correct distribution list
- Descriptive subject line
- Include contact information in the signature
- Let committee members know what to expect from the upcoming meeting
- Be specific in asking for responses

Next meeting date

Next meeting time

Next meeting place

Simplified meeting agenda

What committee members should bring to the meeting

Meeting Follow Up

Synopsis of decisions

Synopsis of new assignments

Synopsis of areas where help is still needed

Next Meeting Date	
Next Meeting Time	
Next Meeting Place	

Monthly Committee Tasks

Jan	Feb	Mar	Apr
May	June	July	Aug
Sept	Oct	Nov	Dec

Check Current Month

Executive Committee Chairman

Project List	Deadline

Accounting

Project List	Deadline

Record Keeping

Project List	Deadline

Communications

Project List	Deadline

Food/Beverage

Project List	Deadline

Souvenirs

Project List	Deadline

Entertainment

Project List	Deadline

www.ReunionSolutions.com

Decorations Cost Sheet

Wall decorations

TOTAL

Table decorations

TOTAL

Ceiling/floor decorations

TOTAL

Free-standing decorations

TOTAL

Setup/Cleanup Supplies List

Setup

- [ ] Tape
- [ ] Pens/Pencils
- [ ] Paintbrushes
- [ ] Glue
- [ ] Stapler
- [ ] Crepe paper
- [ ] Tablecloths
- [ ] Candles
- [ ] Confetti
- [ ] Signs
- [ ] Ribbon

- [ ] String
- [ ] Erasers
- [ ] Fabric markers
- [ ] Sponges
- [ ] Paper clips
- [ ] Tissue paper
- [ ] Table cover clips
- [ ] Banners
- [ ] Bows
- [ ] Dangling cutouts
- [ ] Disposable cameras

- [ ] Scissors
- [ ] Sharpeners
- [ ] Paper/plastic bags
- [ ] Craft knife
- [ ] Balloons
- [ ] Backdrops
- [ ] Napkins/Napkin rings
- [ ] Border trim
- [ ] Bubbles
- [ ] Garlands
- [ ] Lighting

Cleanup

- [ ] Do not throw away list
- [ ] Trasnbags/ties
- [ ] Scissors
- [ ] Stain remover
- [ ] Food containers

- [ ] Transport to next event list
- [ ] Cleaning supplies
- [ ] Tape remover
- [ ] Paper towels
- [ ] Labels

- [ ] Haul away plans
- [ ] Glue remover
- [ ] Sponges
- [ ] Boxes

Balloon Retrieval Tools

- [ ] Water bottle
- [ ] Balloon weights

- [ ] Cherry picker
- [ ] Rake

- [ ] Long string/ribbon

Confetti Removal Tools

- [ ] Static remover
- [ ] Lint brushes
- [ ] Throw-away floor sweeper

Vendor Contact Sheet

Vendor Name   Vendor Service

Address

Contact Name   Phone

Emergency Contact   Phone

Notes

Vendor Name   Vendor Service

Address

Contact Name   Phone

Emergency Contact   Phone

Notes

Vendor Name   Vendor Service

Address

Contact Name   Phone

Emergency Contact   Phone

Notes

Vendor Name   Vendor Service

Address

Contact Name   Phone

Emergency Contact   Phone

Notes

Vendor Name   Vendor Service

Address

Contact Name   Phone

Emergency Contact   Phone

Notes

Vendor Name   Vendor Service

Address

Contact Name   Phone

Emergency Contact   Phone

Notes

Vendor Name   Vendor Service

Address

Contact Name   Phone

Emergency Contact   Phone

Notes

Event Summary

Description

Idea Sketch

Facility

Invitations

Food/Beverage

Souvenirs

Entertainment

Decorations

Expense Ledger

Description of Expense	Date	Deposit	Date	Balance	Date	Deposit Returned

Expense Ledger

Description of Expense	Date	Deposit	Date	Balance	Date	Deposit Returned

Indoor Facility Interview Checklist

Company Name:

Address:

Contact Name: Phone: Fax:

E-mail: URL:

Event Room

Date(s) available

Time available   Starting time   Ending time

Room rental fees   Deposit   Due by   Waived

Cancellation policy

Damage policy   Cleanup fees

Maximum occupancy   Options for add'l rooms

Room dimensions

Room fixtures/obstacles

Room features

Atmosphere   Thermostat control

Lighting   Lighting control

Dance floor   Electrical needs

Other equipment   Wall dividers

Tables   Square   Round   Oval   Rectangle   Condition

Room Setup   Scattered Rounds   Conference Style   U-Shape   Hollow Square

                Banquet Style   Classroom Style   Chevron Style   Reception Style

Table linens   Centerpieces

Condition of the: Chairs   Glassware   Silverware   China

Food service setup

Bar setup

Decoration space: Floor   Walls   Ceiling   Free-standing

Decorating rules

Security   Locked equipment room   Coat/hat check

Handicap accessible

Parties in adjacent rooms   Contract negotiations

Construction plans   Union rules

Billing Data

Deposit date _____ Deposit amount_____

Deposit date _____ Deposit amount_____

Final payment due _____ Final payment amount_____

Payment methods accepted _____

Indoor Facility Interview Checklist

Amenities

Guest rooms	Single	Double	Suite	Family
Group rates	Single	Double	Suite	Family
Guest room condition		Non-Smoking Rooms		Handicap Accessible
Hospitality suite				
Maps/brochures		Driving instructions		
Transportation: to airport		to train/bus	to sites	
Marquee		Cost	Message	
Sign frames		Sign stands	Glass sign cases	
Concierge services		Doorman services		
Freight elevators				
Insurance		Liquor license		
Music license				
Recreation facilities		Cost	Hours	
Parking		Cost	Hours	
Valet Parking		Cost	Hours	
Cleaner		Cost	Hours	
Babysitting		Cost	Hours	
Restaurant		Price range	Hours	
Room Service		Price range	Hours	
Gift shop			Hours	
Check cashing		Fees	Hours	
ATMs				
Emergency facilities		Emergency number		

AV Equipment

Sound System	Loudspeaker	TV	VCR/DVD
Monitor	Flip Chart	Podium	Microphones
Slide Projector	Movie Projector	Computer Projector	
Lighting effects	Laser shows	Robotic lights	
Security	Around the area		Within the facility
Parking			

Notes

Room Setup Styles

Scattered rounds

The scattered round table setup is by far the most common. Scattered rounds are used to put the maximum number of people in a minimal amount of space. Round tables seat anywhere from four to twelve and table sizes can be alternated to give the room a less uniform appearance. If you're going to use scattered rounds and have a presentation, make sure that all dining is finished before the presentation begins because at least one quarter of the audience will have to turn their chairs around in order to see the presentation.

Conference style

Conference style is good if you have a small group and you want everyone to be able to see and communicate with each other. *This style works best with small groups.*

U-shape

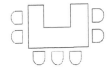

U-Shape is good for presentations because everyone is looking inward and toward the front and no one's view is obstructed. *(If guests will be seated on the inside of the U, allow plenty of space).*

Hollow square

Hollow square style is good if you want to put something on display in the middle of the tables. Sometimes a hollow square is given a small aisle to facilitate service. Guests can be seated within an almost hollow square as long as there is adequate space.

Classroom style

Classroom style easily accommodates a head table or presentations because guests will be able to see without having to turn their chairs around.

Chevron style

Chevron style is also good for presentations because tables are angled toward the center so that no one's view is blocked.

Reception style

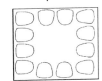

Reception style is ideal if you are planning for cocktails and light hors d'oeuvres where most guests will be standing.

Table Sizing Chart

Table size	Seats/people	Table cloth size
72" round	10-12	132"
60" round	8-10	120"
54" round	6-8	114"
48" round	4-6	108"
36" round	4	96"

Outdoor Facility Interview Checklist

Company Name:

Address:	
Contact Name:	Phone: Fax:
E-mail:	URL:

Atmosphere

Place to prepare food	
Access for caterer	Place for beverage service
Lighting	Electrical needs
Parking	Shade
Running water	Restrooms
Handicap accessible	Construction plans
Parties in adjacent areas	Inclement weather plans

Amenities

Campsites	Boating
Hiking	Biking
Nauture walks	Ranger programs
Store	Signs
Concessions	Souvenirs
Guides	Outfitters

Shelter/Campsite

Date(s) available		Maximum occupancy
Time available	Starting time	Ending time
Cancellation policy	Damage policy	Cleanup fees
Shelter features		

Policies

Decorating rules
Alcohol policy
Cleanup policy
Smoking policy

Emergencies

Security	Access to phones
Access to first aid	Access to rangers/park personnel
Nearest emergency facility	Emergency personnel response time
Notes:	

Billing Data

Deposit date _____ Deposit amount_____

Deposit date _____ Deposit amount_____

Final payment due _____ Final payment amount_____

Payment methods accepted _____

Catering Interview Checklist

Company Name:

Address:

Contact Name: Phone: Fax:

E-mail: URL:

Caterer's experience

Professional association memberships _____

Chef_____   Credentials_____

License_____   Insurance_____

Menus available   Per/person cost

Specialties _____

Taxes_____ Cake-Cutting_____ Coffee/Tea Service_____ Cleanup_____

Kitchen Facilities   Equipment Condition

Sit Down
Room Setup   Staffing needs

Time allotted for service _____

Buffet
Room Setup   Staffing needs

Time allotted for service _____

Light Menu/Snacks
Room Setup   Staffing needs

Time allotted for service _____

Coffee/Tea Service
Room Setup   Staffing needs

Time allotted for service _____

Catering Interview Checklist

Theme Specialties

Serving Tables

Food tray replacement _____

Decorations

Table skirts _____ Centerpieces _____ Seat covers _____

Serving staff

Hourly rate _____ Gratuity _____
Dress code _____ Oversight _____
Hiring requirements _____ Alcohol policy _____

Special services

Food special requests _____
Taste test of your menu _____ Time/date _____

Facility

Familiar with the facility _____
Understands facility policies _____
Available for a facility walk-through _____

Preliminary numbers due

Final numbers due

Client list/references

Billing Data

Deposit date _____ Deposit amount _____
Deposit date _____ Deposit amount _____
Final payment due _____ Final payment amount _____
Payment methods accepted _____

Food Matrix Menu Planner

	Breakfast	Brunch	Lunch	Early Afternoon	Late Afternoon	6PM start	7PM start	8PM start
Hors D'oeuvres	0	0	0	4-6	6-8	10-12	8-10	4-6
Meats	2	3	4	2	4	6	6	2
Soup	0	1	2	2	1	3	1	1
Salads	0	0	3	2	2	4	3	1
Salad Dressing	0	0	3	2	2	3	3	1
Vegetables	0	2	3	3	2	4	3	2
Fruits	4	3	2	2	2	3	4	2
Cheeses	.5	.5	2	1	1	2	1	1
Breads/ Rolls	2	1	1.5	1	1	2	1	1
Crackers	0	3	6	3	3	6	6	3
Butter	2	1.5	1.5	1	1	2	1.5	1
Dessert	.5	1	3	2	2	4	4	5

Are you planning to provide meals without the help of a caterer? This food matrix is a compilation of catering industry recommendations that should help you plan for adequate amounts of food.

Legend

Hors d'oeuvres — pieces per person per hour

Soup — cups per person

Breads, Rolls, Crackers — pieces per person

Dessert — ounces per person

Meats, Vegetables, Salads, Fruits, Cheeses — ounces per person

Salad Dressing — tablespoons per person

Butter — pats per person

Table Settings Equipment List

Plates

- ☐ Show
- ☐ Dinner
- ☐ Salad
- ☐ Dessert
- ☐ Flat
- ☐ Rimmed

- ☐ Soup bowls
- ☐ Cups/saucers
- ☐ Consomme cups/saucers
- ☐ Demitasse cups/saucers
- ☐ Dinner knives
- ☐ Fish knives
- ☐ Dinner forks

- ☐ Fish forks
- ☐ Salad forks
- ☐ Dessert forks
- ☐ Soup spoons
- ☐ Dessert spoons
- ☐ Tea spoons
- ☐ Demitasse spoons

Pot Luck/Picnic Checklist

Assignment List

- ☐ Entrees
- ☐ Salads
- ☐ Side dishes
- ☐ Breads
- ☐ Desserts
- ☐ Appetizers

Cooking Utensils

- ☐ Tongs
- ☐ Sharp knife
- ☐ Whisk
- ☐ Meat fork
- ☐ Spatula
- ☐ Can opener

Serving/Eating Utensils

- ☐ Forks
- ☐ Knives
- ☐ Platters
- ☐ Spoons
- ☐ Bowls

Warmers

- ☐ Chafing dishes
- ☐ Sterno/canned fuel

Coolers

- ☐ Ice chests
- ☐ Ice/dry ice

Cooking

- ☐ Grill
- ☐ Matches/lighter
- ☐ Baking soda (fire safety)
- ☐ Bottle opener/corkscrew
- ☐ Charcoal/wood chips
- ☐ Charcoal starter
- ☐ Oils/seasonings
- ☐ Cutting board

Table

- ☐ Table cloths/blankets
- ☐ Plates
- ☐ Napkins/moist towelettes
- ☐ Cups/glasses

Garnishes

- ☐ Pickles
- ☐ Greens

Condiments

- ☐ Ketchup
- ☐ Onions
- ☐ Mayonnaise
- ☐ Salt/pepper
- ☐ Mustard
- ☐ Relish
- ☐ Salsa
- ☐ Sugar/sugar substitute

Clean Up

- ☐ Food wrap
- ☐ Trash bags
- ☐ Paper towels/rags
- ☐ Food storage/ziplock bags
- ☐ Removal to dump site
- ☐ Water

Bar/Beverage Service Interview Checklist

Company Name:

Address:

Contact Name: _____ Phone: _____ Fax: _____

E-mail: _____ URL: _____

Beverage Service's experience

Professional association memberships _____

Bartenders_____

Credentials_____

Liquor license _____ Liability insurance _____

Policy on serving intoxicated patrons_____

Policy on checking IDs of minors_____

Drink menus available   Per/person cost

Taxes _____ Corking fees_____ Additional equipment_____

Special requests _____ Special equipment _____

Bar supplies _____

Inventory _____

_____

Inventory reconciliation _____

Cash Bar		Open Bar	
Bar Setup	Staffing needs	Bar Setup	Staffing needs

Self-Service Bar		Coffee/Tea Service	
Room Setup	Staffing needs	Room Setup	Staffing needs

Bar/Beverage Service Checklist

Specialties

Theme Specialties

Serving area

Beverage service staff

Hourly rate _____ Gratuity _____

Dress code _____ Oversight _____

Hiring requirements _____ Alcohol policy _____

Special services

Facility

Familiar with the facility _____

Understands facility policies _____

Available for a facility walk-through _____

Preliminary numbers due	Final numbers due

Client list/references

Billing Data

    Deposit date _____ Deposit amount _____

    Deposit date _____ Deposit amount _____

    Final payment due _____ Final payment amount _____

    Payment methods accepted _____

Beverage Matrix

The estimates below are for the first hour's consumption. Amounts fall off significantly in each subsequent hour.

	Breakfast	Brunch	Lunch	Early Afternoon	Late Afternoon	Dinner	Cocktail Hour	Dessert
Coffee/ Tea	3	3	1	0	0	1	2	1-3
Soft Drinks	0	.5-1	2	2	2-3	1-2	1	.5-1
(kids)	0	1	2	2-3	2-3	2	1	0
Fruit Juices	2-3	2-3	0	0	0	0	1	0
(kids)	2-3	2-3	2-3	2-3	2-3	2-3	2-3	1
Beer	0	0	1-2	2-3	2-3	2-3	2-3	1-2
Mixed Drinks	1	2	.5-1	.5-1	.5-1	2-3	2-3	1-2
Wine	0	.5-1	1	.5-1	.5-1	1-2	2-3	1-2
Champagne	1	0	0	0	0	1	1	1

Are you planning to provide beverages without the help of a beverage service? This beverage matrix is a compilation of beverage industry recommendations that should help you plan for adequate beverage amounts.

Champagne Bottle Sizes

Magnum = 2 bottles

Jeroboam = 4 bottles

Rehoboam = 6 bottles

Methuselah = 8 bottles

Salmanazar = 12 bottles

Balthazar = 16 bottles

Nebuchadnezzar = 20 bottles

Bar Setup Checklist

Mixers

- [ ] Clamato/Tomato juice
- [ ] Cola/7-UP
- [ ] Cranberry juice
- [ ] Ginger ale
- [ ] Grapefruit/Orange juice
- [ ] Lemon/Lime juice
- [ ] Sparkling water
- [ ] Tonic water

Garnishes

- [ ] Bitters
- [ ] Black pepper
- [ ] Celery
- [ ] Cinnamon powder/sticks
- [ ] Grenadine syrup
- [ ] Jalapeno peppers
- [ ] Lemon/lime slices
- [ ] Maraschino cherries
- [ ] Margarita salt
- [ ] Mint sprigs
- [ ] Nutmeg
- [ ] Olives
- [ ] Onions
- [ ] Orange/Lemon/Lime slices
- [ ] Sugar
- [ ] Tobasco sauce
- [ ] Worcestershire sauce

Bar Equipment

- [ ] Blender
- [ ] Bottle opener
- [ ] Champagne pliers
- [ ] Citrus reamer
- [ ] Coasters
- [ ] Cocktail napkins
- [ ] Corkscrew
- [ ] Cutting board
- [ ] Funnels
- [ ] Garbage can/bags
- [ ] Garnish bowls
- [ ] Glassware
- [ ] Ice buckets
- [ ] Ice scoops/tongs
- [ ] Jiggers
- [ ] Lemon/lime squeezers
- [ ] Long-handled bar spoons
- [ ] Measuring cups/spoons
- [ ] Mixing glasses/pitchers
- [ ] Nutmeg graters
- [ ] Paper towels
- [ ] Paring knife
- [ ] Pepper mill
- [ ] Shakers
- [ ] Strainers
- [ ] Sponges
- [ ] Serving trays

Entertainer Interview Checklist

Company Name:		
Address:		
Contact Name:	Phone:	Fax:
E-mail:	URL:	

Entertainer's experience

Professional association memberships _____

Entertainer's portfolio/demonstration materials

Typical Program Length

Speaker/Entertainer's Fees

Hourly _____ Total _____ Travel _____ Supplies ____ Per-diem _____

Equipment Needed

Special requirements

Dressing room_____ Back of the room sales_____

Copyrights

Video/audio taping _____

Backup plans

Client list/references

Billing Data

Deposit date _____ Deposit amount_____

Deposit date _____ Deposit amount_____

Final payment due _____ Final payment amount_____

Payment methods accepted _____

Presenter Tip Sheet

Public Speaking Basics

- [ ] Prepare, Prepare, Prepare
- [ ] Check your visual image
- [ ] Take the stage with authority
- [ ] Maintain eye contact
- [ ] Watch your body language
- [ ] Empty your pockets
- [ ] Vary your pace, pitch and volume
- [ ] Speak with confidence
- [ ] Use notes unobtrusively
- [ ] Don't read what's on the screen
- [ ] Plan your exit
- [ ] End memorably

AV Equipment Checklist

- [ ] Amplifier
- [ ] Freight elevator
- [ ] Lecturn
- [ ] Microphones
- [ ] Satellite transmission
- [ ] Slide/Film/Video/Computer Projector
- [ ] Staff for operation
- [ ] Staging
- [ ] Audio mixer
- [ ] Front/Rear Projection
- [ ] Lighting
- [ ] Phone line
- [ ] Screen
- [ ] Sound System
- [ ] Staff for setup
- [ ] VCR/DVD Player

Presenter Supplies List

- [ ] Presentation
- [ ] Hard copy of the presentation
- [ ] Equipment backup
- [ ] Duct tape
- [ ] Flipcharts/Paper
- [ ] Masking tape
- [ ] Pointer/lighted pointer
- [ ] Whiteboards
- [ ] Extra copy of the presentation
- [ ] Extra copy in a different format
- [ ] Chalk
- [ ] Easel
- [ ] Handouts
- [ ] Pens/Pencils
- [ ] Write-on-Wipe-off pens

Technical Rehearsal Checklist

- [ ] Access to staging
- [ ] AV Screen height
- [ ] Cords taped down
- [ ] Lighting dimmed
- [ ] Stage lighting
- [ ] Audio check for dead spots
- [ ] Clear field of vision
- [ ] Equipment working
- [ ] Spotlights off
- [ ] Stairs lighting

Presenter Personal Supplies List

- [ ] Breath mints
- [ ] Wrinkle remover spray
- [ ] Lint brush
- [ ] Static guard

Creative Places to Hold a Celebration

Aircraft Hangar

Amusement Parks/Places

AquariumsPublic

Arboretums/Parks

Arcades/Fun Centers

Arenas/Stadiums

Art Galleries

Auditoriums/Halls

Ballrooms

Banquet Facilities

Bed and Breakfast Inns

Boats/Yachts

Botanic Gardens

Bowling Alleys

Breweries & Brew Pubs

Business Clubs/Sites

Camps/Campgrounds

Casinos

Church Halls

Civic Sites

Comedy Clubs

Community Centers

Conference Centers

Country Clubs/Golf Courses

Cruises

Docks/Marinas

Double Decker Bus

Embassies

Fairgrounds

Farms/Ranches

Fraternal Organizations

Government Buildings

Guest Houses

Guest/Dude Ranches

Historic Homes

Hotels

Houseboats

Libraries

Motels

Movie/Television Set

Museums

National/State Parks

Nature Centers

Night Clubs

Opera Houses

Planetariums

Private Estates

Race Track/Polo Grounds

Railroads

Recreation Centers

Resorts

Restaurants

Retail Centers

Retreat Facilities

RV Parks

Schools — College, Univ, Secondary, Prep

Service Clubs

Skating Rinks

Ski Centers

Steamships

Tea Rooms

Teen Centers

Theaters

Trollies

Vacation Rentals

Vineyards

Visitor Attractions and Information

Waterparks

Wilderness Adventures/ Outfitters

Zoos

Souvenir or Party Favor Ideas

Address Book
Appliques
Athletic Wear
Badges/Patches
Balloons
Balls
Bandanas
Beach Towels
Belt Buckles
Binders
Book Marks
Books
Bumper Stickers
Business Card Wallets or Booklet
Buttons
Calendars
Candy/Chocolate
Cartoons
CD-ROM
Coins
Collectibles
Coloring Book
Commemorative Plates
Computer Games
Cook Book
Cosmetics
Costume Accessories
Decals
Fad Items

Flip Book
Frisbees
Gadgets
Gag Gifts
Games
Glasses
Hats
Headbands/Wristbands
Jerseys
Jewelry
Key Tags or Key Chains
Lapel, Hat or Tie Pins
Letter Openers
Luggage Tags
Magnets
Membership Cards
Memorabilia
Memory Book
Movie DVDs
Mugs
Music CDs
Notepads/Notecards
Paper Weights
Pens/Pencils
Personalized Items
Photographs
Photo Albums/Frames
Plants
Playing Cards
Posters

Post-its
Printed Menus
Prints
Puzzles
Replica Items
Reunion Book
Scarves
Scrapbook
Screen Saver
Shoelaces
Signature Table Cloth
Socks
Stamps
Sunglasses
Sweat Shirts
T-shirts
Table Tents
Ticket Wallets
Ties
Tote/Shopping Bags
Tourist Souvenirs
Toys
Video
Visors
Watches
Wall Hanging
Wine/Beer with Custom Labels

Index

Celebration Solutions

Index

Index

Celebration Solutions

Index

Order Your Copy Today!

Reunion Solutions
IBSN 0-9724975-9-5
$26.95 + $3.75 S&H

_____ _____
Quantity   Cost

Reunion Solutions Planner
ISBN 0-9724975-8-7
$24.95 + $3.75 S&H

_____ _____
Quantity   Cost

Celebration Solutions
ISBN 0-9724975-6-0
$26.95 + $3.75 S&H

_____ _____
Quantity   Cost

Reunion Solutions Idea Deck
ISBN 0-9724975-7-9
$24.95 + $3.75 S&H

_____ _____
Quantity   Cost

Buy all 4 and Save $25.00
All 4 Books for **$75 + $15 S&H**

CO Residents add 3.5% sales tax _____

TOTAL _____

Name: _____

Address: _____

City: _____

ST: _____ Zip: _____

Send payment or purchase order to:
Reunion Solutions Press
P.O. Box 999, Niwot, CO 80544

Place your order online at:
www.ReunionSolutions.com

Order Your Copy Today!

Reunion Solutions
IBSN 0-9724975-9-5
$26.95 + $3.75 S&H

_____ _____
Quantity   Cost

Reunion Solutions Planner
ISBN 0-9724975-8-7
$24.95 + $3.75 S&H

_____ _____
Quantity   Cost

Celebration Solutions
ISBN 0-9724975-6-0
$26.95 + $3.75 S&H

_____ _____
Quantity   Cost

Reunion Solutions Idea Deck
ISBN 0-9724975-7-9
$24.95 + $3.75 S&H

_____ _____
Quantity   Cost

Buy all 4 and Save $25.00
All 4 Books for **$75 + $15 S&H**

CO Residents add 3.5% sales tax _____

TOTAL _____

Name: _____

Address: _____

City: _____

ST: _____ Zip: _____

Send payment or purchase order to:
Reunion Solutions Press
P.O. Box 999, Niwot, CO 80544

Place your order online at:
www.ReunionSolutions.com

Order Your Copy Today!

Reunion Solutions
IBSN 0-9724975-9-5
$26.95 + $3.75 S&H

_____ _____
Quantity   Cost

Reunion Solutions Planner
ISBN 0-9724975-8-7
$24.95 + $3.75 S&H

_____ _____
Quantity   Cost

Celebration Solutions
ISBN 0-9724975-6-0
$26.95 + $3.75 S&H

_____ _____
Quantity   Cost

Reunion Solutions Idea Deck
ISBN 0-9724975-7-9
$24.95 + $3.75 S&H

_____ _____
Quantity   Cost

Buy all 4 and Save $25.00
All 4 Books for **$75 + $15 S&H**

CO Residents add 3.5% sales tax _____

TOTAL _____

Name: _____

Address: _____

City: _____

ST: _____ Zip: _____

Send payment or purchase order to:
Reunion Solutions Press
P.O. Box 999, Niwot, CO 80544

Place your order online at:
www.ReunionSolutions.com

Order Your Copy Today!

Reunion Solutions
IBSN 0-9724975-9-5
$26.95 + $3.75 S&H

_____ _____
Quantity   Cost

Reunion Solutions Planner
ISBN 0-9724975-8-7
$24.95 + $3.75 S&H

_____ _____
Quantity   Cost

Celebration Solutions
ISBN 0-9724975-6-0
$26.95 + $3.75 S&H

_____ _____
Quantity   Cost

Reunion Solutions Idea Deck
ISBN 0-9724975-7-9
$24.95 + $3.75 S&H

_____ _____
Quantity   Cost

Buy all 4 and Save $25.00
All 4 Books for **$75 + $15 S&H**

CO Residents add 3.5% sales tax _____

TOTAL _____

Name: _____

Address: _____

City: _____

ST: _____ Zip: _____

Send payment or purchase order to:
Reunion Solutions Press
P.O. Box 999, Niwot, CO 80544

Place your order online at:
www.ReunionSolutions.com